READERS LOVE DEBBIE MORRISON!

'An absolute delight to read – a beautiful story of family, loyalty, and self discovery'

'Incredibly refreshing . . . I found it hard to put the book down'

'I think Reese Witherspoon would love to option this book for a series or movie'

'This gripping novel will take you on an emotional rollercoaster'

'Perfect for fans of compelling women's fiction'

'A must-read for anyone seeking an engaging story with relatable characters and unexpected twists'

'An entertaining fiction novel that raises so many important, real-life issues'

'Packed with suspense and drama that will keep you hooked until the very end'

Also by Debbie Morrison

*A Perfect Algarve Villa*

*A Perfect Chelsea Townhouse*

*A Perfect Devon Manor*

*A Perfect Devon Farmhouse*

Short Stories

*A Perfect Devon Pub*

# A Perfect Chelsea Townhouse

Debbie Morrison

PROSPERINA PRESS

First published in 2024 by Prosperina Press



Text design by Ellipsis, Glasgow



Produced in United Kingdom

ISBN: 978-1-0686884-3-0 (eBook)
ISBN: 978-1-0686884-4-7 (Paperback)

Cover design: Illustration by Hannah George,
Design by Cherie Chapman

PROSPERINA
PRESS

Prosperina Press,
Grenville House, 9 Boutport Street,
Barnstaple, Devon, EX31 1TZ

*In loving memory of Mrs Wood – the original Lana*

# One

Climbing the stone steps towards the front door, Lana could hear shouting coming from inside the house. 'Loyalty! That's rich, coming from an adulteress,' bellowed a male voice.

Lana frowned. What was he doing here on a Thursday morning? Mr Ellis, the male half of her employers. The half she was wary of. The selfish half. For several months, Lana had suspected his wife, Emily, was having an affair. The hand-washing basket was always full of La Perla lingerie; there were too many Moyses Stevens bouquets delivered without gift cards. And most women don't pack their passport for a yoga weekend in Edinburgh with the girls – not yet anyway.

Lana paused, keys in hand, listening to Mr Ellis's sneering tone. 'I used to think you had taste. What happened? Were all the interesting men uninterested in you?'

Emily didn't miss a beat. 'At least he showed an interest in me! Which is more than you've done for years.' The last word was dragged out, as if to emphasize the passage of time. 'I sometimes think you don't realize I actually live in this house. You just drop by for a shower and a change of clothes. Thank God I've got Svetlana for company.'

Hearing her name, Lana's hand shook; the keys fell, jangling onto the stone doorstep, and she dropped to her knees. The tiles were slick with a hoar frost and cold dampness seeped through her trousers. The shrill sound of the argument still rang out from within. Lana had plenty of experience of marital spats and considered them – like mobs of tipsy football supporters – a hazard best avoided, but she had never heard this couple argue. That would require them to be in the same room, which didn't happen often.

With a shiver, she scooped up the keys and weighed up her options: come back later or let herself in and skirt around the drama.

'Maybe if you did something effing interesting, I would notice you,' scoffed Mr Ellis, still at full volume.

His wife was on cue. 'If you don't find me interesting, why do you care if someone else does?'

Lana could feel the venom in those spiteful words – arrows intended to pierce the heart. She dried the keys on the front of her sweatshirt as a bitter winter wind sliced through her trousers, making her legs feel like they'd been dipped in snow. She gritted her teeth and inserted the key, turning it slowly, quietly, like a teenager letting herself in long past curfew. She nudged the door open a crack and crept in sideways. Her entrance coincided with a fresh salvo of expletives from the sitting room – Mr Ellis was not in a forgiving mood.

Two West Highland terriers scampered towards Lana, claws tapping on the polished parquet flooring, ears flat against their heads, tails tucked under their tummies. Wondering briefly if there'd been a timeout to feed the dogs, she knelt and stroked their wiry hair. 'It's all right, my lovelies,' she whispered.

'Face facts, Emily,' shouted Mr Ellis. 'You caused this.'

Lana pictured Mr Ellis scowling at his wife; no wonder Emily had sought refuge with another man. Lana considered him arrogant, serious, and downright rude, the sort of person you would snigger at, if you saw him trip and spill a takeaway coffee down his shirt. Whereas if Emily did that, there would be a crush of bystanders, tissues in hand, competing to help. Lana only saw him on the occasional Saturday morning. His favourite place to spend Saturdays – and every other day – was the office. She tip-toed down the hallway, listening to Emily's raised voice, surprisingly loud for someone only five foot, three inches tall. 'Stop blaming me! I didn't fire you, Paul did.'

*Fired!* Lana stopped instantly, as if a policeman had shouted 'freeze'. Her heart was beating faster than rain drumming against her greenhouse roof in a winter storm. So, that's why he wasn't at the office. Was he going to be here all day? Every day? Getting underfoot, messing up rooms she'd just tidied and demanding cups of coffee as if she were a vending machine. She had a fleeting memory of her school days and a strict supply teacher who'd taught her German for a month when lovely Mrs Ambrose was off sick. The replacement teacher made the class learn all the vocabulary from the "supermarket" chapter of the textbook, rather than teaching them nursery rhymes and carols. Lana could still sing the first verse of *Silent Night*' in German, but she also still knew the vocabulary from *die selbstbedienungsladen*. All of it.

An alarming question popped into her mind. Could they still afford her wages? She stepped closer to the sitting room and leaned towards the wall. The dogs moved with her as if joined by elastic.

'But you caused it,' snapped Mr Ellis. 'Paul loved spelling that one out.'

'Paul fired you because you've had a running feud with him for years.'

There was a bitter laugh from Mr Ellis. 'If you don't stop dancing on that pinhead, you'll fall off. You try working with that stuck-up prat. Oh, wait, but you've never worked, have you? Well, now's your chance. I'm setting up on my own. Paul's spread rumours, and the headhunters won't touch me. You went to secretarial college, you're hired.'

'No way!' screamed Emily. 'I'm not working for *you*.'

'And here we are, back at Go. Effing Paul. So, we fire Svetlana, and replace her with a PA.'

Lana's stomach lurched. Thoughts were whipping through her mind so fast she couldn't separate them. It was like trying to catch one of those white butterflies that threatened her brassicas, chasing it around the plants, snapping her hands in vain. What was her notice period; what would she do about Janet; where would they live? And who was this Paul they kept mentioning?

'You will *not* fire her. Svetlana has worked here for fifteen years, she has earned this family's loyalty,' shouted Emily. Lana crossed herself as Emily lowered her voice. 'I will not lead my mother's life. I'm not running this house like Mary does. Her housekeeper only comes in a few hours a week.'

Grasping her lifeline, Lana concluded she had heard enough. A constant refrain from her childhood was playing on a loop in her mind: *eavesdroppers never hear good of themselves*. She retraced her steps – the dogs following obediently – opened the front door and slammed it shut, then raised her voice and cried out, 'Tosca, Floria, come'. At her feet, the dogs cocked their heads to one side and whined, their tails giving a half-hearted, confused wag.

Emily burst into the entrance hall, the folds of a heavy silk dressing gown flapping around her legs, and like a ghost, glided silently up the stairs. Heedful that Mr Ellis might pursue his wife, Lana grasped two collars and trooped downstairs.

She let the dogs into the garden, flicked the kettle on, her mind spinning with the implications of what she'd overheard. Securing another position as a housekeeper wouldn't be tricky, but finding one that provided "all found" accommodation – rent, utility bills, and council tax paid by the employer – in a flat in Knightsbridge, within her notice period? Lana wasn't obsessed with the area, but she didn't live alone, and the other resident of the basement flat in Ovington Square had a super glue-like attachment to the Knightsbridge postcode. Which was why, despite Mr Ellis and his mean-spirited insistence that, irrespective of the temperature, her heating only went on for six hours a day, Lana had stayed for fifteen years. Should she be concerned, or was her loyalty about to be repaid?

She marched to the freezer, flicking her thick, black framed glasses off her face. Lana had been short-sighted since childhood, but her close-up vision was perfect. She sometimes questioned if that would still be true if she had followed her dream to become a PA, and for the last thirty years stared at computer screens rather than the inside of toilet bowls. The cord securing her glasses tugged against her neck, reminding her she was also shackled . . . to Janet.

It might be a Thursday, but no doubt Mr Ellis would expect a cooked breakfast. She removed a neatly wrapped package, recognizing her own writing, "*Breakfast X1*", and briefly wishing it said "X2"; if the Ellis's son Alex was here, Lana would be serving breakfast informally in the kitchen, and the couple would have been more discreet. Acrimony would have been limited to Alex and his father, and their rows resembled English summer storms - occurring frequently, often savage and unpleasant, but short-lived.

She stared at the frosty air, seeing not cartons of homemade soup and casseroles, but the basement flat behind the wall against which the freezer rested. Would Mr Ellis alter her package? Was this the opportunity he had been waiting for to evict her?

A warning beeping noise sounded – *was that prescient?* Her chest tightened as if someone was kneeling on it. What if she did lose this job? To rent a one-bed flat in Chelsea would cost more than her monthly salary. She banged the freezer door shut, telling herself not to fret – she had her own guardian angel. For the last fifteen years, Emily had paid someone to wash her hair twice a week; those manicured hands weren't going anywhere near a bottle of bleach.

Half an hour later, Lana was puffing her way up the stairs with a loaded tray. Although the same age and height as Emily, with a penchant for sweet treats rather than exercise Lana was stockier and unfit. She rapped on the dining room door.

'Come in,' said Emily in a clipped voice.

Inside, Emily had her back to Lana, but was sitting unnaturally upright, as if someone had warned her there was a wasp crawling over her back. Mr Ellis was at the other end of the table, his face puce, his lips drawn and tight. Both were rigid with tension, sitting like a pair of dogs waiting for the fetch command after their favourite toy has been thrown. Lana tried to muster some sympathy – imagine discovering your spouse was having an affair *and* losing your job on the same day – but she couldn't. She'd never been married, nor lost her job, and it was tough to empathize with someone so haughty.

Keeping her eyes down, Lana strode to the sideboard. She heard Mr Ellis ask if there were any weekend commitments, but without a hint of interest in his voice, and Emily started talking about her Pilates class in a forced jolly lilt. Lana picked up the cooked food, thinking to herself, *all three of us are trying to appear natural, as if we're pushing a luggage trolley through an airport's "nothing to declare" channel, hoping not to be searched.*

Lana put a plate in front of Mr Ellis, her thanks for delivering an unplanned cooked meal a sharp *sotto voce*: 'Tell her, Emily. You're not being fair.'

From the other end of the table, Emily spoke in an equally hushed voice. '*Not now.*'

Lana put a platter of fruit beside Emily – mango, pineapple, de-stoned cherries and a sprinkling of berries. 'Thank you, Svetlana,' said Emily, without glancing up.

'Emily.'

'Not *now*, Mark!' snipped his wife.

The housekeeper picked up a mug of green tea.

'We've always been good employers, and I'm not about to take a leaf out of the bank's book,' said Mr Ellis. 'You may think you are being kind, but you are not. Tell her, or I will.'

The mug wobbled, hot tea slopped over Lana's wrist, and she flinched. Today, she was going to lose her job. Today. And this was Mr Ellis's idea of being kind. Hateful man. She set the mug on Emily's coaster, then picked it up again and used the end of her apron to wipe the handle dry.

'NOW!' snapped Mr Ellis.

Beside Lana, there was a faint grunting noise. 'All right,' said Emily. 'Svetlana . . .'

Lana wiped her hands on her apron and crossed her arms, feeling her heart hammering against her wrist. A blonde coiffed head turned her way, the face arranged into a strained smile. Emily was toying with her linen napkin, rubbing it through her fingers as if testing the material. 'We need to have a chat about your position,' she said.

Lana tried to dislodge her tongue. It was stuck to the roof of her mouth, which was so dry it felt as if someone had taken a sponge and mopped out all the moisture. Her voice came out in a croak. 'Now?'

'When we've finished in here,' said Mr Ellis.

Of course, thought Lana, he hadn't meant *right* now. He'd keep her sweating – why let your housekeeper's life interrupt breakfast? She stalked to the sideboard and collected the tray; fifteen years of loyalty didn't seem to buy you much slack from the Ellis family.

In a basement kitchen on the opposite side of the square to Lana, a woman called Mary was hunched over twelve scraps of paper. Despite often using the word to describe herself, Mary's life wasn't average. She was average height, build, weight and complexion, and without carefully spaced out twice yearly trips to the salon, she claimed her hair would be a typical mousy colour, not dark blonde. But Mary was born a Standerwick, and they – she learned at an early age – were not average. She was raised on a childhood diet of restricted fatherly praise, limited to the rare occasions when he acknowledged that she'd lived up to what he thought the name required of her.

The Standerwick kitchen bore little resemblance to the one in which Lana cooked with its concealed appliances, and sleek storage units. Mary's kitchen had originally been the housekeeper's room, and there was still a bank of linen cupboards along one wall, thickly painted in matt cream, the internal slatted shelves now filled with crockery, pots and pans, and groceries. Opposite the cupboards in the old fireplace stood an ancient Aga – which had started life coal-fired, now converted to run on gas – with a sleeping mat on the floor in front of it. A black Labrador languished on the bedding like a diva on a sun lounger; Biscuit lifted a back leg in the air, and the sloppy sound of slurping could be heard above the rhythmic purring of the oven.

In Mary's kitchen, instead of a marble island, the centre of the room was dominated by a long, wide pine table, above which was a wooden drying rack, suspended from the ceiling, festooned with sheets, shirts, and socks. The yeasty smell of baking bread hung in the air, mixed with the unmistakable sour odour of damp dog.

Mary shuffled the scraps of paper, isolating her own name and that of her husband Charles – a marriage of which her long-dead father had approved, especially when he adopted the Standerwick name – and placed them at either end of her imaginary table before shunting the others into two piles: men and women. She plugged in a whisk, stuck it into a bowl of egg whites, and pressed go, drowning out the sound of Biscuit's licking. Her eyes flickered between the frothing eggs, the laundry on the hanging rack – wondering if it would be dry before this evening – and the names on the table. Who did she want to sit next to tonight? If she chose Paul, he might amuse her with ex-army stories, but on the other hand, he might talk about work, and she didn't want to discuss money with anyone, let alone with someone as rich as Paul. Which is why she hadn't invited Barry. She liked Barry, with his impish smile and carefree manner, and he and Charles were good friends, but like Paul, Barry worked in the City – initially for her father – and it was January. If both men were together, they'd be puffing out their chests, claiming that their "daddy" – AKA *bonus* – was bigger than anyone else's, and she'd spend her entire evening diverting them from that vulgar topic. The EU may have capped bankers' bonuses, but the investment banks still paid their top earners egregious sums. They had to. Charles had explained this to her. If the banks didn't pay, all their star earners would decamp to the shadow banking industry. Wealthy investors funded those deep pools of capital and were unconstrained by the regulatory controls on bonuses. She shunted Paul's name tag beside her own – there was another reason she wanted to keep an eye on him tonight.

The eggs now beaten into stiff peaks, she unplugged the whisk and riffled through the remaining names, dismissing Mark with a little titter, then picking up his name and screwing it into a ball.

It was a Thursday. Mark didn't do midweek suppers. He never cancelled himself, his assistant always called with profuse apologies, and he sent a huge bouquet of flowers. Dumping the dirty whisk near the sink, Mary wondered if those deliveries were organized as soon as a social engagement appeared in his diary.

Who was strong enough to place opposite Paul? What about Tom? She didn't know him well, but he was an investigative journalist; Tom could conversation-wrestle with a rhino. She slotted Tom's name into place.

'Hmm, lunch smells good.'

She glanced up at the sound of the familiar voice. Charles was only slightly taller than Mary, with a thatch of brown hair which hung just below his protruding ears, camouflaging their size. His face was not classically handsome, the nose a bit too small, as if it had stopped growing in childhood, the jawline starting to sag, but it was the eyes that had first attracted her. They were steely-blue, both kind and filled with purpose. They matched the person.

'Here's the birthday boy. That's not lunch, darling. The bread is for tonight. You'll have to fend for yourself today.'

'The birthday boy has the day off. Need any help? Shall I lay the table?' he offered.

She shot him a loving look. 'Have a look at the seating plan while I check the bread.'

He sidled over and gave her shoulder a squeeze. 'Why are you baking bread? Buy a baguette like everyone else.'

'That's expensive, and anyway, I like making an effort for your friends.'

'They're your friends too,' he said.

She smiled inwardly. She liked Charles's friends, and it was Mary who invited them for dinner or supper, but they were his friends, not hers; Mary only had one friend.

'You're a funny woman. Buying bread isn't extravagant. Don't exhaust yourself.'

'We're serving champagne.'

'Why? It's my party, and I don't even drink the damn stuff.'

'It's the right thing to do.'

'According to *whom*?' he said emphasizing the last word.

'Yes . . . well.' She tugged the oven gloves off the Aga rail and gently nudged the Labrador with a foot. 'Biscuit, out of the way now, boy.'

'Because it's the Standerwick way: what your father would expect.'

She ignored the jibe. 'Champagne means I must economize somewhere. This house is expensive to run in winter, did you see the last gas bill?'

'I paid it, and the electricity bill. This house is expensive to run all year round.' Behind her, she heard Charles groan. 'I like Emily,' he said, 'and I know she's your only real friend, but I sat next to her last time.'

Mary opened the oven door, releasing a blast of heat that stung her cheeks. She didn't need reminding. Charles had a wide circle of friends, but Mary worked from home and didn't have time to form new friendships. She reached into the Aga, the warmth seeping through her oven gloves, an earlier conversation with Emily replaying in her mind. Her friend had called to check Mary was still joining the Thursday Pilates class.

'Of course, I'm going to Pilates,' said Mary, 'but, Emily, are you sure you want to come tonight, with Paul on the guest list?'

'I have to get used to seeing him, and I wouldn't want to disappoint Charles.'

Was it too soon, wondered Mary, putting the loaf tin on the chopping board and pecking her husband's cheek. 'They're your guests, darling, you choose who you want to sit next to.'

Bending over the seating plan, Charles chuckled. After a moment, he raised his head and gave an exaggerated sniff. 'Phew. The dog's not going to be in here tonight, is he?'

'Biscuit will be wherever he wants to be. This is his home too.'

'Can't he be outside? He's a bit whiffy. Some of the guests don't like dogs as much as you do.'

'If they don't like the smell of Biscuit, our guests are welcome to go outside whenever they want.'

Gripping the tin with an oven-gloved hand, Mary ran a knife around the inside, and tipped out the loaf. It bounced, landing on its side.

'He's not my closest mate, but where's Mark's name?' asked Charles.

'He won't show on a Thursday. Tom is Emily's "date" for tonight.'

'Lucky Tom!' Charles said, swapping Emily's name with another and putting her beside Paul. Mary stifled a laugh and swapped the girls back. She was surprised Charles hadn't guessed and impressed that Paul hadn't told him. Unbeknown to you, darling, she thought, your oldest friend has been having an affair with my best mate for the last year. Funny that Emily's husband and her lover both did the same job; if Paul could make it to midweek dinner engagements, why couldn't Mark? Was Paul better organized or just better at the job?

Mary tapped the bottom of the loaf. It rang hollow. Success, she thought, recalling another triumphant midweek supper party, which Mark had reliably absented himself from, when the evening was electrified by Paul and Emily's flirtations. That night, Paul's eyes had followed Emily's every move, like Biscuit tracking his food bowl from the pantry to the kitchen floor. She wondered why Charles hadn't noticed Paul listening to everything Emily said with the same rapt attention as a newly confirmed parishioner to the vicar's sermon.

But a few weeks ago, Emily had ended the affair. The last place her friend would want to sit tonight was beside Paul.

Mary ran water into the empty loaf tin, which hissed in protest, then spread the meringue mixture onto a baking tray, wondering when she would find time to lay the table. 'Must dash, darling,' she said. 'Pilates with Emily. My turn to drive, you don't need the car, do you? Stay away from the Aga, I've a casserole slow cooking for next week.' She pointed a finger – like all its neighbours, filed short – at the bread. And don't snack on that.'

'I wasn't planning to do either,' huffed Charles. 'Do you want me to do anything while you're out? Why don't I lay the table?'

'Just sort the wine, please. Everything else is under control,' she said, before kissing him and rushing upstairs.

'It always is,' muttered Charles.

Rain spattered on Mary's jacket; she put up her hood, dashed down the steps, and flung herself into the car. Ovington Square was built around a rectangular communal garden, currently a winter smudge of dark evergreen bushes among the statuesque leafless plane trees with their tall, mottled trunks. Over the bushes, Mary could see Emily standing on her doorstep, hands stuffed inside jacket pockets, staring at her feet.

Starting the car, Mary wondered if Emily regretted ending the affair. She wasn't completely surprised when Emily had succumbed to the attractions of bachelor Paul – wealthy, impeccable manners, charming, and without the complications of a former wife or children. Plus it must be lonely being Mark's wife. The man virtually lived in the office.

Emily had told Mary about the affair within days of it starting, but Mary would have guessed anyway. The glowing skin, the ready smile, the lightheartedness. Paul put the sparkle back into

Emily; it was as if he had found the trip switch fused by workaholic Mark's absence and flicked it back upright. Classically, the affair started at the office Christmas party, which Mark – caught up in a completion meeting – never reached. Paul looked after Mark's abandoned wife, escorted her back to her empty house, accepted the suggestion of a nightcap, and made love to her on the sofa, to the glow of the Christmas tree lights. Mary could've managed without that last detail.

That was just over a year ago, twelve months of conniving and deceit, with girlie weekends invented as cover stories for romantic trips to Paris, or cosy Cotswold cottages. Emily and Mary were each other's secret-keeper; neither would reveal a confidence, even to their spouse.

A year of Charles telling Mary that his mate Paul was having an affair with a married woman that was turning serious, that Paul had fallen deeply in love, and was begging his girlfriend to leave her husband. Tonight would be the first time Mary had seen Paul since Emily ended the affair. She must look after him.

Mary checked for traffic, pulled out and raced round the square, then took her foot off the pedal, coasting to a halt outside her friend's house. Emily didn't move. She was rooted to her doorstep as if on guard duty. Mary tooted the horn, and Emily looked up. Her hair hung in limp bedraggled tendrils, like seaweed stuck to her face. *Why didn't she put her hood up?*

Mary depressed the window switch and leaned across the passenger seat. 'Come on, girl, you're getting soaked, and we'll be late!'

Her friend plodded down the steps, got in, fastened her seat belt and faced forwards, tucking her damp hair behind her ears. Mary felt a rush of sympathy; Emily must be feeling wretched. Probably drowning in guilt. Guilt for betraying Mark, guilt for repeatedly lying to her husband, guilt for locking up her secret to prevent the pain it would cause him if Mark learned the truth, and guilt at the pain she was now causing Paul by ending their affair.

'You OK?' asked Mary.

'Not really,' grunted Emily.

They pulled up to a set of lights, and Mary glanced once more at her friend, taking in the bloodshot eyes and flushed cheeks. Emily only had Mary to lean on; no one else knew about the affair. Her friend was fiddling with the strap of her handbag as if she didn't trust her hands to be left idle. How was she hiding this fragile state from Mark? It was a godsend the man was never at home.

Above the gentle hum of the electric car, Mary heard a throat being cleared.

'Mark knows about Paul.'

Mary's hands tightened round the steering wheel. *A discarded toy regains its allure if another child shows interest*. A mental picture of Mark came to her. Physically not dissimilar to Paul; both were tall, slim and fit, with dark hair, Mark's curly, Paul's straight and cut military short. She didn't like Mark much; he was a bit full of himself, always talking about work, blathering on about bond yields or articles that had caught his eye in *The Economist*. Nothing ever caught Mary's eye in that magazine.

She flicked a sideways glance at the sorry figure beside her. 'Ouch,' she said. 'Are you up to Pilates?'

'I've got to get out.'

'I don't suppose the affair being over helps.'

Emily slouched over the dashboard. 'Not a lot. How do you think Charles would take it?'

Unfair question, thought Mary. She couldn't imagine how her husband would react because she would never be unfaithful.

A horn blared. Mary squinted up at the lights – green – poked her tongue out at the rear-view mirror, and accelerated round into Sloane Avenue, pulling up behind a stationary taxi. 'How is Mark taking it?'

'How do you think?' Emily groaned. 'He's spent most of the morning shouting at me. He says I've humiliated him. I've tried to explain how lonely I get with him stuck at the office, but he won't discuss it.' Emily blew out a sigh, her lips quivering. 'I think a lot of his anger is because it was Paul.'

Mary clicked her tongue; Paul and Mark's work feud was notorious. But then, she thought, there's more testosterone in a square foot of an investment bank office than the entire changing room of a men's rugby team. Imagine having to see your spouse's former lover at the office every day. 'You've crushed his ego . . .' she said.

'I hated seeing the hurt in his eyes.'

'Give him time.'

'The thing is, Mark's being so nasty, saying he's not sure if he can ever forgive me, and . . . I'm beginning to wonder if I've parted with the wrong man.'

Mary slammed her foot on the brake. Shoppers dawdled across the zebra crossing. She peeked across at her friend. 'Wow. That's a bolt from the blue.'

'I shouldn't have said that.' Emily whispered.

'Even to me? Does Paul know you're having second thoughts?'

There was a pause. Mary switched her attention to the shoppers, spying a gap, and shooting off around Sloane Square. Eventually, Emily broke the silence, saying, 'Paul knows that Mark knows.'

*How?* Mary thought. Suddenly, she realized why Emily had dodged her earlier question. 'You're still seeing him,' she said, in as even a tone as she could summon.

'No,' Emily said adamantly. 'I haven't seen him since before Christmas.'

Mary adopted her *mother* voice. 'Emily,' she scolded, 'that was very carefully worded. You may not have physically seen him, but you're still in contact, aren't you?'

Emily didn't reply.

Mary gasped. 'You *are*, aren't you?'

'Yes,' whispered Emily.

'Oh, Emily,' said Mary, in the tone she reserved for Biscuit when she found him curled up on the bed upstairs. 'Is it the attention you miss?'

Emily let out a soft whimper. 'I'm so mixed up. I don't know what to do.'

What a mess, thought Mary, but she had to let her friend think this through for herself; this must be Emily's decision.

'What can I do to help?'

'Keep my glass topped up tonight?' said Emily, laughing.

'Are you sure you want to come? Remember, Paul will be there.'

'I must get out. I can't stand another night in watching TV.'

Mary wondered if Emily was telling the truth, or if Paul was the lure. She had a sudden thought. 'I haven't had any flowers yet . . . Mark isn't going to show up too, is he?'

Emily gave a short laugh. 'No chance. He's too busy working on a business plan.'

To one side of the Ellis kitchen was a pantry where Lana stowed floral-patterned housecoats and aprons in a drawer she suspected Emily had never opened. Lana removed an apron decorated with little daisies, pulling it over her comfortable workday clothes of elasticated trousers and sweatshirt. It looked more cheerful than she felt.

One more task.

The two terriers followed her to the breakfast bar. Ordinarily on Thursday afternoons, Emily would sit opposite Lana, rescheduling a weekend disrupted by Mark's sudden insistence that he was required in the office. This Thursday, however, there was no sign of her employer.

She started hulling strawberries, dropping the refuse alternately left and right, her actions punctuated by the sound of snapping jaws. It was like feeding two Venus flytraps. Once she'd covered the fruit platter with cling film, she could leave before anyone fired her, and start her job search. The chat about her position had been postponed in favour of a Pilates class followed by a shopping expedition, and Mr Ellis had been out all day. Hurrah!

But then Emily walked in, dressed in a cream cashmere trouser suit. Lana pulled the stalk out of the last strawberry and, picking up a paring knife, sliced the fruit in half lengthways.

'Tea?' she offered, putting down the knife.

Emily didn't answer. The silence lasted a beat too long to be companionable. Lana slid the chopped fruit onto the plate and glanced up. Emily was rubbing her hands up and down her trouser legs as if smoothing away creases. This looked bad, but Emily wasn't here to fire her, she'd insist on Mr Ellis doing that dirty work.

'Let's sit down. We need to talk,' said Emily.

There was a blank expression on her employer's face, and she was pulling out a chair at the kitchen table. Why? When Emily wanted a chat, she usually plonked herself on a stool at the breakfast bar. Lana heard a throat being cleared and she turned towards the sound to find a frowning Mr Ellis. Lana glanced at her Fitbit – heart rate over 90. 'What's this about?' she asked, trying to keep her voice neutral.

It was Mr Ellis who spoke. 'I've got something to say to you.'

Mr Ellis rarely spoke to her. Outside of a Saturday morning, Lana didn't see him, just plenty of evidence of his existence: T-shirts on the treadmill, sweaty sports towels on the gym floor, discarded shirts in the shower room. He dumped soggy towels on the bathroom floor and scattered half-eaten midnight snacks and half-drunk mugs of coffee around the kitchen as if setting the trail for a treasure hunt. There was only one thing he might have to say to her. She tried to banish that idea.

'Sit,' commanded Mr Ellis, as if Lana was one of the terriers. No please, no suggestion of making herself comfortable, just the command, but then she wasn't sure Mr Ellis ever said please or thank you to anyone.

The threesome gathered around the kitchen table. No one sat. It was like an empty fireplace in summer that still acts as a focal point for a room. Mr Ellis leaned against one of the bi-fold doors, and Emily put a hand on the chair she'd pulled away from the table. Lana wasn't going to sit like a naughty child looking up at the adults.

'Something has come up,' said Emily in a slightly squeaky voice.

Lana didn't need to look at her Fitbit; her heartbeat was in overdrive.

'You went to secretarial college, like me, didn't you?' asked Emily.

Decades ago, before her father had gone on that business trip to Manchester, back when her dreams still mattered. Lana nodded.

'The thing is,' said Emily, the ghost of a smile twitching at the corners of her mouth, 'Mark has decided to leave the bank and set up on his own.'

Lana stayed silent. Was she expected to pretend she hadn't overheard this morning's screaming match, despite it being so loud it might have been audible in Hyde Park?

Emily coughed and then continued in an excited, high-pitched voice. 'A sort of boutique advice business. He's had enough of working in a big office.'

Lana tried to take in what was being said about Mr Ellis's new business, something about needing an assistant . . .

'So, what do you think?' asked Emily.

'What do I think about what?' asked Lana, her eyebrows wrinkling.

'About helping Mark out with a bit of secretarial work?'

She was being asked to work as an assistant. For Mr Ellis? Was that on top of the housekeeping or instead of? But she wasn't being fired, Lana told herself, and she wasn't losing her home. Neither was Janet.

Mr Ellis cut into her thoughts. 'No, this won't work,' he said in a resigned voice. 'I need someone with experience. I'll get a temp until Anne can join me, and you'll have to replace Svetlana with a part-time cleaner until the business takes off.'

How could he talk like this in front of Lana, as if she were a nineteenth-century maid, unworthy of being acknowledged? Irrelevant, despite standing a few feet away. Before she could say anything, Emily leapt to Lana's defence, her face flushed.

'No, Mark, we agreed! I won't have Svetlana become a casualty. She's not put a foot wrong for fifteen years. And there's Janet, we can't make her homeless too.' Emily switched her gaze to Lana. 'Please give it a go, or at least say you'll think about it over the weekend.'

Lana shuffled her feet. The thought of being in the same room as Mr Ellis was unpleasant enough, but what would being his assistant involve? She ran her tongue over her teeth and asked, 'what would I be doing?'

'Mark?' asked Emily.

'Assisting me.'

'Like . . . how?' demanded Lana.

'I don't know yet,' said Mark, rolling his eyes at Emily. 'But I do know I'll need help. She can shadow me and learn on the job.'

He's not exactly selling it to me, thought Lana.

Upstairs, a clock chimed. Five long beats. 'Right, I'll leave you to it.' Mr Ellis turned and headed for the stairs.

'Well' said Emily, her voice soft. 'It's time you went home. Good luck at the dentist tomorrow. She put a hand on Lana's arm, adding gently, 'I'll get Mark to jot down a job spec over the weekend.'

Lana pursed her lips. In a hushed tone, Emily continued 'Just do it, Svetlana. You need to learn to move on. Forget about what happened to Janet in March. Anyway, working for Mark will only be temporary.'

# Two

Banging the gate shut behind her, Lana told herself she shouldn't be surprised; the very rich often treat employees like pawns in a chess game: unimportant, ignored, to be sacrificed to suit their whims. The reason Mr Ellis wanted her to work as his PA was to avoid paying for one, using her as a quasi-buy one,-get one free worker until his new business got going. The arrogance of the man!

Oblivious to the rain lashing her jacket, Lana reached down and ran her fingers through the leaves of a plant growing in a pot on her top step, raised her hand, and sniffed the fragrant scent of rosemary, switching her thoughts to gardening. On the bottom step, she bent over and tucked a loose piece of bubble wrap around a tub, then took a few moments to inspect the tiny courtyard.

Angled to make the most of the sliver of winter sun, her raised bed was dominated by a Brussels sprout plant, the bottom half of the stalk bare, the top still sporting tiny green helmets. Beside it were other vegetables, a few cabbages shorn of their outer leaves, a celeriac, all ringed by crushed eggshells to deter slugs. She shoved her jacket sleeve up to the elbow and pulled a yellowing leaf off a swede. She would do what Emily asked. She would think about it, but she was trapped – it was winter, and there was Janet.

Set against the wall opposite the front door was a slim plastic greenhouse. Lana punched in the key code and unfastened the lock. The door slid open, making a grating noise against the cement base, and she peered in at trays of pak choi, rocket and pots of parsley. She dipped a finger into each container. The soil was springy but moist. With each prod the tightness in her muscles dissipated, like sand slipping through an egg timer. There might be scores of vacancies for live-in housekeepers in Knightsbridge. She pulled out a little bag of pale brown granules from her pocket – a homemade fertilizer of ground, dried-out eggshells – and showered a handful over each tray.

Once inside the flat, she shut the door behind her with the faintest click. It was dark, but she didn't switch on a light. She sagged against the wall, breathing in the habitual smell of incense mixed with mothballs. Behind the closed door at the end of the entrance hall came the sound of scratchy tinny voices from a television. This had been home for fifteen years, but she wouldn't mind packing up her plants and moving to the country. Maybe Janet was ready to move.

The door squeaked open, and a white-haired woman peered around the side. 'Why are you standing in the dark?' The head disappeared, the door clicked shut, and a voice floated out to her from within. 'You're late. Emily shouldn't expect you to work overtime. You have other responsibilities.'

Lana reached out a hand, fumbling her way past her blouses and trousers suspended from a black metal rail that filled most of the hallway, following the voice, the smell of incense growing stronger with each step. She shrugged off her jacket, hung it on a peg, and as she opened the door she was hit by a fug of heat, like stepping into her greenhouse in mid-August.

For London, the reception room wasn't small, but it was multifunctional. It housed a sofa bed – Lana's bed – and a galley kitchen, the worktop doubling as the dining table. The space was also an informal shrine; on a chest of drawers stood a white alabaster statue of the Virgin Mary, and scattered at the base like presents beneath a Christmas tree was a prayer book, a Bible, hymn book, and a set of rosary beads. Behind the statue, reflecting Lana's image back at her, was a mirror. Tucking a stray grey hair behind her ear, she wondered when she had ballooned from being a short slim woman, like Janet still was, to this stocky creature with a craggy face. Maybe Janet's condition kept her slim.

'It's only ten past, hardly overtime,' Lana quipped, peeling off her top layer. 'It's roasting in here. I hope you haven't had the fan heater on all day, we're close to meter reading time.'

'What does he expect if the heating's only on for a few hours a day?'

'Mum don't start. My contract says reasonable use of gas and electricity. I've offered to pay to keep it on longer, but Emily says he won't listen.'

'I bet Emily has the heating on upstairs all day, that's her interpretation of reasonable use. I spend more time with Father Paul than I do here in winter.'

And Lana was pleased Janet did, she didn't want to come home to her mother huddled over the stove for warmth like she had in that cold snap last March.

'Well switch the lights off if you've got the heater on,' scolded Lana.

Lana tossed her sweatshirt onto the side chair, picked up the remote control, stabbing the buttons until the volume from the TV was tolerable.

Her mother reached for a sofa arm, staggered, then lowered herself into the seat. 'Don't turn that off, I'm watching it. And you mind your hours. Once they start expecting you to stay on, you'll never see the end of it, mark my words.'

*As if you'd know – when did you ever work?*

Lana bustled past her mother. A thin hand picked up the remote control and the sound of a choir filled the room. Lana tried to blank it out. She had plenty to occupy her mind, but she couldn't think with her mother moaning, and people singing about Jesus. Flicking the lights on in the kitchen area, she said, 'homemade cauliflower soup for supper. Do you want toast with it?'

'Soup?' There was a pause, then her mother whined, 'Again? And I had toast for breakfast.'

'Yes, I can tell,' said Lana, sweeping crumbs into the palm of her hand. She squirted washing-up liquid into the basin and turned on the tap. Maybe her mother was ready for a country way of life, she thought; the two of them could be happy in a little cottage. 'Mum, how would you feel about moving out of London?'

'What?' came the instantaneous reply, in a voice that made it sound as if her mother was being strangled. 'Don't say such things! You know stress is bad for me.'

Lana shook the suds off her hands, patting them dry on her trousers. She walked around the counter and sat down, taking her mother's bony hands in hers. Janet was trying to tug herself free, her eyes staring at the Madonna. Lana recognized the trance-like expression on Janet's face, spotted the quivering mouth as her mother whispered the comforting words of the Rosary. This intense expression had dominated Janet's face for most of Lana's life, although she did have a few early memories of a smiling, more relaxed mother. She recalled those very early days as happy ones – picnic blankets in a park or on a beach, her father playing with her, laughing his deep-throated laugh. It had always been the two of them running about, while Janet lay reading a book or just *resting*. Her mother had never been active, not after the diagnosis.

Looking at her mother's wrinkled profile, Lana tutted, and gave one more push. 'Yes. Out to the country where the air is cleaner. A cottage with a garden for you to potter about or relax in when I'm at work.'

Janet's chanting stopped. 'I spent nearly twenty years of my life in the countryside, living with a man I wouldn't have had to put up with if it wasn't for you. I won't go back.'

Lana's eyes fell on Janet's evening tablets, lined up like incriminating evidence, and she sensed the familiar stab of guilt. Her mother had played the ace of trumps, killing the idea of moving to the country as efficiently as Lana's trowel dispatching a weed. Her mother was still talking. Lana listened – her penance for "causing distress". She knew the story, she'd heard it often enough, how it was Lana's fault her parents were hustled into marriage by their Catholic grandparents, dismayed by the sin of premarital sex, united in preventing the greater sin of a birth out of wedlock. How that birth ruined her mother's life, mentally and physically, by locking her into an unhappy marriage and irreparably damaging her heart.

'If it wasn't for you, I wouldn't have a weak heart. And I wouldn't have been forced to live with that sinner, your father.'

Lana let it wash over her. Janet was in no rush, trotting out each complaint like a salesperson running through their catalogue, but Lana knew that, like her mother repeating The Lord's Prayer, she would reach the end, they would both say *Amen*, and move on.

The climax arrived. 'There won't be a church I can walk to in the countryside.'

'There might be,' said Lana, without enthusiasm – her heart wasn't in this discussion anymore.

'But it wouldn't be a proper church.'

'As a fellow Christian you would be welcome in any Anglican church.'

'Pah! We haven't been welcome in an English church for nearly five hundred years.' Janet smiled at Lana. 'I like it here. Why move? You get on well with that Emily, don't you? She sounds like a nice lady.'

But her husband wasn't so nice. If the heating had been on during that March cold snap, Janet wouldn't have been rushed to hospital. And to stay in this flat, a convenient distance from her mother's Catholic church, it was Mr Ellis – not his wife – Lana would have to work for.

In Mary's kitchen, the stage was set for Charles's birthday party. The table was covered with a grey tablecloth patterned with brightly coloured cock pheasants – Mary didn't own a white one, such an impractical colour – and laid with intricately patterned, antique solid silver cutlery and mismatched wine glasses. Unlit candles sat in the centre of the table like attentive waiters ready to be summoned for duty.

The hostess was dressed in jeans, a jumper, and scruffy, low-heeled ankle boots, her top half protected by an apron which matched the tablecloth. She was wrapping bacon around prunes left soaking in tea all afternoon.

Charles burst into the kitchen, muttering, 'There's always one, isn't there?'

Mary speared a bacon-wrapped prune with a toothpick then looked up. 'What's wrong, darling?'

He flashed her an uneven smile, making her laugh. Her father had never understood why Charles had captured his daughter's heart; he hadn't valued traits such as kind eyes. But her father did spot Charles's purposefulness and scooped him up from his job at an accountancy firm, finding him a role in the family business. If only Charles were closer to the coalface, like her cousins were, he could be earning the footballer sized packages needed to finance their home. Mary didn't hanker after an Emily-style makeover. Double storey basement digs for a swimming pool and gym, ensuite bathrooms and lifts weren't her dream. It would be enough just to restore the house to its splendour and stop worrying about leaking roofs, draughty windows or putting the heating on.

She felt his arms wind round her waist, and he nuzzled her ear. She leaned back against his solidity; Charles wouldn't be Charles if he was as stressed as Paul, Mark or Barry. She wouldn't swap his contented nature for a fat bonus. The house was a drain, though, and Charles was a dear for putting up with living in her family home, scrabbling to keep the old place ticking. He'd probably be happier somewhere smaller on the outskirts of London, in a house they owned, instead of living as family-trust tenants in Ovington Square.

He nibbled at her ear lobe, saying, 'Tom wants a glass of red. Says he's gone off champagne.'

She shook herself free and fished around for the last prune. 'Must get these in the Aga. Well, he's your friend. More bubbles for me. Is Emily upstairs?'

She picked up the piece of paper which scheduled her evening in minute detail – when to clear soup bowls, put vegetables on, pull the homemade ice cream out of the freezer.

Charles was standing in front of her, a large glass of red wine in one hand. 'No Emily yet. Coming?'

She blew him a kiss. 'Two ticks. Be a dear and look after Emily when she arrives. Keep her glass topped up, she's going through a rough patch.'

He ran a hand through his hair, his eyes twinkling attentively. 'Are you going to elaborate?'

'You know better than to ask.' She waggled her fingers at him, dripping tea back into the bowl. 'Up you go, I'm right behind you.' As he ducked out of the room, she raised her voice, calling after him, 'But when you bring everyone downstairs, the soup is in that saucepan . . .'

He took a step backwards into the kitchen. 'Got it. Anything else?'

'And I've sliced the bread.'

'Right.' He turned to go. 'Am I dismissed now, ma'am?'

She laughed, listening to the gentle clumping of his feet on the uncarpeted stairs. Mary checked the timer – seven minutes – picked up the cold canapés and headed for the stairs.

Outside the closed sitting room door stood a fit looking man wearing a white shirt with contrasting scarlet braces and a matching bow tie, reminding her of a soldier on sentry duty. 'At ease, Paul,' Mary said lightly, kissing him on one cheek. She could smell his cologne, sharp and citrusy. It was a confident scent. *Did Emily find it sexy?*

He took the platter from her and set it down on a small side table. 'Is she coming?'

Mary bit her lip. Where *was* Emily? It was unlike her to be late.

Paul reached for her hand and held it tightly, crushing it. 'She's not answering my calls. Please, I must see her. I need to explain, tell her why . . .' He tailed off.

Mary tugged her hand free. Seeing the pain etched on his face, she took pity. 'She *is* coming.'

Above the bow tie, Paul's face softened, and Mary felt a twitch of alarm, wishing she had told Emily to stay away. She raised a warning finger. 'She's feeling fragile. Don't ambush her.'

'I only want to talk to her,' he said eagerly, leaning closer, bringing the lime and lavender smell with him and grasping her hands. 'How do you think I should handle this?' he asked conspiratorially.

Mary shook herself free. 'Not now, Paul,' she whispered, picking up the canapés and opening the sitting room door. Inside, the guests were gathered on saggy sofas arranged in a horseshoe shape. The heavy curtains were carefully drawn to hide the edges, frayed from decades of sun. There was an oil-fired radiator in the empty fireplace, and a couple of table lamps with battered shades stood on elegant antique side tables, along with several flickering candles that filled the room with the tangy aroma of orange blossoms. A husky voice was singing jazz softly in the background.

Charles had his back to Mary, facing a sofa where Biscuit lounged like a *prima donna*, keeping a droopy eye on proceedings, tail thumping a welcome. Charles looked over his shoulder, and his eyes shone.

'Told you she wouldn't be long. Everyone wanted to come down and help, darling.'

Mary placed the platter on a stained leather-topped footstool and circled the room pecking guests on the cheek. She stopped in front of a man sitting beside Biscuit, stroking the dog's side. He was short and slim – she always thought of him as Emily-sized – and dressed, in complete contrast to Paul, in a grey roll-necked sweater which hung loose over jeans and soft shoes.

'Paul,' she said, 'come and meet Tom Withers. He's a journalist. This is Paul Williams,' she continued when Paul joined them. 'He works in the City, frightfully high-powered.'

'Interesting,' said Tom, taking a gulp of red wine. 'I'm working on an investigative piece about the City.'

'Ah-ah, Tom, don't snoop for stories, else you won't be invited again,' Mary warned.

Paul grimaced. 'What are you looking into, and for which paper?'

'Not sure who will publish it yet. I'm freelance. I'd like to shine a light on some of the more salubrious parts I'm convinced are more common than we laymen realize. Could I come and talk to you?'

Beside her, Paul shot his hostess a worried glance.

'Tom,' Mary explained, 'is widely published, so watch what you say! Now, what's happened to my drink?' she asked, directing the question at Paul.

'I'll fetch you a glass,' he offered.

As she sat down beside Biscuit, a spring squeaked, poking into her bottom. She wriggled sideways to avoid it. 'Now, I don't want serious, Tom . . . I want scandalous gossip.'

Tom smiled. 'All right then. The question on everyone's lips is, will the West stand up to Putin if he invades Ukraine? We should've done it when he marched into Crimea.'

'Not that sort of gossip,' said Mary with a low throaty laugh.

She heard the ring of the doorbell. *Phew, Emily!*

'I'll go,' Paul offered, handing Mary her glass of champagne.

But Mary rose quickly. 'Stay where you are,' she said, picking up the canapés and handing him the tray. 'Would you mind doing the rounds?' She didn't want him following her.

Carrying her flute of champagne, she slipped out of the sitting room, closing the door and muffling the voices to the level of a babbling brook. Her eyes darted to the hallway's faded wallpaper, noticing that there was now an area close to the ceiling where a strip had come loose and was folded over, a flop of beige against the green. She looked up at the gaps in the cornicing, then down to the cracks in the floor tiles; one day she'd get this repaired. Her father would've expected her to find the money; it hadn't looked like this when she was a child.

Walking towards the front door, her boots sounding like clogs clopping on the ancient floor tiles, she decided to warn Emily that Paul was behaving like a jilted teenager. She depressed the latch and pulled it open. 'A quick word . . .'

Icy air hit her, her jaw dropped, and she clenched the stem of her glass. Champagne slopped onto her hand.

'Hi,' said Emily, bending forward for a kiss. 'Sorry we're late.'

'Hello,' said Mark.

Mary stared at her unexpected guest; his face looked drawn, and he was fidgeting with his hair as if unsure of his welcome. Her mind spun through the challenges. *Was there enough food? Where to set the extra place – better if Charles slipped down, she would have her hands full with another problem. How to ensure Emily's two lovers behaved.*

Mary pulled herself together. 'Mark! So kind of you to make a special effort for Charles's birthday.'

'We brought him a little pressie,' said Emily, holding out a flat package and taking off her coat to reveal a short, figure-hugging black dress. Paul would be panting. Mary debated hustling her friend downstairs and covering the outfit with one of her dog-walking raincoats, preferably with the hood up.

Emily pecked her on the cheek, whispering, 'didn't you get my text?'

'Nope,' Mary murmured into her friend's hair. Clamping a smile on her face, she said, 'Come on through. Champagne?'

'Beer for me,' said Mark.

*Good excuse for Charles to sort the table.* Mary hurried to the sitting room, announcing loudly, 'Charles, we have an honoured guest. Look who's come to celebrate your birthday.' She pulled Charles aside, speaking in a voice she suspected might be trembling. 'Darling, Mark would like a beer. Could you bring up the hot canapés too?' Then, with her mouth pressed to his ear, 'And lay another place!'

He winked at her and trotted out. Over by the fireplace, Mary saw Paul's eyes pop open as if he'd been slapped. Biscuit sat up and barked.

She drained her glass of champagne and spun round. 'Mark, come and meet Tom. You two will get on well.' She grabbed Mark's hand. It was stiff, as if frozen, and she could hear him breathing heavily. He glared at Paul and wrenched his hand free, like a dog escaping a slip-leash. Mary's gaze swivelled between her friend's husband and lover. She took hold of Mark's elbow and steered him towards the journalist, keeping one eye on Paul, who was sidling towards his quarry like a fox stalking its prey. 'It's your lucky night tonight, Tom. Mark is one of the most highly regarded M&A specialists in the City. Frightfully high-powered, works on all the big deals.'

By now, Paul had reached Emily, a pleading expression on his face. With her eyes shut and lips puckered, Emily looked close to tears. Beside Mary, Mark's fists were balled and his jaw jutted. Mary's eyes circled her other guests – was she the only person feeling goosebumps at the friction between these two men? She sloshed champagne into a clean glass and rushed across the room to claim her friend.

'Paul, piss off,' snipped Mary in a low voice. She thrust the glass at Emily. 'Drink that,' she ordered. Behind her, she heard Mark's firm voice. 'A word please, Paul.'

'I tried to call you,' said Emily, 'but it went to voicemail. Mark guessed Paul would be here tonight and didn't want him thinking he was hiding. He said it was important to face the enemy with his head held high.'

Once in the military, always in the military, thought Mary, recognizing the phrase she'd heard Emily's ex-army father use so often. Mark's pride? Or was he just wanting to keep an eye on his wife, wondered Mary.

Emily drank her champagne greedily. Mary turned around; Mark was standing inches from his rival with his thumbs hooked inside his belt. 'Leave her alone!' he spat.

As if someone had pressed the mute button, the room fell

silent. Mary glanced at each of the guests. She felt dizzy. How could she rescue this?

'She's capable of making her own decisions,' said Paul with a sly expression.

The husky soloist sang on, reminding Mary of the lyrics from one of her favourite jazz tracks, which described a woman's plan to be reincarnated as a man. Maybe not such a brilliant aspiration. The music stopped, and she could almost hear the candles flickering.

'What a fascinating group of guests!' said Tom, chuckling.

'Anyone for a top-up?' asked Charles, reentering the sitting room. He bounded around, dispensing champagne, seemingly oblivious to the charged atmosphere. Slowly, conversations stuttered back into life. Charles filled Mary's glass last, whispering, 'Panic officially over, darling.'

Mary wasn't so sure.

Twenty minutes later, Mary asked her husband to escort their guests downstairs, then sidled over to her friend, hissing, 'Leave first, I'll delay Paul.' Emily tottered off, banging into the door frame. Oh dear, thought Mary, as a smiling Paul moved towards her friend, a helping arm extended. Mary caught Mark's eye and saw him stiffen. 'Paul, could you give me a hand with the empties, please?' she called lightly, picking up a glass.

As Mary loaded a tray, she gave Paul a pep talk, asking him to remember it was Charles's birthday party. 'I'm relying on you to prevent a scene.'

'I love her,' he said wistfully.

Mary looked him in the eye. 'But she doesn't love you. She loves her husband.'

Carrying the laden tray, Paul stomped down the stairs behind her. The metal Blakey's on the base of his brogues rang on the wooden steps, seeming to echo his melancholy mood.

Opening the kitchen door to the gentle roar of well-lubricated guests, she smiled at Biscuit who was standing, whiskers twitching, an inch away from the Aga door.

Charles had been super-efficient. Steam was rising from the cauldron of soup, the candles were lit, and there was a slice of homemade bread on each side plate. Six chairs were arranged down one side of the table, facing the Aga. Emily and Mark were on that side, Mark next to Charles – well, she did introduce him as the honoured guest, and Charles would've interpreted that as "put him on your right" – and Emily down Mary's end. Charles had moved Emily next to Paul, shielded from Mark's immediate view by the three guests sitting between him and his wife. *This didn't look good.*

She spun round. Paul was grinning. He rubbed the palms of his hands down the sides of his trousers. 'Great seating plan. Cheers.'

'Don't try anything!' she hissed. 'My table's not that long.'

'To the birthday boy,' announced Emily, raising her glass and taking a large gulp.

Mary sat down. Paul refilled Emily's glass.

Tom leaned over the table towards Paul. 'Can I call your assistant and arrange an interview?'

'Bit busy this month,' grunted Paul.

'It's an investigative piece, slow burn. It can wait.'

Mary risked a tiny sip of wine, noticing Emily's glass was already empty. Relax, she told herself, it'll be fine. Tom reached across the table and refilled Emily's glass.

The party stumbled on, drinking their way through the first two courses. Mary got up and started collecting crockery. Charles was hovering beside Emily, a bottle of wine in his hand. Mary tried to catch her husband's eye. He inclined his head at her, then filled Emily's glass. *He's doing what you asked him, but why can't he tell she's drunk?* The plates clattered against each other as Mary dumped them in the sink, then resumed her place at the head of the table.

Paul's face was close to Emily's. Mary heard her friend giggle and kicked Paul on the shin. He winced, and she wondered – *hoped* – briefly if she'd left a bruise. Emily stretched in front of Paul, towards Mary, her eyes glassy. 'Aren't we shinging – oops,' she giggled, sending several blasts of wine-breath Mary's way, 'shinging . . .' She steadied herself and spoke slowly. '. . . shinging . . . happy birthday?'

'Shush,' said Mary, smiling. She got up to take the ice cream out of the freezer.

Charles handed her a bottle of wine. 'No one's heard of dry January!' he said. 'There's a fresh white for you, I'll go and get another red.'

Mary kissed him. 'It's a good party, are you enjoying it . . .?' She heard a crash and spun round. With his back to her, Paul thumped his palms against the table; his side plate jolted up, crashing back down. There was a guffaw of laughter from Tom. Mary's eyes flickered between the two men.

Charles raised his eyes at her, gave a loud tut, and stepped towards Paul, placing a hand on his shoulder, and addressing both Paul and Tom. 'Come on, guys, it's a party . . .'

'In my world, you eat what you kill,' said Paul, shrugging off his host's hand.

There was a cackle of laughter from the other side of the table. 'That's a joke. You guys with your fat corporate salaries and nest egg pensions. You've no idea what it's like being self-employed.'

'Tom,' warned Charles.

'You're not exactly traumatized by the cost of your utility bills, are you? The word banker still makes me think *wanker*,' taunted Tom.

'That's enough, Tom,' Mary said, shooing Charles aside and resuming her place.

Paul's face was scarlet. He picked up his glass and waggled his eyebrows at Tom. 'Some *bankers* might soon be fretting about bills, actually,' he said. 'I just fired a few.' He leaned over and whispered in Mary's ear, 'Including Mark.'

Mary's breath caught in her throat. She gasped, shooting a look down the table towards Paul's victim – he'd been working on his *own* business plan, not a client's. Why hadn't Emily told her when they were at Pilates? Thankfully, the other guests seemed oblivious to Tom and Paul's exchange and were talking about Ukraine. 'Paul, you didn't . . .!' she muttered.

Paul's expression was smug. The question circling Mary's mind was his motive – was the sacking revenge for being scorned by Emily?

Tom wriggled in his chair, causing the legs to scratch against the floor. 'Who got the chop, Paul? Anyone we know?' he probed, before giving Mary a hard look. 'Tell me, Mary, you clearly know . . . Who did Paul let go?'

She felt her cheeks flush, shook herself, and said brightly, 'Who needs a top-up?'

Tom wasn't deflected. 'Come on, big boy, tell us who you fired? Must be someone we know, or why mention it?'

Don't do it, Mary willed, shaking her head at Paul. Don't fall into this trap. Tom's smile was wily, reminding her of childhood games of Monopoly, landing on Mayfair, and her father gleefully demanding rent.

There was a screeching sound; Mary looked left. Emily had nudged her chair backwards, and was standing, wobbling. She started singing, 'Happy birfday to you . . .' Soon Paul's slurred voice joined in, and he too rose. One by one, the other guests stood up. *'Happy birthday, dear Charles . . .'*

Mark was last to rise, moving round to Charles's empty place at the foot of the table.

The guests sang on: *'Happy birthday to . . .'*

Mary saw Paul trace a finger down Emily's bare arm. Above the singing, Mark shouted, 'Get your fucking hands off my wife.'

The singing petered out. Paul spoke above the dying notes. 'Just being friendly. She doesn't mind, do you, Ems?'

The other guests studied their hands, their food, each other, anywhere but at Mark, Emily, or Paul.

'Emily, we're going home,' spat Mark. 'NOW!'

Emily lowered her head. Silence. Mary dredged her mind for finishing school tips on how to deal with awkward situations. Mark stalked out, thundering up the stairs. Seconds later, the front door banged.

Mary glowered at Tom; was he intrigued? Did she need to protect her friend from Tom's vicious pen? Plenty of people had affairs, and employees got fired every day of the week. Nothing to see here. Except, how many bosses fired their mistress's husband?

Live-in housekeepers were in demand. Especially those with excellent references, and Lana was certain Emily would give her a glowing report. Lana was sitting in the Kew Gardens Conservatory – the shape of which always reminded her of a beached submarine – scrutinizing the "situations vacant" section of *The Lady* magazine's website. There were columns of adverts. She celebrated her discovery by tearing the wrapper off a bar of chocolate. Nibbling her treat, she listened to the rain hammering on the glass roof, but the sound failed to dent her optimism. Lana ate the whole bar, then wiped her sticky fingers with a tissue, picked up her phone, and scrolled through the adverts.

Outside the capital, there were titled families who employed "other staff", seeking housekeepers to join their team, which made Lana think of Carson in *Downton Abbey*. All these positions came with cottages but were in the country, and most involved Sunday work, another of her mother's red flags. The Sabbath was reserved for God. Lana may have wriggled out of the services which commandeered her teenage Sundays, but her mother's faith was still omnipresent in Lana's life.

It hadn't always been.

Initially, childhood Sundays involved family outings. There was one engraved on her memory for all the wrong reasons. It had started so well, a magical day at the beach when her father took her swimming, holding her around the middle while she thrashed her little legs about, tossing her up, catching her as she fell squealing, and dipping her toes into the icy waves. Later he'd bought ice creams and split his chocolate flake in two, giving half each to his ladies. In the car on the way home, Lana fell asleep and woke up cuddled in her father's arms. She kept her eyes closed, inhaling his spicy aftershave; it was so comfortable listening to his heavy breathing as he climbed the stairs to her bedroom. He removed her shoes and lay her under the blankets, fully clothed, tucking her toys around her, and she was soon asleep again, dreaming of chocolate cake.

She remembered waking, and feeling frightened, but not knowing why. She could hear shouting. It was coming from downstairs. She crept out of her room, baby comforter tucked under her armpit, and sat shaking on the top step, looking at the brown carpet covered in a pattern of orange swirls, sucking her thumb, the comforter doing overtime. Suddenly, the door below burst open, and her father stormed out. His eyes shot upwards, hard dots, but then he smiled and jogged upwards, the stairs creaking with each step, and sat down beside her.

'I thought you'd stopped that,' he said, removing her thumb.

'Don't worry, Lana.' She stared at the face she loved, huge eyebrows above gentle eyes. 'I will always take care of you.'

And he had. Until . . . he wasn't there to look after her anymore.

After that day, Janet started leaving the house each Sunday morning, smartly dressed, wearing a sombre expression, and Sundays became "special time with daddy". The September Lana started secondary school, Sundays took a turn for the worse; her father told her she was to start accompanying her mother to church. Roast dinners with a fizzy drink in a smoky pub were replaced by cups of tea and bourbon biscuits – Janet's new commitments meant she didn't have time to cook on a Sunday. The smell of her father's aftershave was replaced by that of incense, his jokes by homilies, prayers and hymns. After a couple of years, Lana begged her father to let her spend Sundays with him again. 'When you are eighteen, you can choose your own path,' he said. 'It'll all turn out fine.'

It was a false prophecy. When Lana went to college and started working evenings and Saturdays in a café, she regained control of her Sundays, but her life was still ruled by the Scriptures – Janet deducted 10 per cent from Lana's wages for the Church. That amount doubled after her father's extended business trip. Janet had no income of her own; she'd never been a burden on the state, always contributed to her Church family, and was determined not to let a bad Catholic – meaning Lana's father – affect her equilibrium. So, Lana agreed to meet her mother's church donations as well as continuing her own. She'd been doing that now for almost thirty years.

Lana scanned the adverts for positions in London. There were agencies promoting glamorous-sounding jobs working for professional couples, offering the opportunity to travel – that wouldn't suit Janet – nor would the idea of North London or Wimbledon. No one wanted a live-in housekeeper in Knightsbridge.

She emailed a couple of the agencies – they wouldn't advertise every job, and there must be vacancies in Central London. There had to be.

# Three

To Gwen, the best thing about her home was that it was owned by her son, not the council or an unresponsive landlord. The house was in Chalkwell, not too far from Colchester, where Gwen had spent most of her adult life in a tiny bungalow with poor insulation and damp walls.

Standing in her front room, Gwen twitched the net curtain aside. Mark was coming alone today – apparently Emily was busy, and Alex was in Devon. Her Mark had done so well. Unlike her, he was still married, with stories of exotic holidays, not day trips to Chalkwell. It was comforting to think her son was living his life to the full. Despite his background, she'd propelled him into a better life than her own. A happy one.

She dropped the curtain. She'd check the tea tray. In the kitchen she poked out a finger, counted the Welsh cakes, then opened the biscuit tin, releasing a sweet smell that made her mouth salivate and promptly replaced the lid. Gwen patted her girth, loosened the belt on her brown-checked housecoat and turned away to prevent her lingering fingers from jumping the gun.

The doorbell chimed. She turned on the gas underneath the old-fashioned metal kettle, gave the tea tray a quick glance as if telling it to prepare for action, and bustled down the corridor, limping a little from her arthritic hip, her little corgi, Romeo, yapping at her heels.

'Hello, love. Good journey?' asked Gwen. 'Proper nobbling it is out there. Get yourself inside.'

Mark slipped past her. She closed the door, bending to replace a long, scarlet crocheted dog that guarded the entrance against chilly gusts of sea wind.

'Mum, it's no warmer in here. Turn the blinking thermostat up.'

'Waste not, want not. I've plenty of jumpers and a good thick pair of tights.' She grinned at her son. 'Layers, that's what you need to keep you warm, boyo – layers.'

They'd had the same conversation last Sunday, and they would probably have it next Sunday too. She lived for these visits. He couldn't make every Sunday, not with his high-powered job and busy social life, but he made most and often stayed for lunch, although sadly not today.

'I pay the bills!' he said. 'You don't need to be cold.'

She didn't reply, watching him remove his coat, while holding a wooden hanger in one hand, her other extended for the garment. She stroked the fabric: cashmere, her son wore such expensive clothes.

'Come on in, I'll get the tray,' she said, wheezing off down the corridor, listening to the uplifting sound of her son's footsteps drumming on the carpet behind her. The kettle was singing. She turned off the gas and poured water onto the tea bags, then picked up the tray. 'So, how's work? How's that lovely wife? What's Alex doing with himself?'

'Let me carry that, Mum,' said Mark, taking the tray from her. 'Front room?'

He led the way, setting down the tray on a glass-topped table. Gwen poured tea and pushed the plate of Welsh cakes his way. 'Take two, love. I know you can't get them at home.' *He might be happily married, but Emily didn't even cook, let alone bake!*

Grasping one in her hand, she took a bite, then dropped a chunk onto the floor for Romeo.

Mark leaned forward and folded his arms across his knees. 'Mum, I've got something to tell you.'

She peered across at him. 'What's that, boyo?'

'I've decided to set up on my own.'

She whistled. 'Your own bank?'

He blew on his tea. 'Not exactly.'

'But you work at a bank.'

'Yes, but I don't need to.'

She tilted her head to one side. 'So, you're changing career?'

'Sort of. I'm setting up a boutique,' he said brightly.

She screwed up her face – this sounded peculiar. 'Like a shop?'

'Nothing like a shop,' he said, pushing a whole Welsh cake into his mouth. He chewed for a moment, then said, 'That's the whole point. I'll just be selling my advice. Not trying to flog other products, some of which, to be honest, we aren't very good at.'

'Well, as long as it's what you want. Just be happy, that's all I ask of you. Be happy.'

He slurped his tea, reaching for another Welsh cake. 'I will be,' he mumbled around the biscuit. 'The thing is, I'm going to be flat out. I won't be able to visit you as often.'

He was avoiding something; he couldn't hide it from her, something was wrong. But if he didn't want to talk about it, she wouldn't probe. 'I'll miss you. Just come when you can spare the time, but keep in touch, eh? Don't be a stranger.'

He grunted.

'And how's young Alex?' she asked.

'Hiding in Devon. Surfing. Wasting his time and my money,' said Mark.

No change there, thought Gwen. Why did Mark have such a

fractious relationship with his only child, especially when she and her son enjoyed such a strong bond. Not for the first time, she questioned if it was the lack of a father figure in Mark's upbringing which was the root cause of Alex and Mark's bickering. The strange thing was, both Mark and Alex were physically so similar, and just like her ex-husband. If Steve had been part of Mark's life for longer, would Mark have learned how to interact with his own son? Was the breakdown in Gwen's marriage responsible for the tense relationship between her son and grandson? Was she to blame?

The doorbell chimed once more. Gwen looked at her watch and heaved herself upright, a jolt of pain shooting through her hip. 'That'll be Deidre. You know she likes to pop round when you're here, she's always had a soft spot for you! Drink your tea. I'll be there now in a minute, mind.'

Gwen opened the door to a tall lean lady with a long face, who rushed inside bringing the familiar scent of lily of the valley with her. Deidre, Gwen's friend of over forty years.

'Ooh it's horrid out there!' panted Deidre. 'Wasn't raining when I left home. I shan't stay long, but I wanted to ask Mark's advice about that bit of money my uncle left me.'

'Mind how you go now, Deidre. He's in a funny sort of mood. He's a bit preoccupied with work.'

'Isn't he always? You got a pot on the go, girl?' she asked, squeezing droplets of water from her ponytail of grey hair. 'I'm gasping for a cuppa.'

Gwen thought about what her son had just told her. He wouldn't want it kept secret; Mark knew she always shared his triumphs with Deidre. 'Says he wants to start running his own bank,' she said, with a little chuckle.

'His own bank?' said Deidre, hanging her limp ponytail over one shoulder. 'Well, I never. Whatever next, eh?'

'As long as he's happy.'

Deidre gave her a penetrating look. 'Take care of your own happiness, Gwen, let Mark take care of his.'

When the women walked in, Mark got up, saying, 'Can you tell Mum to turn the damn heating up – it's January! I don't want her sitting in the cold with that hip of hers.'

'Your mother sets her own thermostat. She doesn't like waste.'

'I pay the bills, Deidre,' said Mark.

'No, you don't. She pays them, she doesn't touch the money you send her,' said Deidre. Gwen winced; Deidre could be a bit outspoken if challenged. Was Mark going to ask how she could afford such a big house on a state pension? Deidre winked at Gwen, and she relaxed; her friend wouldn't let slip that Gwen still worked for a few of her regulars. She didn't do much anymore, just ironing and polishing silver for the major, and she enjoyed beeswaxing the antiques at the Old Rectory, but she didn't think Mark would be pleased if he knew.

The two women faced Mark, and Gwen thought it looked a little like they were interviewing him. 'So, what's this about you setting up a bank? What's it called?' asked Deidre. Gwen saw her son's face stiffen. Why hadn't he asked her to keep shtum if it was a secret? 'Can your mum and I move our accounts? Will you have a branch in Colchester, with someone we can talk to?'

'It's not a bank, Deidre, it's a boutique. Not a shop,' Gwen added, passing her friend a cup of tea.

'That's right, Mum,' said Mark. 'I'm calling the business Ovington Advisory.'

Whatever he wanted to call it, Gwen could tell there was something troubling her son. If he would not come to Essex, she would have to call him; when he was ready, he would tell her what was wrong.

*

With her hands on her hips, Lana announced to the empty Ovington Square dining room, 'I'm not working in this mess.' Her temples were throbbing; she hoped this wasn't the start of a migraine. From the head of the table, his face hidden behind a screen, came Mr Ellis's voice, 'Good morning, Svetlana. How was your weekend?'

Lana closed her eyes, telling herself there were no flashing lights dancing in her head, and that until she secured another position, she must become Mr Ellis's temporary assistant. Maybe if she kept emphasizing the word temporary it would sound better.

What she was currently determined to ensure was temporary was the chaos in the dining room. Unopened boxes were balanced on chairs or dumped on the floor, the table was strewn with books, cartons of pens, and pads of paper. There was a peculiar dark grey flattish object – resembling a mini starship – with a protruding wire snaking through the mess and disappearing underneath the sideboard, forming a permanent trip hazard on the right-hand side of the room between her and the new boss. Not that she would often venture to his end of the table.

Where Emily normally sat was a pile of papers, the top one headed:

Svetlana task list

Sitting next to which was a slim rose-gold coloured laptop.

She picked up a mug and, choosing the less encumbered side of the table, dumped it by the boss, noticing how, in contrast to her elasticated trousers and sweatshirt, he was wearing a suit and tie.

She stalked back and picked up her task list. Her thoughts strayed. Would Emily feed and walk the dogs? And what about the housework? Emily had mastered the skill of swilling out a mug and popping it in the dishwasher, and frequently rinsed and reused the same mug, but just like every other winter Monday morning, Svetlana had turned on the kitchen lights when she arrived and been greeted by the remains of Mr Ellis's weekend snacks.

She heard a snapping noise and looked up. Mr Ellis's laptop was shut. 'I've spoken to Anne,' he said. 'She was my PA for ten years, and she's happy to help you. I've written her number on your task list. Until she's reassigned, she's not busy.'

Lucky her, thought Lana, scanning her list. She got no further than item one before her brow furrowed. *Set up printer*, words that brought back memories of college days, of the technical sessions, and a classroom of gabbling teenagers struggling to match their word processors to the printer – all those language options – and attempting to pair to the right operating system. No wonder this was on her list. There would be someone at the bank who did everything like that for Anne; her new helpmate wouldn't solve this one.

She read on:

Set up email addresses for new business. Mark@Ovingtonadvisory. Try for dot com.

There was a second suggested email address for herself. She'd start with that one; last year she'd had to change her own email address after downloading a virus and had suceeded. Her eyes danced down her list. She was tasked with calling important sounding people and arranging lunches. Where? *Ask Anne!* Further down the page, she hit a roadblock that made setting up the printer look attractive:

Call Magic Circle for quotes to act in dismissal claim.

A picture of Harry Potter and his wand floated into her mind. Would Anne be able to help with that one?

She looked over the top of the page at Mr Ellis, at the taut expression on his face. 'Any questions?' he asked in a tone that prevented her from asking any.

'You need to tidy up. I won't work in this mess,' she grunted, thinking Anne must be a saint to have worked for this slob. His mouth opened, and there was the faintest gasp.

'Just this once, I'll straighten things, then you must keep it neat,' she instructed, adding Anne's phone number to her contacts list.

A hint of a smile lightened her boss's expression. 'We're going to be a team,' he said. 'Chill a little, eh?'

A phone rang, and he snatched it up. Lana left, shutting the door behind her and muttering to herself, 'Chill a bit . . . says the man enthroned at the head of the table.' She stomped down to the kitchen. Emily was sitting at the breakfast bar, dressed in a baggy yoga outfit, filing a nail, and watching the TV where the presenter was delivering the weather forecast. It sounded grim – rain, lots of it. But wet and warm was better for Janet than dry and chilly. Lana gathered up the mugs scattered around the work surfaces, clattering them against each other and stalked into the pantry. Something had to give – Mr Ellis's list would take all week; she wasn't going to become a full-time PA on top of all the housekeeping. She strode back to the kitchen, picked up a cloth and attacked the water stains on the counter, vowing to find a new job immediately. Anywhere!

Emily was recounting her standard Monday agenda of a dog walk with her friend Mary – if the rain stopped – followed by yoga and lunch at the gym. Lana was never expected to cook lunch for Emily on a Monday, there was too much housework. If Mr Ellis wanted lunch, he would be making it himself.

'How's it going?' asked Emily.

Lana put down her polishing cloth and scowled.

'Lean on Anne,' suggested Emily, smiling and getting up. 'How's Janet? I hope she's warm enough, I don't want her rushed to hospital again.'

Lana's mind flooded with the horror of last March, opening the door, and finding Janet with her coat on, huddled over the stove, shaking. She'd called an ambulance and spent that night in the emergency department of the Chelsea and Westminster hospital. Lana used the incident as a prompt to get Mr Ellis to change his mind about her contributing to the heating cost, but the reply – delivered with some sugarcoating by Emily – was a firm no.

'I've bought a fan heater,' admitted Lana, trying to dispel a sudden image of a spinning meter.

'I'll offer to take your reading,' suggested Emily with a wink. She fiddled with a lock of hair. 'Look, I must warn you. He's a bit out of sorts and . . . and . . .' Emily stammered to a stop, lowered her gaze, and added, 'I'm sorry to add to your load, but just for now, he's sleeping in his dressing room. We're working through a few issues.'

Lana stared at Emily, who blushed under her gaze. *So, I'm to pretend I don't know about the affair?*

'Shall I pop the dishwasher on once I've stowed my things?' suggested Emily. Brilliant, very flexible, thought Lana. That would save her thirty seconds.

Back in the dining room, there was a note lying on her laptop: "*Gone out. There's a meeting at two thirty. You're joining.*" She crumpled it up and tossed it in the bin, then checked her phone for emails. Two recruitment agencies had replied. Neither had any suitable positions on their books but encouraged her to submit her resume; they would let her know if a job came up. She didn't like the use of the word *if* – why hadn't they said *when*? She might have to make this work . . . temporarily.

The printer box loomed like a like a caged lion, ready to attack. She'd have a go while the boss wasn't watching. Using scissors, she slit open the box, pulling out the protective chunks of cardboard, and frowned. There was an instruction leaflet entitled: *"Plug and Play"*. Haha, that innocent sounding phrase didn't fool her.

She heard the familiar high-pitched sound of an opera singer – the Ellis's distinctive doorbell – and went to answer it. In the corridor, Emily dashed past, saying, 'I'll get that!' Over Emily's head, Lana saw a young woman holding a bouquet and a turquoise Fortnum & Mason bag. 'Delivery for Emily Ellis,' said the woman, checking her device. There was a rustling noise, and Emily staggered backwards, clutching her bounty.

'Put those in water, please,' Emily said to Lana, tearing the delivery card from the cellophane wrapper. 'All in one vase, in my bathroom.'

'Bathroom?' quizzed Lana, inhaling the sugary scent of hyacinths and white oriental lilies. *How much did a bouquet this size cost?*

'Yes. Quickly, please, before Mark gets home.'

Lana had heard Emily's tales of cardio tennis sessions; that morning, she invented her own workout – cardio housekeeping. She bustled up the stairs, tidied the master bedroom in a fraction of the time she normally took, accelerated out and down to the pantry with a bundle of washing stuffed in a pillowcase stained with lipstick – *this would have to stop, she wouldn't have time for Monday linen changes*. She raced back up to the dressing room, picking her way around an obstacle course of shoes, belts and jumpers, collecting dirty socks and boxer shorts, and tucking them inside a handmade shirt. There was a shower of biscuit crumbs on the carpet by the bedside table. She ran downstairs, laundry in hand, for the handheld vacuum cleaner. Lana heard a sharp yap. The glass door had two snouts pressed up against it. The rain had only recently stopped. Had they been walked yet?

By two o'clock, the dogs had been walked and the house was looking shipshape. The vacuum cleaner was humming, Lana's sweatshirt was tied round her waist by the arms, and with the cord in one hand – as if holding up a long dress – she was moving round the sitting room in an imaginary dance, plotting how to maximize space for this year's tomatoes. Could she squeeze in another growbag if she ran the bags sideways?

The room fell silent. She swung around. Mr Ellis was standing by the socket, the plug in his hand. She glared at him.

'Is the printer working?'

'Yes,' she said curtly. *If you'd realized how easy it was, you could have done it yourself over the weekend, you selfish brute.* She'd followed the instructions and got Emily to tap in Mr Ellis's computer password. 'And the email addresses work. I sent a test from my phone.'

'Good. What about the quotes? Who have you called so far?'

'I must finish in here . . .' Lana said, trying not to sound defensive. She wasn't admitting she had no idea how to get in touch with the magicians.

'You haven't called anyone?'

'I haven't been in since Thursday . . . and there's an extra bedroom to clean now . . .' she said forcefully.

He ran a hand over his face. 'It's not your fault,' he muttered. 'I knew this was a bad idea. Have you spoken to Anne?' Lana hadn't. When Anne had offered to help, Lana suspected she was expecting envisaged tips on sandwich preferences and how the boss liked his coffee, not the basics of the job. Lana had the qualifications but had never tested them.

He was scowling. She must buy time until she found a new job. 'Why don't I make you a sandwich?'

He spoke gently. 'That would be kind.'

She had to grasp this reprieve; it might take weeks to find a new position. She would message Anne as soon as the sandwich was ready.

The afternoon meeting was attended by a man who didn't introduce himself. He was shorter than her boss, dressed in the same uniform of dark suit, white shirt, and coordinating tie, with light-brown hair and stubble on his cheeks. Lana was given a copy of the agenda, but she felt as relevant as the carafe of coffee. She was present, with a purpose – to take notes – but wasn't invited to speak. Which was a godsend: she didn't understand a word of what she wrote, but hopefully Anne would. Earlier, the former PA had replied promptly to Lana's message: *Been waiting for your call. Let's meet tonight; can you come here?* Lana would have caught a train to Scotland, let alone Canary Wharf.

Both men spoke confidently. This was their world – as natural to them as herding sheep was to a collie dog.

'The bank's made a derisory offer, Mark: after tax, you'll only get £60k,' said the stranger. *Sixty thousand pounds, after tax, derisory! It was a huge sum of money*. 'This isn't my area, but no harm seeing if there's a bit more in the tank.'

Mr Ellis gave a tight laugh. 'I'm not accepting that. I'll see the bastard in court. I'm sure I've got a case for unfair dismissal.'

The guest raised a warning finger. 'Be careful. Take advice, but I think you'll find the comp for unfair dismissal is capped.'

'Svetlana is on it. We'll hire someone top-notch. What about the non-compete clause in my contract? I'm setting up on my own, I can't twiddle my thumbs for six months.'

'It's probably unenforceable, and the bank knows it.'

'Unlikely to stop them threatening me with an injunction.'

'The courts recognize you would've been forced to sign a standard employment contract. And they dismissed you – it's unfair for them to be able to stop you working for such a long time. But don't get revenge by nicking existing mandates.'

This time, Mr Ellis laughed properly. 'That would be fun, but no, I have a much better plan for revenge.'

*Should she minute that?*

The guest started talking about a shelf company, then PI insurance. She screwed up her face. *Did he say a clean reference, and who was that from?* She scribbled fast; she'd google later. Mr Ellis was being advised to find someone to deal with compliance. She added another question mark. Lana shook her hand, then gave it a quick massage. Now they were discussing website design. Did the guest know anyone he could recommend? He didn't, but he threw out another acronym. She picked up her pen, scribbling down GDPR.

'Svetlana can deal with that,' said Mr Ellis.

Her task list was growing, but the men might as well have been speaking Mandarin. Lana's mantra of *temporary* wasn't dislodging a gathering sense of gloom – this job would be more temporary than she needed unless she could decipher her role. She scanned her notes; tonight's meeting with Anne would be a long session.

She thought she was going to get away with it, but shortly before five o'clock Mr Ellis asked the question Lana couldn't answer, the one she was sure would get her fired. She was printing off her typewritten notes, allowing the hum of the machine to cast her mind back thirty years to when that sound was familiar.

'When do you expect the quotes?' he asked.

She closed her eyes, fingering the printed pages, trying to force the smoothness of the paper to soothe her thoughts. Temporary . . . this is temporary, she told herself.

'You haven't called anyone, have you?'

'No.'

'Come on then,' he said in a resigned voice. 'I'll make the first call. You can listen, then make the others. How's that sound?'

She pulled up a chair next to his and listened. He asked to speak to a partner who specialized in employment law. He was put through to an assistant, confirming that he wanted a quote for a "new matter". He needed advice on suing his former employer. Hearing his authoritative voice, Lana was surprised by the tingle of respect that shot through her.

'My assistant Svetlana will be dealing with this,' he said, giving out Lana's phone number before ending the call. He spoke to Lana kindly, 'I need to concentrate on setting up the business. There's a tonne of stuff to do, and you can't do much of it because you don't understand the business yet. But you can make the other calls, just copy what I said. Once you've got the quotes, we'll choose together. I'll help brief them, but I'm relying on you to run this project.'

The room fell silent. His eyebrows crunched together. She willed herself to ask who else she should call, but her mouth stayed clamped shut, like a terrier with its jaws around a slipper.

Mr Ellis scrunched up his face. 'We'll give it a code name. Let's call it . . .' – he smiled at her, his eyes shining – 'Project Revenge . . . and here's the deal,' he said, running a hand over his jawline. 'I'm going to incentivize you. I'll pay you a percentage. I'll draw up a contract so that it's all documented. Do whatever it takes, spend whatever . . . just wipe that smile off Paul's face. Let's win.'

Another item chalked onto Lana's to-do list. A percentage of his compensation sounded great, but she was a housekeeper, how was she going to win against a major investment bank?

# Four

As Lana caught the Jubilee line from Green Park, she didn't realize she was en route to a London as different to her familiar surroundings of Knightsbridge as her new role was to her old. She was meeting Anne at a bar in Canary Wharf called The Parlour. Given the name, Lana imagined a small pub with dimmed lights, a dark wood interior, and tiny tables; but Lana had never been to Canary Wharf.

Alighting into the sleek modernity of the Canary Wharf tube station, her eyes widened. She'd seen pictures of these towering office blocks, but assumed they were tightly knit, like the buildings in Central London. There was so much empty space – the pavements were wider than her flat, vast areas carved out for nothingness, where she imagined office workers could sit and eat lunch or just take in the view, like a compact Hyde Park. For several minutes, she stood in a bewildered fug, gawking at her surroundings. She heard a jet engine and looked up, her eyes skimming the sides of the office buildings, up, up, up – they were so much taller than in the West End – eventually catching sight of the plane streaking through the sky.

After following Anne's directions to the bar, she pulled open the glass door and hesitated in the doorway, her stomach churning. She didn't belong here. The Parlour was a large open-plan room with banks of lights shining from the ceiling, steel supports, and marble floors. The air inside pulsated with music. She'd expected it to be busy, but there was a vibrancy, almost as if the pulse of the financial markets had somehow been recreated in entertainment form. The customers oozed a sense of a shared bond: they were part of the Canary Wharf working tribe. The room, and everyone in it, screamed success. In a West End pub, she'd have expected a murmur of voices; here she heard a roar. It was like one big party. Groups of men had their sleeves rolled up, pint glasses in hand, and women in sharply-cut dark suits were laughing, and waving glasses of wine so large Lana could imagine arranging flowers in them. She had a flashback to arranging that bouquet in the master bathroom, quickly, keeping a furtive eye out for Mr Ellis. She didn't like being part of the duplicity and she certainly didn't want to be caught.

Lana looked around the spacious, light-filled room. She had spent so long studying the picture Anne messaged her, she could've picked her out in an identity parade. Anne wasn't here. But then Anne was used to meeting up for after-work drinks, and her job wasn't in peril. Anne wouldn't be twenty minutes early. Lana spotted an empty table, rushed over, unzipping her coat and tossing it onto one chair while sitting in another. She listened to the beat of unfamiliar music and the cackles of laughter, imagining herself belonging here – is this what her life could've been like?

In the final few weeks of her secretarial course, Lana's focus had been on her upcoming exams, dreaming of forging a life away from the constrictions of her mother's devotion to the Church. With her mind preoccupied, Lana hadn't registered which day her father was due home from his business trip. Back then, home was a small two bedroomed terraced house on the outskirts of Bristol, where the lives of the occupants were organized to fit around Janet's Church commitments. No change there, thought Lana; she could only meet Anne tonight because her mother was at choir practice and had left Lana's dinner in the oven.

Thirty years ago, as usual, she'd gone straight home from college, her thoughts on applying for a job she'd seen advertised in London. At 5.15 p.m. promptly she had rung the doorbell, since she wasn't allowed her own key, and Janet answered, her face so wet with tears that she might have just got out of the shower. Lana remembered the smell of fish clogging the entrance hall – so it must have been a Friday. Her mother gave a long, drawn-out sniff.

'Your father isn't coming home.'

Initially, Lana's spirits rose. Like a curtain pulled on a lightning storm, her father's absence allowed peace to settle in the Bristol house; no raised voices, no sharp words, and she wasn't in a hurry to alter that. But Lana didn't realize her father wasn't just delayed, nor how significantly his absence would affect her life. She soon discovered.

Janet retreated into religion, finding solace through her faith, leaving Lana to resolve practicalities. Her father had given notice on the rented Bristol house, forcing Lana to scramble to find additional work and somewhere affordable for them to live. She supplemented her café income with ad hoc cleaning jobs, discovering the physicality of the work provided a channel for her own hurt. Her father hadn't even left a note explaining why he'd left. She missed him terribly and scoured the post every day for three months. Nothing.

Bizarrely, it was Janet's faith that indirectly came to their rescue. The priest knew of a rich couple looking for a live-in housekeeper on the other side of Bristol. Lana swapped six jobs – where each employer expected her to perform six hours of work in just four – to care for a beautiful six bedroomed house where she was trusted to ensure boilers were serviced, the linen rotated and meals cooked, rather than simply scrub bathrooms and mop floors. She and her mother lived in the couple's attic flat until the house was sold ten years later, when they moved to London to another position found by Janet.

A cheerful voice calling, 'Svetlana', interrupted Lana's thoughts, making her sit upright.

So, this was Anne. She looked a little like a younger version of Emily. She had long ash-blonde hair and wore a short, red tartan skirt, white blouse and thick black tights. Lana glanced down at her own outfit. She should've changed; she couldn't have looked more out of place if she'd come in fancy dress.

'It's Lana.'

'That's pretty. I expected you to have an accent.'

'My grandfather was Polish. A fighter pilot in the Battle of Britain. He married an English girl. He chose my name.'

'Wow. Do you speak any Polish?'

'Not a word.'

It was Anne's local, and she insisted on buying the drinks. 'Got a bottle,' she said, plonking down a plastic wine bucket and two glasses. 'Cheaper in the long run.' She sloshed white wine into both glasses, raised hers, and said, 'Cheers. So, how's it going? I miss him already and he's only been gone a week. How can I help? Nothing I don't know about that man.'

What on earth did this cheerful lady miss about Mr Ellis? Lana took a sip of wine. Were they having an affair? Was that why he wanted Anne working for him? Convenient, having your mistress working in your home office.

Lana laughed. 'How long have you got?'

'That bad, huh? Take a tip from me – keep his diary full, and make sure he has coffee. He can be a bit snappy if he's bored or craving caffeine.'

Deciding she liked Anne, Lana confessed, 'I'm out of my depth. I went to secretarial college but . . .' she paused, peering into her glass.

'But what? Life can deal us a bum card sometimes. What happened?'

Lana clicked her tongue. 'How true! I had to get a job which came with accommodation. I'm a housekeeper . . . but then Mr Ellis will have told you that.'

Anne shook her head. 'No. He just said you didn't have as much experience as me and asked me to help you.' Anne reached a hand across the table, tapping Lana gently on the arm. 'A lot of this job is about planning, multi-tasking, and I'm sure you've got heaps of experience of that from housekeeping. You'll be fine. Now, what's top of your worry list?'

'How do I contact the Magic Circle?' Lana blurted out. Anne took a swig of wine, cackling round the side of the glass. 'Seriously, I have to get a quote from them,' said Lana.

Anne swallowed a mouthful of wine. 'It's a nickname for the top London law firms. I can give you a list and telephone numbers. What else?'

'He might've told me!'

'He wasn't trying to catch you out. He's a very smart man and he assumes everyone else is as smart as him. Come on, what else?'

Lana pulled a piece of paper out of her handbag. 'I made a list.' Anne got up and pushed her chair round, so the two women were sitting side by side.

Half an hour later, a combination of wine, discovering that Anne had grown up in Bristol like herself, and Anne rattling out explanations in her reassuring voice was making Lana believe she was more than up to this job.

'I never do anything like this after work,' said Lana.

'What would you normally do on a Monday night?'

'Bit of gardening?'

'In January? Kenny and I - that's my husband - we can't seem to grow anything.' A wistful look came over Anne's face. 'Well, we can't keep anything alive for long.'

'I could help. Everything's easy if you know what you're doing.'

Anne changed the subject. 'Tell me, where's he going? I don't mind switching banks.'

'He's not going anywhere. He's setting up on his own.'

'Wow, that's brave. But that's Mark. He'll make a go of it.'

Tuesday morning started badly. Lana arrived early, cleaned the kitchen, and was slicing Emily's breakfast fruit when she walked in, chattering about her packed schedule. The fridge purred as Emily opened the door. She nudged it shut with her bottom, pulling the lid off a carton of yoghurt. 'Glad I've caught you,' she said, whisking the freshly cut fruit off Lana and spooning yoghurt over it. 'A few errands, please. I'm jolly busy this week.'

The tasks piled up like damp days in summer. Could she bake a chocolate cake for a fundraiser, order more dog food, and take Tosca to the vets to have her nails clipped? The appointment was at noon, so Lana could do it during her lunch break. Lana's stomach growled. She'd skipped breakfast – when would she have time to eat? The Ellises were taking advantage of her.

'Have you agreed all of this with your husband?'

Emily, head down and rummaging in her purse, didn't seem to have heard the question. 'I tried to collect the dry cleaning for you,' she said, smiling brightly at Lana, 'but it wasn't ready. I don't need anything before Friday evening.' She handed over the receipt.

*Vissi d'arte* started playing upstairs, the soprano's voice reaching the high notes effortlessly. Emily's spoon clattered against the plate. 'Leave that to me,' she offered, dashing out.

When Lana walked back into the dining room, Mr Ellis didn't look up. He grunted, 'You're a bit late.'

'Emily had a few errands for me.'

'Emily can run her own errands. Your priorities are in here now,' he mumbled.

'Who's going to tell Emily?' she demanded.

He looked up and pointed at the mug in her hand. 'That for me?'

'No,' she replied, taking a noisy slurp.

'Where's mine?'

'Where's mine . . . please,' said Lana.

His eyes widened in shock, and inwardly Lana groaned, thinking she must rein in her temper. Then he started laughing. Sighing, he said, 'Give Emily time to adjust. I'm off to meet a website designer, then I've got a lunch meeting, so I'll see you about three o'clock.'

'See you at three, Mr Ellis,' she replied neutrally; she really must try not to resent this man so much.

Shortly after three, the front door slammed, and Lana heard her boss talking in the hallway. 'I think we've found the website designer. How did you get on?' he asked, walking in, removing his jacket and arranging it on the back of a chair. 'Got those quotes?'

Lana pushed her glasses firmly against her face. She had called all the lawyers while making Emily's cake. 'I called them. They won't be quoting.'

'Why not?'

'They're conflicted.'

It was another term Lana hadn't heard before. The first lawyer to return her call had explained, couching it in legalese that Lana translated into money – the firm wouldn't earn much from

Mr Ellis's case and risked losing lucrative business from the bank. The response was the same from all the "Magic Circle" firms.

Her boss tutted. 'My fault. I should've guessed. We're on the outside now. We need a mid-sized law firm, someone too small for the bank to instruct, but who knows how the City works. Let me think . . . While I do that, take a squint at this. It's the contract to incentivize you on Project Revenge.'

She waved a hand dismissively. 'I don't need that.'

'Lana, the days of "my word is my bond" are with the dinosaurs. Agreements must be written down, no matter how friendly the two parties are, as a record if the relationship sours.' He tossed the piece of paper at her. 'Go on, read . . .' – he waggled a finger at her – 'and make sure you understand.'

She reached for the single page, letting her glasses drop to her chest. The top half was headed up "Definitions", and underneath was a series of words in capitals, followed by an explanation of what each one meant. She learned that she was to be paid a "PROPORTION" (defined term, the amount left blank) of the "SETTLEMENT" (the gross amount of cash paid by the bank to Mr Ellis). She got the gist: she was to be paid part of whatever the current offer ended up at. What proportion though?

'Any questions?' he asked.

'Just the obvious one.'

He sat back in his chair, his hands behind his head, cupping it. 'What do you want?'

She shrugged.

'Tell me, what will motivate you?' he asked, looking at her so intently she felt as if he was pinning her down before attacking.

She lowered her eyes. How much was on offer? *The heating on in winter? He wouldn't go for that idea, and anyway, she wasn't planning to stay long enough to see the full benefit.* 'A month's salary?'

'No way!'

She screwed up her face. 'A week?'

He stood up, laughing. 'You're going in the wrong direction. The idea is to incentivize you to maximize my payout. To align our interests. What proportion of the prize do you want for putting your heart and soul into this project?'

She chewed her lip unsure where he was going with this.

'1 per cent?' he suggested.

'OK.'

He threw up his hands. 'Noooo,' he said, drawing out the word. 'Don't just accept the first number. Negotiate.'

'2 per cent,' she shot back.

He was laughing again. 'I can't do this. I don't want to be like the fox in a hen house. I can see I'm going to have to teach you the art of negotiation. Right, I'm going to fill this in. You sign, then give me a copy. By tomorrow, I want you to find us a lawyer,' he said, jabbing a finger at her. 'Meanwhile, I've got to get on with the brief for the website.' He scrawled a number onto the page, initialled it, signed the bottom, and passed it to her.

Her eyes bulged.

10 per cent. She would earn 10 per cent of whatever he settled for; even the current offer would give her an enormous amount of money – especially if she didn't tell Janet.

Ovington Advisory's second guest was Barry Hitchens. He was a wisp of a man: short and slim, with close-cropped black hair, and a cheerful, almost childlike disposition. Standing on the doorstep, rocking back and forth on his heels, he introduced himself and asked Lana her name with an infectious grin.

'So, go on, what's he said? Tarred my name already, has he?'

'No,' she said, finding herself returning his smile.

'How's he taking this?' asked Barry, giving her a conspiratorial wink. 'I still can't believe it. Your boss is one of the best, and I owe him big time. He got me promoted.'

She could hear Mr Ellis thundering up the stairs from the kitchen, shouting, 'Don't trust a word that man says, he's only interested in money!' Stopping halfway up, he waved something in his hands at Barry, 'In you go, Baz.'

At the dining table, Barry peeled off his coat, then his jacket, throwing both carelessly onto a chair, then sat down on top of the pile. He was dressed in chinos and a button-down shirt.

Mr Ellis followed them in, bringing the aroma of chocolate with him. 'Baz is a foreign exchange trader,' he informed Lana, setting down on the sideboard what looked suspiciously like the chocolate cake Lana had baked that morning. 'He works the other side of the firewall from me.'

Lana looked at Barry, who chuckled. 'Do you know what a firewall is?' he asked, and she shook her head. 'That man' – he pointed at Mr Ellis – 'works on huge international deals. I could make enough money to retire if I knew about them ahead of the market. All I needed was a camera in the M&A department.'

'That's not much of an explanation to a novice, Baz,' said Mr Ellis, turning around and waving a chocolate-smeared knife at Barry. 'Some M&A deals move share prices when they're announced. Some can move currencies – say if there's a large, cross-border mining deal involving the South African rand. Banks have firewalls to ensure trading floors – where the Barrys of this world work – can't discover what smart folk like me are working on.' He went back to the cake, saying, 'If we need to work together, as Baz and I often did, there's a formal process to bring him over the firewall, make him an insider to that deal.'

Mr Ellis was holding two plates. He gave one to Lana and the other to Barry. 'Understand now?' he asked.

Lana bit into her slice of cake, letting the gooey chocolate fill her mouth and recharge her confidence. She had no idea what a firewall was but wasn't going to admit it. She'd ask Anne. 'Sort of,' she mumbled.

'Why?' asked Barry. 'Why did Paul do it?'

'Revenge.'

'Hmmm, that's a powerful motivator,' said Barry, taking a mouthful of cake. 'Delicious . . .'

'The bastard has spread rumours with the headhunters. They won't tell me what he said, but they won't touch me. I've got to set up on my own.'

Barry took a large mouthful of tea then asked, 'How can I help?'

Mr Ellis scrunched up the remains of his napkin, sliding the rubbish underneath his plate. Lana raised a finger at him. 'In the bin, Mr Ellis.'

Her boss rolled his eyes at her, removed the napkin, and made a show of putting it in the bin, then turned his attention back to Barry. 'I'm going to need to staff up. You were always brilliant at spotting talent at other banks – keep your eye out for juniors who'd like to move.' Mr Ellis had a determined look on his face. 'Watch me. I'll get that effing bastard.'

'There's always someone pissed off with their bonus at this time of year.' Barry dipped his head and slurped his tea. 'Need any investment advice? How much capital have you got?'

'We've got a reserve fund,' said Mr Ellis.

Lana thought of her own rainy day fund. Saving £100 a month, a little more in summer when her garden was in peak production, she had scraped together £10,000. Her reserve fund was sitting in the bank earning zero.

Barry tipped his saucer, pouring the slops into his cup, then waved the saucer at the other man. 'I can give you some tips, bolster your return rate,' he offered, swilling his tea. 'Become a shadow investor until the business takes off.'

Mr Ellis laughed. 'What, like a remora fish attaching itself to a whale, hitching a lift off your giant expertise? One more favour. Can you add my new email address to the list for the bank's research?'

'Sure. Choppy times, eh, but once the Ruskies pull back, things will settle down. It's always the same, markets hate uncertainty.'

The men discussed bond yields, interest rates, swaps, and something called "cable" which, according to Baz, was driving up the oil price and fuelling the UK's inflation rate. Lana's thoughts drifted to her task list. She was hopeful she'd cracked finding a lawyer to advise on Project Revenge. She'd researched online and found firms who specialized in employment law, and she also now knew that GDPR was about protecting data.

A grin appeared on Barry's face. He told Mark he was spending the weekend in Paris, 'Taking my friend in compliance for a frolic at the Ritz.'

Mark grunted. 'That doesn't sound cheap!'

'Some of us got a bonus. I've got my eye on a new yearling at a stud in the south of France. Lovely little mover. My trainer's just running through the bloodline. If it checks out, I'll nab him.'

Barry stood up and collected his crumpled jacket. 'Good to see you again, mate. Ta for the cake. I'll come back with some investment ideas.'

'I'll be all ears. Have fun in Paris.' Mr Ellis handed Barry his coat. The men left the room, leaving Lana wondering if Mr Ellis might share those investment tips with her.

Emily's torso bent around the door. 'I'm off for a shower – where did you put that cake?'

Lana's gaze instinctively flicked to the sideboard. Smiling, Emily walked in, looked at the remains of the cake then at her housekeeper; her body stiffened, and her smile slipped. Lana ran her tongue over her teeth, dislodging a piece of cake, filling her mouth again with the taste of chocolate and her mind with guilt.

Mr Ellis strolled in asking cheerfully, 'What did you make of Bazza then?' When he saw his wife, his tone switched to sarcastic. 'Come to help out, Emily?'

'Mark, what am I supposed to do with that?' She pointed at the half-eaten cake.

'Help yourself. It's a great cake.'

'Which was baked for a fundraiser!'

'OK, we've had ours, take the rest,' he said with a deadpan expression.

'Haha. You can't sell half a cake. Svetlana baked that for *me*.'

He put his hands on his hips. 'Svetlana's priority is to Ovington Advisory. You agreed. If she has time to bake cakes, we get first dibs.'

'Oh, don't be so childish!' shouted Emily.

'If that's all, we've got work to do, and it sounds like you have a pressing social engagement.' His eyes met Lana's, and for the briefest moment, she thought he was smiling at her.

'Is this going to be expensive?' asked Mary. She was standing in her hallway, looking down at a woman dressed in navy-blue dungarees, crouched on all fours, scraping her fingernails over a chipped floor tile. The decorator had long brown hair secured in a high ponytail, which shook as she scrubbed. 'I'll never be able to match these.' She looked up at Mary. 'They're beautiful - original Georgian.'

She had come highly recommended by Emily, but Mary needed to communicate that her friend's approach to redecorating wasn't like her own. Emily's primary goal was to minimize inconvenience.

'I reckon if I give them a thorough clean and reseal them, you won't notice the chips,' the woman said.

'Is that cheaper than replacing them?'

'It's . . . labour intensive.'

So that's a no, thought Mary. 'I don't mind you fitting me in around other jobs, I work from home. Come and do a few hours when you can, if that helps bring down the cost,' suggested Mary, wanting to ask if she could pay in instalments.

The ponytail was shaking again. 'That doesn't make any sense. I could split the work into three parts. Tiles, wallpaper, and the work on the cornicing,' said the decorator.

Three stages. That sounded promising, thought Mary, tracking the other woman's gaze up to the ceiling. 'I'll have to make a mould for the missing pieces of plaster. I'll send you a quote.'

'Thank you.'

The decorator cast a look around the hallway. 'You're so lucky to live here.'

After letting the woman out, Mary stood in her unheated hallway, oblivious to the cold, trying to see it through a decorator's experienced eyes. The space was like a beautiful woman who has shunned delaying the ravages of time, allowing wrinkles and liver spots to pepper her face, her hair to be streaked with grey, then turn silver and eventually white, but whose fine bone structure still shone through.

Mary's daydream was disturbed by the doorbell. It was Tom.

'Time for a chat?' he asked.

What did he want? He'd never popped in for a chat before. 'It'll have to be quick,' she said. 'I'm due at the gym soon.' She showed him downstairs into the kitchen and closed the door to stop the warmth escaping; it made a grinding noise as she wrestled it shut.

'What's that noise?' quizzed Tom.

She tutted. 'A house gremlin . . . Can I get you tea?'

'Please. Look, I've got a proposition. I bet your address book is full of City contacts.'

'It is,' she said warily.

There was a piercing scream from the Aga. Tom's head jerked, his eyes circling the room. 'What the . . .' His face wore a puzzled expression. 'Another house gremlin?'

Mary huffed and walked to the Aga, giving the back of the oven a sharp tap. 'I'm going to have to get this one sorted, this is the only warm room in the house.' *How much would that cost?*

'I'd pay you . . . once I get a backer,' Tom offered.

She looked at the journalist, aghast. She would not be Tom's source for some hideous article. 'My address book is not for sale.'

'It's an investigative piece. I'm not asking you to shop anyone - although I think there might be something interesting going on between your friends Paul, Mark and Emily,' he said, sniggering. 'Think about it, you won't be doing any harm, just helping me.'

Mary wrinkled her nose. She didn't know Tom that well, wasn't sure she could trust him. The Aga let out an encouraging scream. 'Let me think about it,' she said -noncommittally.

Unlike Emily, Mary couldn't afford to pay £100 an hour for a personal trainer, so Emily trained her. They usually met on Wednesdays, mid-morning, at a gym where Emily was a member – despite having a fully stocked gym in her own basement. Emily always signed Mary in as a guest. It was never busy. Today, there were a handful of fellow fitness enthusiasts. A woman walking on a treadmill inclined to maximum, her body straining to keep pace with the moving belt. Another was cycling, her arms resting on the handlebars, feet spinning the pedals, and two others sitting on rowing machines, fan belts whooshing out warm air as they heaved backwards on the handles.

Mary was lying on her back on a padded bench, her arms stretched above her head, each hand clasped around a dumbbell. She was mulling over Tom's offer, not because she was tempted, but to divert her thoughts from Emily droning on about her love life. They hadn't seen each other since Charles's birthday party.

Emily was standing behind the bench, hands splayed in a claw-like position ready to grab the weights if Mary faltered. Mary lowered the dumbbells to her chest, exhaled and pushed them up.

'Ten,' she gasped. 'Two to go.'

'What do you think I should do?' asked Emily.

Mary let the weights sink, resting them on her chest, and peered up at Emily's pinched face. She wasn't surprised to hear that the atmosphere in the Ellis house was strained 'How bad is it?' she asked. 'Mark sulked for two days, then went to see his mother on Sunday. He's ignoring me. If I walk into a room, he leaves. We're never going to return to planet normal if he won't talk to me.'

Mary puffed out her last two bench presses and sat up, an image flashing into her mind of Emily in her slinky black dress being embraced by Paul when she finally left Charles's party. She dropped the dumbbells, which thudded onto the floor either side of her. Mark was proud. He'd worked his way up from a council house to the pinnacle of his profession, and Paul had humiliated him: sacking him and cavorting with his wife in public. And then Emily had refused to leave the party with her husband. Of course Mark was angry. Sending Emily to Coventry was a bit childish, but Mark was using the only available weapon to hurt her.

Sitting up, Mary ran a towel over her sweaty face, waiting for one of the trainers to walk out of earshot. 'Do you need time apart?' she whispered. 'Let him experience life without you, force him to think. Why not go to Devon for a bit?'

'Come with me. You haven't seen the new house yet,' wheedled her friend, picking up the dumbbells. 'One set of bench presses to go, then it's chest flies. Come on, girl, dig deep.'

Mary wiped her towel over the bench, then lay back; she wouldn't mind getting away from the Aga's peculiar noises for a while. Added to the push was the allure of a centrally heated house. Looking up into Emily's face as her friend placed the weights into Mary's gloved hands, she said, 'I'd love to get away. What about next week? Tell me, how's Mark's new business going?'

'Well, he's got a diary full of lunches, and he's suing the bank.'

Sitting up, Mary rested the weights on her legs and whispered, 'He's suing the bank?'

Emily's eyes were wide. 'Don't say a word,' she warned. 'It's called Project Revenge.'

Rounding the corner, Romeo trotting beside her, Gwen noticed a short, skinny man in casual clothes lounging against her front door. She stopped, tucking a handful of hair back under her hat. The man beamed at her.

'Mrs Ellis,' he called out in a friendly voice.

She kept her distance. 'Who's asking?' she said, checking Romeo's lead.

He approached her, arm outstretched. 'Tom Withers. I'm a friend of Charles and Mary Standerwick. They live opposite your son Mark.'

Romeo sniffed the stranger's shoes. Gwen looked down at the scruffy trainers, then back up at the smiling face. Mark often mentioned Emily's friend Mary, who sounded very grand. She was descended from the family that built Ovington Square – generations of the Standerwick family had lived in her house. According to Alex, they were Labour Party activists like him, and their house didn't look like it had altered much in the last forty years, resembling a stage set for a London period drama.

'What do you want?' she asked.

'I'm a journalist. I wanted to ask a few questions about your son, Mark,' he said, smiling warmly.

'What sort of questions?'

'Mostly background stuff for an article I'm writing about the City.'

'I don't know anything about the City. Why not ask Mark?'

'He claims he's too busy.' That would be true, thought Gwen. 'And I'm pretty sure you can help me; I'd like to know how someone like Mark got to where he is now.'

Gwen felt a drop of rain on her wrist, then another. 'Well, let's do this inside,' she said. 'Come on, Romeo.'

As Gwen talked about Mark, how hard he worked, how successful he was, the journalist ate his way through a plate of Welsh cakes, jotting notes all the while in a little book balanced on his skinny legs.

'He's worked in the same bank for over twenty years,' said Gwen.

'It must have been tough, leaving?'

Finishing her cup of tea, Gwen pondered the question. 'He'll know what he's doing. Always been a plotter, my lad; he says that's why he's good at strategy. He isn't put off by roadblocks. He's always got a plan B in mind.'

The journalist rose and walked around the room. He picked up a picture of Emily and Alex taken on the balcony of the Devon house, the sea in the background a shimmering, hazy grey-blue. Emily was wearing a pink bikini, and her son was in a wetsuit, grinning out at the camera, one hand resting on a surfboard, the other holding a small trophy.

'Your grandson?'

'That's right. Alex, and my daughter-in-law Emily. He's an excellent surfer. He was privately educated . . . just finished university.'

'I've met Emily at Charles and Mary's. She's very pretty.'

'She is.'

'Shouldn't think your son sees much of his family. Work kind of takes over some men, doesn't it?'

Gwen bristled and leaned over to stroke behind one of Romeo's ears, letting the soft silky fur settle her. 'He finds time for what's important. He comes up to see me most Sundays. I don't expect him for a while though, now he's busy getting this new bank going.' Her eyes shone. 'A new bank! But then he's always done well for himself, my boy. He studied hard, worked hard, why shouldn't he set up his own bank if he wants to? It's a boutique, not a shop.'

The journalist replaced the picture on the sideboard. 'Young Alex is the spit of Mark, isn't he. Do they get their height from your husband's genes?'

Gwen gave a short laugh. 'It's not from me, is it!' They'd got both their height and their looks from Steve, but thankfully they didn't seem to have inherited any of his less attractive traits.

'Is Mr Ellis senior still around?'

She huffed. 'No. I divorced that useless bugger when Mark was still a nipper.'

'So, Mark grew up without a father. That gives some men drive, doesn't it? Not butting up against another man's pride can enable them to scramble up the success ladder faster.'

She thought about what the journalist was saying. Was that what Mark was doing to Alex? Was her son inadvertently protecting his own ego by thwarting Alex's progress? Was that why Alex spent so much time surfing in Devon? Was that why the two always bickered? She got up. Her hip clicked, and she let out a tiny gasp, staggered, and gripped the back of the chair.

'You OK?' asked the journalist, approaching.

She shuffled to the pot on the sideboard and poured more tea. 'Hip giving me a bit of jip.'

'But why now?' he continued. 'What made Mark decide to start a bank now?'

It was a question Gwen had asked herself. Was that what was bothering Mark – was he having second thoughts? Gwen passed the journalist his cup, then sat down again, picking up her own. 'He didn't say.'

'Did he tell you he'd been fired?'

Gwen spluttered over her mouthful of tea, droplets splashing her hand. Mark, fired? For what? She wiped her hand on her apron. 'You've made a mistake.'

'I haven't,' the journalist said, gently. 'Mark was fired, but what I'm trying to find out is why. Could you ask him?'

Why hadn't Mark told her? She'd been right: there was something wrong. Something terribly wrong.

# Five

Halfway down the steps, Lana paused, sniffed, and wrinkled her nose. Every Friday, that same smell greeted her, but tonight she didn't want to reek of fish: she was meeting Anne in half an hour, this time closer to home, for them both. At their first meeting, Anne had mentioned that she and her husband Kenny lived in a tiny flat inherited from a rich uncle, only a stone's throw from Lana. The flat was in a purpose-built 1950s tower block, on one of the many West End sites levelled by a German bomb that had missed its target of Buckingham Palace.

She contemplated leaving her coat outside, but instead hung it on the peg in the hallway and opened the door to the sitting room. Plates were on the breakfast bar, glasses of water beside them. There was no steam rising from the food. She glanced at her wrist: twelve minutes past five.

'You're late again,' said Janet, climbing onto a stool by the counter. Her voice was wistful; it wasn't a reprimand, more a complaint against life than her daughter. Yes, a whole ten minutes late, thought Lana, sitting down. Her mother wore a pair of sparkly orange trousers and a fawn-coloured silk blouse. Lana had seen both before – they were by Roberto Cavalli, hand-me-downs from Emily. Closer to the food, Lana's stomach turned, but she picked up her fork and jabbed it into the tepid congealed mush.

Janet tucked a napkin into the top of her blouse, letting it dangle like an oversized retro kipper-tie. 'I have Mass,' she said. 'They shouldn't be keeping you late.'

'Mum, I can't plan my days like I used to. Not now I'm helping Mr Ellis.'

'Hmm. Have they increased your wages?'

Lana shook her head. *If they did, should she admit it?*

'Is that right, luv? Expecting you to do more for the same wage?'

Lana put down her cutlery and rubbed her brow, wanting to scream. She was suffocating, squeezed like a tube of toothpaste with the cap still on, between her mother's needs and the Ellises' expectations, both trying to extract what they wanted while she gasped for breath. The solution was to resign, but she couldn't do that until she found another post. And there was no point discussing any of this with Janet!

'Mum, they're going through a sticky patch. I can't ask for a raise now.'

'Don't be a doormat, Lana. And you might say thank you for this meal. You're just like your father, he never said thank you either, expected his meals cooked and his clean shirts ironed. A little gratitude and punctuality isn't too much to ask for, is it?'

Lana ate in silence, listening to a catalogue of her deficiencies – just like her father used to. No wonder he'd scarpered. Janet finished her meal, downed her glass of water, and stood up. 'Right, you made me late, so you can clear away,' said her mother, removing the napkin and shrugging on a bright red Millets waterproof jacket. Lana winced. *With orange trousers?*

'I'm off,' Janet announced, draping an Hermès handbag over her arm.

'Have a good evening,' chirped Lana, who had every intention of enjoying her own.

*

The Enterprise was very different from the last bar. Both were warm, rowdy and welcoming – as the best pubs are – the soft hum of group chatter, the occasional raised voice, bursts of laughter. But The Enterprise was a fraction of the size of The Parlour. A polished wooden bar ran along one side, while the other was filled with small tables squashed so close together that Lana suspected if you asked the person sitting opposite if they were enjoying their meal, you might get multiple responses. Like their last meeting place, it too was full of off-duty workers, but the atmosphere was more sedate; there was no pulsing sense of power.

The room was crowded with people in shirtsleeves, their top buttons undone, a beer or glass of wine in hand. In the centre, a small group had gathered around a floor-to-ceiling pole, with a six-inch circumference of wood where customers could balance their drinks. Just another Friday at the local. Everyone wore their work clothes . . . Apart from Lana. Tonight she was wearing jeans and her best blouse. It was bat-winged, with three quarter length sleeves, made from pale blue chiffon that hung loosely over her body to disguise her large tummy. It had been too big for Emily, and swamped Janet, allowing Lana to claim it.

Was Anne here yet? She brushed past shirt backs, and the sour smell of wine, jostling her way along the bar, elbows pinned – she didn't want anything spilled on this blouse – until she saw Anne sitting on a stool at the far end, in front of the largest gilt-framed mirror Lana had ever seen. Anne waved at Lana, then towards the bar, at a bottle of wine with a third missing. 'Guess what? I've been reassigned,' she said as Lana approached. 'It's a promotion, really. I'm working for the head of department now!'

Lana took off her coat. 'Congratulations. Good new boss?'

There was a cackle of laughter. 'Not sure yet. So, how's *your* week been?' Anne removed her suit jacket from a stool beside her, and Lana swung herself onto it. 'Found your feet?' asked Anne, pouring wine into an empty glass, and topping up her own.

'I met someone nice.' She looked up at Anne. 'Barry?'

'Bazza! Yes, he's great fun. He and Mark worked together a lot; you'll like him.'

'He said Mark got him promoted. How? They didn't work in the same department, did they?'

'We do annual 360° reviews,' Anne explained. 'Juniors rate the seniors, and people from one department review people they've worked with in another. Mark probably gave him a glowing reference and he kept asking for Bazza to work on lucrative deals. Fees are the key to promotion at banks. How did you get on with the lawyers? Who has Mark chosen?'

Lana sipped her wine. She was hoping Anne would ask that question. Lawyers had dominated her week and looked set to dominate the next one too. 'None of the big firms will act,' she said. 'They don't want to risk upsetting the bank. So how do I find a different lawyer? Any ideas?'

Anne took a gulp of wine, while Lana mentally crossed her fingers.

'Google?'

Lana huffed, recalling how Mark shredded the results of her online research, claiming none of them would understand how pay worked in the City; they'd all believe what they'd read – that bankers' bonuses were capped. Apparently not for everyone. 'Not good enough. Any other ideas?'

Anne lubricated her thoughts with more wine. 'Well,' she said eventually, 'the big firms may not act, but if he calls one of his old contacts, I bet they could recommend someone who did a decent job against them. Below the radar, they'll want to help. He'll soon be hiring lawyers to act for him on mega deals.'

'Brilliant!' said Lana. Except, she doubted Mr Ellis would make that call. Would Anne?

Before she could ask, Anne launched into a tale about a journalist who was pestering her. 'He's very chatty, sounds lovely. Says he wants to write a piece about time management skills. Offering me lunch or dinner. Sounds awfully glamorous, doesn't it?'

Lana scrunched up her face. 'Sounds a bit creepy to me. What does Kenny think?'

'No, it's OK, I've checked him out. He's a real journalist. Kenny won't mind, but you're right, better not to go alone.' She batted her eyes at Lana. 'Why don't you come too?'

'Me? He won't be interested in anything I have to say,' scoffed Lana.

Anne tutted and changed the topic. 'My new boss was in a foul mood today, because he lost one of Mark's clients to a competitor and he reckons it's you lot, Ovington Advisory, who poached them.'

Lana felt a stab of pride at the use of the words "you lot".

'He said Mark isn't supposed to work for months, but you and I both know he's out pitching under the guise of having lunch. I gave you the names of his favourite restaurants, didn't I?' Suddenly, Anne's eyes lit up. 'Fancy eating here?'

Lana shook her head. She rarely ate out; after paying the church, food, bills and her mother's allowance, there was little left for luxuries. 'I've already eaten. Why not order a bar snack?' she suggested, then added, 'Do you think Mr Ellis will mind calling one of his lawyer contacts?'

Anne barked a laugh, her tiny frame shaking. 'He'll hate it. Phoning without his calling card of being an MD at the big bank.'

Just as Lana had thought.

Anne furrowed her brow. 'Why do you always call him Mr Ellis, and not Mark?'

'He's always been Mr Ellis, I can't call him Mark.'

'Why not?'

'I dunno, we don't have that sort of relationship. It's too . . . chummy.'

'Silly you!'

'Anne, would you mind calling one of those lawyers for me? You know, for a recommendation of someone who would act for Mr Ellis.'

'I'll get a name for you,' promised Anne.

Her employers' routines hadn't changed much. Emily still popped in and out to tennis games, exercise classes, girls' lunches, shopping trips and the dogs home where she volunteered occasionally. Lana didn't see much of her anymore, and Emily started leaving instructions on sheets of pale blue Smythson notepaper.

Mr Ellis still donned a suit and tie, left a soggy mess in the bathroom, and headed for the office, albeit now relocated to the dining room. Telling herself she was only putting up with this until she secured a new post, Lana started arriving at 8 a.m.

On the Wednesday of her second week, Lana modified the housekeeping regime. Instead of cleaning upstairs, she telephoned the three employment lawyers Anne had recommended. Lana had rewarded Anne with advice on how to germinate rocket. 'I've gone through three packets of seeds already. Nothing.'

'Where are these experiments taking place?' asked Lana.

'On my balcony.'

'In January!' snorted Lana. 'No chance. Try inside, somewhere warm with sunlight, like your kitchen windowsill.'

After speaking to the lawyers, Lana identified her favourite, a woman called Clare Hetherington, who returned her call promptly and laughed loudly when told who had recommended her. 'Enjoyed every minute of that case against them last year,' she said. 'I made them pay up.' Clare sounded like the sort of lawyer Mr Ellis would choose. She typed a list for her boss highlighting Clare's name in bold.

'Have you spoken to this Clare Hetherington?' asked Mr Ellis.

Lana didn't hesitate. 'Yes. You'll like her. She's a tough nut.'

'Get her in for a meeting,' he said. Then, looking Lana's way, added, 'Well done.'

She felt a smile twitching at the corners of her lips. 'I've got her on hold for three o'clock this afternoon.'

Hearing a knock on the door, Lana twisted around. It was Emily, encased in Barbie-pink Lycra. She spoke directly to her husband, as if Lana wasn't present. 'I'm sorry to disturb, but could I have a word with Svetlana please?'

Lana rose. Was this a clandestine task like the bouquet of flowers?

'No, stay where you are,' said Emily, looking Lana's way. 'I'm off out. Tosca and Floria are looking a bit peaky, and one of them has been sick. Could you keep an eye on them please? And I don't want to take them in the car to Devon tomorrow, so I'll leave them here.'

*Sole dog walker on top of everything else!* Lana opened her mouth, then clamped it shut, focusing her mind on her mantra – this is temporary. Emily started to shut the door, but changed her mind, adding, 'And I thought I'd take a casserole with me. Please rustle one up, then Mary and I won't have to cook on the first night.'

Lana's jaw tightened, but Mr Ellis spoke first. 'Hold on,' he said in a clipped voice. 'Svetlana doesn't have time for that.'

Emily stalked into the room. 'Making a casserole isn't much to ask.'

'No,' said Mr Ellis, his eyes drilling into his wife. 'This won't work. Svetlana has an important meeting this afternoon at three o'clock.'

Emily pouted and made a sad face. 'I'm sorry, but it was the only Ocado slot I could get, and I need the stuff for Devon.'

'When?' asked Lana.

'Three o'clock,' said Emily, shutting the door softly behind her.

Across the Square, an elegantly dressed woman stood in front of Mary, wafting her fingers, widening her eyes, and wiggling her chin in the way the French do so well. 'You must be harder on Francois,' she said, gripping a ten-year-old boy by the hand, and dragging him into the corridor.

'Mrs Dubois, I can't force your child to speak English if he doesn't want to,' explained Mary.

Some days, this was a tough way to earn £20 an hour. Mary watched her pupil slouch towards the front door. Poor lamb. In Paris, when it was just another school subject, Francois had probably been perfectly adequate at English, but "Daddy's" promotion to the London office necessitated the child mastering the language, and she didn't blame him for putting up a protest.

Mary's eyes flickered between the chipped floor tiles and the crumbling cornicing. With inflation galloping at 10 per cent, she must pin down that decorator for a quote and tackle Charles before the price shot up.

Mary opened her front door. Behind her, she heard a crashing noise and spun around. Mrs Dubois jumped. Francois started laughing. There was a clump of cornicing lying on the floor tiles, surrounded by white shards of plaster like a stationary planet with its accompanying moons. That was close. She must check she was insured if something hit a pupil.

*

Later, Mary was chopping onions, her eyes watering, as she watched the rain lashing against the windows. In the courtyard Biscuit's water bowl had been blown against the fence and gusts of wind were rattling through the gaps in the window frames. February's weather was wild; this was the third named storm. She put down the knife and dabbed at her eyes with her sleeves.

She didn't want to look – not after the hallway incident – but she must.

Mary plodded upwards. The staircase narrowed, the height of the steps decreased and as she climbed the elaborate cornicing became plainer. On the fourth floor her pace slowed. Should she just ask Charles to investigate? She forced her legs up the last flight of stairs and stood staring at the closed doors either side of the cramped landing. Slowly she opened the first . . . *plop* . . . *plop* . . . Her eyes circled the room, fixing in turn on three puddles on the bare polished floorboards then shooting upwards; water dripped steadily as if there were three leaky taps attached to the ceiling. 'Oh shit,' she muttered.

An hour later, the front door slammed, Biscuit barked and Mary counted to ten. Footsteps rang out on the stairs. 'I'm home,' called out Charles, walking in and tossing the *Evening Standard* on the table. 'Yum, supper smells good.'

'Not for you,' said Mary, picking up the paper and flicking through it. 'It's for me to take to Devon tomorrow.'

'Ah, yes, how long are you going for?'

'Not sure. I'm doing next week's tutorials by Zoom. No one minds; they got so used to it during the pandemic.'

'No one would dare say they minded, even if they did. No one teaches English as a second language like my wife.'

'Did you talk to the trustees about the roof today?'

Charles groaned. 'It's year-end.'

'Charles!'

'I know.' He patted the air with his hands. 'I promised . . . I will talk to them.'

Mary bit back her temper. 'Things have escalated. It's not just blotches on the ceiling anymore; it's leaking. That's got to be the sort of emergency they pay for – we can't fund a new roof, and there's all the red tape to navigate with this being Grade II listed.'

'Shit,' he groaned, undoing his tie, and pulling it free. 'Let's cover all the bad news – did you get the estimate for the front entrance hall?'

Mary chewed a fingernail. 'It's nearly ten grand.'

'Wow. Your father should have sent you to a decorating school, not finishing school.'

'Anything left in our kitty?'

He winced. 'We could manage half. Does it make sense to do half the work now, the rest another time? I was hoping to take you away to Tenerife for a bit of winter sun. Wouldn't you rather do that?'

'Needs must,' said Mary with a huff, wondering if Charles was starting to resent paying for the house. She must try to make more money herself. 'Did you post the thank-you notes for your presents?'

'Yes, Mummy,' he said, winking at her. 'Come here, Biscuit.' Over by the Aga, the dog sat up, then ambled over, his tail wagging languidly, and plopped his snout on Charles's lap. He rubbed his hands over Biscuit's whiskers. 'How was your day, Biscuit? Busy?'

'Can we talk about the gas contract?' asked Mary.

'Must we?'

'If the Russians invade Ukraine, the price will shoot up. Tom says they're going to do it. So, please look at the quotes and let's decide before it's too late.'

'Tom hasn't got a clue. He's just sensationalizing, trying to frighten you. He's a gutter press journalist, not the Eastern European correspondent for the *Times*.'

'That's a bit mean. He's doing a big investigative piece on the City. That's not gutter press.'

Charles closed his eyes and started counting. 'One . . . two . . . three . . .'

What is he counting for, wondered Mary, pouring the casserole into an empty ice cream carton.

'. . . four . . . five . . . six . . .'

'And could you—'

His eyes opened. 'Bingo!' shouted Charles, sitting up and laughing. 'What's my next instruction, darling?'

Lana skipped breakfast and, while walking the dogs, did a Facetime interview with a woman called Alice from one of the recruitment agencies. Alice was about the same age as Janet and wore a caramel-coloured, polo-necked jumper, and large framed glasses that seemed to magnify her smile.

'Svetlana, I'll be frank. I've been in this industry for decades, and if you want me to find you a new position, you must be more flexible.'

'How flexible?'

'It's not that I don't currently have the sort of position you are looking for on my books, I've *never* had one. Most Central London employers don't want live-in staff, and those that do, don't offer a flat, just a room, or a bedsit in the attic at best.'

'Where's the closest job with proper accommodation?'

'I have a lovely family in Kent . . .'

Lana felt a vice-like pressure on her temples. *Kent!* Floria bounded over, dropping a grubby tennis ball at Lana's feet. She jammed her phone between her neck and shoulder, knelt and clipped a leash on the terrier, pocketed the ball, then secured the other dog.

'Sorry, dog duty,' she said, retrieving the phone. 'Nowhere closer?' she asked, trying to keep the note of desperation out of her voice.

'Someone did call me from North London. I'm speaking to her later today; I can check if it's an all-found position.'

Lana felt a jerk on the leashes, reminding her it was time to get back, and that she too was tethered; Janet wouldn't move to North London. Which meant she must use Emily's absence to convince Mr Ellis that she was a capable assistant.

By the time she'd reached the top of Ovington Gardens, Lana was feeling optimistic – she could make this work. She squinted. There was someone on the doorstep of the Ellis house. Holding both leads in one hand, she slid her glasses back up her nose and picked up the pace. It was a tall man, wearing a suit. Had her boss arranged a breakfast meeting, forgotten, and gone for his jog? The stranger was walking back down the steps.

'Hello,' she called out. 'Can I help you?'

He didn't look her way.

'Sir,' she cried, but he turned left onto Walton Street without turning around.

She huffed. She'd checked her emails before she took the dogs out; her boss couldn't blame her if she didn't know about the visitor. From the bottom step, she spotted a small, turquoise paper bag, fastened with an elaborate orange ribbon, pushed hard up against the front door. The dogs strained forwards, and she felt a stabbing pain in her elbows.

'Heel!' she said, yanking them backwards. 'Tosca, Floria!'

The threesome panted their way up the steps and over to the package. Both dogs' snouts were twitching like snuffling truffle hounds in an autumn wood. She looped the end of the leads over a spike in the railing and picked up the bag. There was a tiny white envelope stuck to the outside. She didn't recognize the handwriting, but she did recognize danger:

For My Darling Emily.

With the washing-up done, Lana rootled through the kitchen for a sheet of Smythson paper, fantasizing. Bankers earn a fortune. Imagine if she and Ms Hetherington won £500,000 for Mr Ellis. £50k would set her up, especially if it was earning a healthy return from Bazza's tips. She decided to explore how to buy shares.

There was no chore list, which meant that Lana could concentrate on Ovington Advisory. Good.

A stony-faced Mr Ellis appeared in the kitchen doorway.

'Is the coffee ready?' he asked. 'We've got a meeting with the lawyer at nine, rescheduled, so you could sort out Emily's food delivery. We'll need refreshments.' Lana huffed; she hadn't scheduled the clashing Ocado delivery! 'And my towels were still wet this morning.'

'They won't dry if you leave them on the floor.'

'So, it wasn't a mistake. OK, you've made your point. Get my room cleaned today.'

'If I've got time,' she muttered. The coffee machine pinged.

'Make time, and yes to coffee.'

'Yes . . .' she said, pausing before adding a sarcastic '. . . please.'

He hung his head. 'Sorry, my day got off to a bad start. *Please* could you find time to clean my room, and *please* may I have a cup of coffee when it's convenient.'

Lana wanted to ask what was wrong. It had been a good apology, the sort that made you feel the person was genuinely contrite not just ticking a box, but she didn't think his day could have started as badly as hers. Not unless he'd found the Fortnum & Mason bag she'd hidden upstairs. Confining the dangerous bag to the back of her mind, she announced brightly, 'Coffee in a jiffy,' then offered, 'toast?'

Mr Ellis ran a hand over his face. 'Thanks. Yes please.'

*A please and a thank you in the same sentence!*

Slotting bread into the toaster, Lana decided her boss was a bit like a porcupine, from the outside, bristling with defences and unapproachable, but she was starting to think that once he let you past that prickly armour, he could be quite fun to work with.

On the drive to Devon, Mary had dozed off shortly after Stonehenge – which she thought looked like an army huddling in the cloak of a winter mist – and woke up to find they were on Exmoor. The fields were brown – winter-scorched – and the trees seemed stunted. It was easy to forget how high up the moor was, forcing vegetation to adapt to the hardy climate. Despite her bleak surroundings, Mary felt elated. Tom with his nagging about her City contacts, and her Aga – still making a peculiar screeching noise – were both in London, as were the three metal buckets in the attic that, given the relentless winter storms, required regular emptying.

Emily drove through Barnstaple along the coast and pulled into a long layby perched on the edge of a cliff. 'That's the house down there,' she said.

Mary opened her window, smelled the tangy breeze and gazed around her. On her right was a small sandy beach: Croyde Bay. When Alex told surfing stories, Mary had always imagined it to be so much bigger, but it was only a few hundred metres long, backed by boulders, surmounted by dark jagged rocks culminating in a steep but short cliff. Dog walkers were trekking across the sand, some of their charges perched on the nearby rocks, snouts down, pawing at tempting smells. A few brave souls were standing with waves whipping past their waists, clutching boards.

By the time they arrived it was drizzling. Mary ran behind her friend with a jacket over her head, and the pair huddled in the porch, stamping their feet to keep warm. Emily unlocked the door, and the women dashed inside, shaking off the water. Mary removed her dripping jacket and stood spellbound. The house exuded the sort of warmth she had to hug the Aga to enjoy in her own home. And the contrast between the two houses didn't stop there. In front of her, instead of a dark hallway, was a wide double-storey window, a picture frame for the wild exterior. Between the house and the sea was a single barren field, dotted with spiky clumps of marram grass, then craggy rocks, and finally the Atlantic Ocean, which stretched out like an enormous grey rug that someone had grasped the corner of and given a good tug, creating deep wrinkles. On the horizon, the sea merged into a misty oneness with the sky.

The entrance hall separated two rooms – on her right was the kitchen-dining area, and on the left a sitting room where a wood-burning stove glowed. Neither was particularly tall, there were no decorative features to compare to the intricate Ovington Square cornicing, but instead of the restricted view from her sash windows, both rooms were flooded with light by floor to ceiling glass doors which opened on to a balcony stretching the entire width of the house.

Rain was spitting against the wall of glass and Mary could hear the wind howling, even from inside. But looking out at the drizzle drifting sideways in the onshore breeze, and the dark damp decking of the balcony, Mary felt a tingle of childlike excitement.

Emily hollered out, 'Alex!'

There was no answering call.

'Perhaps he's out surfing,' said Mary, hanging up her coat and pointing out at the choppy waves. 'Shall I fetch Biscuit, or do you think this rain will let up?'

'Let's get the kettle on first, then unpack.' Emily tracked right, and Mary followed. Behind her, she heard footsteps on the stairs leading to the lower floor, and Alex – the spitting image of his father – jogged into the room. Shortly afterwards, another man appeared. He was shorter, with straggly ginger hair and a matching beard that stretched from his earlobes to six inches below his chin. Both men were barefoot and wore surfing shorts and sweatshirts.

'Hi, Mum,' said Alex. 'Good drive down?'

'Hello, darling.' Emily embraced her son.

Alex gestured at his companion. 'This is Sam, but we all call him Ginge.'

'Nice to meet you, Sam,' said Emily.

Mary smiled a greeting at both men. 'Don't suppose you fancy unloading the car for us? We're a bit shattered after the drive.'

'We were just going to catch a few waves; surf's been flat for days. But we can help you first,' said Alex. 'Dad not with you?'

'No, he isn't. I told you he wasn't coming,' said Emily, ruffling her son's hair.

'Phew,' said Alex.

'Your father isn't very happy just now. You might try being nicer to him.'

'Hmm,' huffed Alex. 'Why doesn't he try being nicer to me?'

'Alex. It takes two to keep a feud running, and only one of you to call a truce.'

Mary listened to this advice. Alex was an only child. You'd think he and his father would have a shared interest in football or rugby, but the only hobby they seemed to share was insulting each other. She couldn't imagine Charles not getting on with either of their daughters, both away in Australia until Christmas. Part of her wished they hadn't decided to take their gap year together, although it was reassuring to think of them looking after each other. She and Charles missed them terribly. They kept in regular touch, but a WhatsApp video couldn't replace a hug.

'There's a cool box in the boot,' said Emily. 'Mary made a casserole, so if you bring that in first, I can get supper on the go while you two frolic in the sea.'

'And bring Biscuit in too please,' added Mary.

They ate dinner on their knees in the sitting room, around the wood-burning stove. Alex spoke of his and Sam's business, but Mary was exhausted, the wine was delicious, the fire soporific, and she wasn't really listening. She let the strange terms wash over her: "cold wallet", "cyber security" and something about "AI-powered crypto trading bots". What were they? She asked if the business steered clear of energy intensive blockchain but was met with arched eyebrows. Ginge said gently, 'Not an issue these days. Apart from Bitcoin, most cryptos use proof of stake to add blocks to the chain instead of proof of work.'

'Right, good, I get it,' she replied.

She had no idea what the business did and cared even less. It was keeping the pair out of mischief. She and Charles always feared Alex would end up a surfing bum to spite his father, and this venture sounded like it might prove them wrong.

Puccini started playing shortly before nine the next morning, and Lana got her first glimpse of Clare Hetherington. She was nearly as tall as Mr Ellis and dressed similarly in a midnight-blue trouser suit with flat, grey suede ankle boots. Clare's blonde hair was so short it looked like the straw stubble Lana used to see in the Somerset fields of her childhood. A hand – short unvarnished nails

– shot out, and Lana detected a whiff of Imperial Leather soap. Lana extended her own hand, which was crushed in a firm grip.

'Svetlana Smith?'

Lana flexed the fingers, restoring circulation. 'Yes. Very nice to meet you, Ms Hetherington.'

'Call me Clare.'

'Mr Ellis is on the phone. I'll let him know you're here.'

'It's an unusual name for a Ms Smith, Svetlana.'

Lana recounted the story about her Polish grandfather. 'I use my mother's maiden name – it's a lot easier than Adamczyk.'

'Fascinating,' said Clare in a tone that implied she would love to chat more.

Lana showed the lawyer into the sitting room, pointing to the tray set up with freshly brewed coffee, a jug of iced water and sparkling clean glasses and cups. 'Help yourself. I'll be right back.'

Outside the dining room, she could hear her employer on the phone, voice raised. She nudged the door open. Mr Ellis's face was a shade paler than a radish, and he was fidgeting with his tie as if trying to wrestle his neck free. He looked up and frowned. 'Hang on a tick,' he said, lowering his phone then hissed, 'Start without me. Here.' He slid a pile of papers across the table towards her. 'Utility bills and my passport. She'll need them for her regulatory checks, "know your client" and the money laundering malarky.' Without waiting for a response, he hollered into the phone, 'Tell me who's on the Board.'

She pulled the door shut and returned to Clare, who was sitting on one of three beige sofas, legs crossed, with her suit jacket folded on the cushion beside her. On the table in front of the lawyer was a legal notebook, a pen and a glass of water. Lana handed over the papers, and Clare shuffled through them. 'He's done this before, hasn't he?'

'I suspect so.'

A silence fell. Lana fiddled with her glasses, unable to think of any small talk. After a few awkward moments, she said, 'Mr Ellis said to start without him. I know what has happened.'

Clare smiled. 'But it didn't happen to you.'

Lana fidgeted with her glasses, Mr Ellis would expect the meeting to have progressed by the time he joined. 'I'm sure he won't be long. Can we please try?'

'Fine. Client's name.'

Lana answered the questions, each one fired off while Clare was still noting the answer to the previous one. Lana knew the bank's name, how long her boss had worked there, and his previous job title. She passed Clare a copy of his employment contract and confirmed that he had never been part of any disciplinary process.

The door opened, and a composed Mr Ellis came in. Clare stood up, extending her hand. 'Ms Hetherington,' he said, shaking her hand. 'Sorry to keep you waiting.' He sat down, placing his phone on the table.

'Why don't you walk me through what happened the day you were told to leave?' suggested Clare.

Mr Ellis's phone vibrated on the table. He glanced at the screen, stood up, and his eyebrows clenched together in a line. 'Sorry, I must take this. Carry on without me . . .' Speaking urgently into the phone, he left the room.

Lana passed Clare a copy of the letter her boss had been given the day he left the bank. She hadn't read it. She couldn't – it was too private.

'This says he's been made redundant,' said Clare, folding the letter in half after reading it. 'Is there any proof the bank has replaced him?'

An image of Anne – holding a glass of wine – bounced into Lana's mind. 'I can find out.'

'That would be useful.' Clare scanned the letter a second time. 'He's being paid in lieu of notice *and* given redundancy. He's also being offered an additional sum to go quietly. Has he accepted these terms? They're still on offer.'

'Definitely not. He says the offer is way too low.'

'Is that what this is about? There's probably a bit of slack; the bank won't want bad publicity, and they won't want senior management tied up fighting a claim. Does he have a figure in mind?'

'I don't know what his target is. But I know his motive.'

'Which is?'

'The codename for this project is "Revenge".'

Clare laughed. 'Ah. That tells me a lot.' She leaned over and picked up her glass of water. 'How much do you know about employment law?'

'Assume nothing,' said Lana.

Clare drank then replaced the glass. 'This is a fair settlement, unless he can prove one of four things.' She ticked them off on her fingers. 'His redundancy was a sham, he was either unfairly or wrongly dismissed, or lastly, that he suffered discrimination.'

Lana gave Clare a blank look.

'Let's consider the possibilities,' suggested the lawyer. 'Unfair dismissal . . .'

Lana interrupted. 'What's unfair dismissal?'

'When your employer doesn't have proper grounds for terminating your employment. Wrongful dismissal means they haven't gone about things correctly, like ignoring disciplinary processes or notice periods. A claim for unfair dismissal is capped at approximately £105k; wrongful dismissal is considerably lower. All the big banks cull staff annually. They know the drill. The only place they may have tripped up is by using redundancy as a cloak to sack him, say if someone else is now doing his old job. But you said you can check that for me?'

'Yes, I will. What about discrimination?'

'Mr Ellis is a middle-aged white male. I didn't ask but,' she added, casting a look around the sitting room, 'there are several pictures of what I presume are his wife and child, so I presume he's heterosexual and either agnostic or Church of England?'

'I expect so. I've never seen him cross himself, so he's not Catholic.'

'An employer must not discriminate on the grounds of race, gender, sexual orientation, religion, or marital status. I don't see promising ground for a discrimination claim.'

Lana's brow furrowed. There must be an angle. She needed her 10 per cent bonus. Once Ovington Advisory was established, a trained PA – probably Anne – would replace Lana, a cleaning lady would be looking after Emily, and she and her mother would be evicted. The best angle seemed to be sham redundancy. This called for another meeting with Anne.

# Six

After a peaceful night, Mary woke to the sharp screeching of seagulls. She rolled out of bed, stretched, slipped on her dressing gown and drew the curtains. The low front had blown through; the sea looked blue not grey, and gentler, with little ripples like the top of a cottage pie rather than the yawning peaks and troughs of yesterday. She was close enough to watch the gulls circling and swooping, jabbing their beaks into the water, silvery fish reflected in the sun as they flapped away clutching a breakfast feast. She switched her gaze to Croyde Bay. This morning, dogs were capering at the water's edge, plunging into the sea after unseen toys hurled by wellie-wearing owners bundled up in waterproof jackets. She was itching to join them, could imagine Biscuit in those waves.

There was a knock on the door. Emily's face appeared, the eyebrows arched. 'Dog walk on Exmoor, then pub lunch?' she suggested, passing Mary a mug of tea.

'Sounds lovely,' Mary said, the warmth seeping through the mug adding to her chirpy feeling. Life was different with the central heating on; this morning she hadn't woken to her breath forming foggy clouds above the duvet, nor steeled herself to throw back the covers and step into the icy chill of an unheated bedroom. 'I'll nip out with Biscuit for a quick beach walk, then join you for breakfast. Are the boys coming with us?'

'Too busy. They're out trying to surf now, then they're working.'

'What *is* this business?' asked Mary.

Emily shrugged. 'Fintech.' She grimaced. 'Something to do with artificial intelligence. Sam is quite nerdy, isn't he? But I like him.'

Mary laughed. 'Me too. I didn't want to bring his name up, but if you want to understand what your son is doing, you should ask Paul. I gather from Charles he's become an overnight bore on the fintech sector. He's pitching to advise a hot startup.'

Emily shrugged. 'As long as it's legal and keeps him out of mischief, who cares what the business does? Alex's attention won't last long . . . I still reckon he'll end up doing something in the surfing world.'

'Don't write him off!'

'I'm not,' said Emily. 'But you know his politics, he doesn't want to lead his father's life. Toast and more tea upstairs in half an hour.'

Mary clambered back into bed and picked up her phone. There was a message from Tom:

I've got a backer for my City piece, so I can pay for your sources . . . tempting?

To reach Exmoor, Emily drove inland while Mary admired the view from her elevated position in the Bentley. It was a slow, silent journey, but they were good friends, and the silence was comfortable, so neither stirred to break it. Emily steered down single-track lanes, lined with hedges long since parted from greenery, a few stubborn brown leaves still clinging to branches waiting for a storm to blow them free. When they reached the moor, Mary expected the sheep and cattle she'd seen to be replaced by ponies, but there were no animals, just miles and miles of fields, with an occasional distant clump of white indicating a remote farm building.

Closer to the road were prickly gorse bushes, heather and

bracken. She hoped they wouldn't have to tramp across any of that to reach the path Emily had chosen. The car rounded a sharp corner and in front of them, beneath a cliff that appeared to be at least five hundred feet tall, was the Bristol Channel and the distant Welsh coast. On the other side of the road, out of Emily's window, Mary could see a V-shaped valley, the side closest to the road almost vertical. She'd never seen anything so dramatic, nor so invigorating. Her legs twitched – she wanted to get out and walk. There was a short stretch of wooden fencing fixed to the edge of the narrow road; it didn't look up to the job of preventing a sheep tumbling over, let alone a car.

'I hope we don't meet anyone coming up the hill.' said Mary.

'Nearly there.'

They pulled off the road onto a strip of tarmac and bumped to a stop under a beech tree. They were on the edge of a forest. Leafless branches overhung the shiny, dark-green leaves of holly trees. Mary opened the tailgate, and Biscuit hopped out of the boot with a whimper of excitement, circling the car, his snout snuffling the ground.

'This way,' said Emily. 'It's a steep climb, but my legs could do with a workout.'

Mary called Biscuit to heel. They hadn't passed a single car, bicycle, or person for miles, and in the silence, surrounded by the tangled forest, she felt a peace she never felt in London. They tramped down a narrow muddy road littered with twigs, listening to their boots ringing on the tarmac. Biscuit dipped his head, lapping at a pool of water in a pothole.

'This place is magical,' said Mary, relaxing the lead and letting her dog pull ahead.

'It's busier in summer, but I like it all year round. You and Charles should come together next time. We can bring Svetlana to help.'

'How's your angel coping with Mark? You don't want to lose *her*!'

Emily huffed. 'He was all for letting her go under an economy drive. I had to beg him to let her stay. And now I hardly see her anymore. She's helping Mark, and I miss having someone to run errands and chat to.'

Mary could hear water. She peered down the steep valley side, through what looked like a massed army of tree trunks advancing up the hill, but she couldn't see the bottom. She checked Biscuit's lead; if either of them slipped, only a tree trunk would halt their fall.

'What budget has he trimmed instead?'

'Oh no, he's not on that warpath anymore. Barry is going to give him investment advice.'

Mary pictured the impish Bazza, his charming smile. She hadn't seen him for a while. 'Of all Charles's friends, he's the most fun, always makes me laugh,' she said. 'But Barry's a foreign exchange trader. How comes he's such a whiz at investing?'

'Mark says Barry knows what he's doing. Your father taught him well.' Emily grabbed Mary's hand, saying, 'Up here on the right.'

Ahead of them, by the side of the road, was a waist-high wooden sign fashioned as a hand pointing up a vertiginous hill:

LADIES MILE ¼ MILE

The pair walked in single file, Mary leading, stepping over tree roots, bracken brushing her sides, all the while the front of her legs burning with the effort. Biscuit was butting against her ankles, so she let him past, and he gently tugged her upwards, like a little engine.

'Emily, you haven't started seeing Paul again, have you?'

Behind her, she heard Emily huff. 'He won't back off. I keep finding little presents on the doorstep like a secret Santa. I'm so worried Mark will find them, I've taken to stalking the front door.'

Mary grimaced. 'Seriously, that's got to stop. How does he find the time?'

'Sometimes it's a courier, but lots of clients are based in the West End, so I guess he drops things off on his way back to the bank. He's got a chauffeur, easy enough to get him to swing by and wait.'

Mary spun round. 'Have you blocked his number?'

'That seems a bit harsh. He doesn't call, just sends emojis of beating hearts.'

Mary thought her friend was being flippant; she was behaving more like a teenager flirting in the school playground, than the married woman she was. 'And do you reply? Are you encouraging him?' asked Mary, giving her friend a stern look. 'Emily, be careful. I don't think it makes a hoot of difference if it's a woman or a man being scorned. The culprit can still get scorched.'

At the top of the hill, they stopped. Mary looked Emily full in the face, stroking a finger across her friend's cheek. 'You do look better after a night here. Fresher, fewer lines.'

'It's sleep . . . I sleep better in Devon. Mark has moved into his dressing room. That's not healthy, is it? In London, him not being next to me, it's a nightly reminder of my . . .'

Mary didn't fill the gap, curious to know how Emily viewed her affair. Did she regret being unfaithful? Was she working her way through guilt or grief?

'Come on, this way,' said Emily, pushing in front.

'Why is it called "Ladies Mile"?' asked Mary.

'Good question, certainly not because it's a mile long!'

They walked on in silence, the sound of the bracken swishing as they pushed past. A few minutes passed, then Emily said, 'I miss the attention Paul gave me.' She turned and started walking backwards, facing Mary, chewing her lip. 'It can be a bit lonely being married to Mark. He spends all his time in the office.'

'Not now, surely!'

'Yes!' said Emily turning around the right way. Her voice floated back to Mary, 'He's working seven days a week on this new business, even if it is in the dining room. He says he must, to get it going but . . .' She sighed. 'It all sounds *very* familiar.'

Mary took a long breath. The air smelled cleaner, fresher, and made her feel bolder. 'But to fund your lifestyle he has to find a way to replace a gargantuan City package.'

'Paul made time for me . . .' snapped Emily.

'Ouch. Don't say that to Mark. Why not tell him you want more of his time?'

'I've tried. I asked him to take me out for dinner, or a drink, but he just says not yet, and I don't feel I can push. He doesn't trust me anymore.'

Why should he trust you, thought Mary, when you've proved that he can't. But she didn't think Emily was ready for that message and didn't want to upset her friend a second time.

'He won't even go to see his mother. He says he's got work to do, but that's not why he won't go. Every time I try to slip out of the house, his head pokes out of that dining room like a cuckoo clock, asking me where I'm going, who I'm meeting, and how long I'll be.'

'It'll take time to rebuild his trust,' soothed Mary.

'How much time?'

In the "office", Mr Ellis looked up from his screen. 'How did it go with Ms Hetherington?' he asked.

Lana sat down. 'Work in Progress,' she said breezily.

'Questions for me?'

'A few points of detail – I'll email you a list.'

He wagged a finger at her. 'You're a fast learner,' he said, passing her a Post-it note. 'Do some research on these two companies, please. Ideas from Bazza.'

She looked at the slip of paper. She'd found out how to buy shares, here was her opportunity.

'Another piece of admin for you. Can you take a photo of your meters this weekend?'

Lana dropped her gaze. The previous reading was before Christmas, two months ago. She had a sudden image of her mother, warm air gushing over her feet from the fan heater, but it was soon replaced by one of Janet huddled over the stove. She nodded. It was a shame her guardian angel was in Devon; Lana couldn't dislodge the feeling her boss wanted her out of the flat without paying her redundancy and asked herself why she was helping him win money from his former employer when he was such a bad one himself.

'Hold the fort, I'm popping upstairs,' said Mr Ellis, rushing out just as his phone started dancing on the tabletop. 'Answer that. Tell whoever it is I'll call back.'

Pulling a face and murmuring 'Please' in a sarcastic voice, Lana scooped up the device, saying, 'Mr Ellis's phone.'

There was a scratchy sound, then a few heavy breaths. 'Hello, is he there?' shouted a female with a Welsh accent. 'He told me I could call him on his mobile.'

Lana suppressed a giggle. 'I think you may have the wrong number. This one belongs to Mr Ellis.'

'Oh, sorry, love,' said the sing-song voice, that Lana now recognized. Although she'd worked for them for fifteen years, Lana had yet to meet Mr Ellis's mother. She never came to stay, and rarely called Emily. 'Have I called when he's busy? I'm just worried, you see. I know there's something wrong, and now this man, who came to my house – well, he's got me worried too. I want to check he's all right, that my boy is OK.'

'What has this man said?'

The voice dropped to a whisper. 'He says that Mark lost his job.'

Lana hesitated. That was mean. It was up to Mr Ellis to tell his family what had happened, not a stranger. Who had done this? She tried to sound confident. 'He's a bit tied up at the minute. Can I get him to call you back?'

'No, don't worry. I've never called him at the bank before. Don't disturb him, love.'

She had a nasty thought – was this mysterious man Effing Paul? Was that who was upsetting Mr Ellis's mother? 'What was this man's name?' she asked.

'Tom, I think. Or was it Tim? He left me a card. I've put it down somewhere, but I think Romeo might have eaten it.'

*Tom, or Tim, not Paul.*

'Tell you what, Mrs Ellis, my name is Svetlana Smith. I'll give you my number. If that man gets in touch again, if he bothers you, let me know.' Slowly, she called out her number and made the other woman repeat it back.

'Oh, you are a dear. Thank you.' Lana heard pounding footsteps on the stairs. Should she tell Mrs Ellis to hold on? 'He's lucky to have a lass like you. Bye now, love.'

The door crashed open with Mr Ellis clutching the Fortnum's bag Lana had found on the doorstep. 'This wasn't in the master bathroom last night. Who delivered it?' He was struggling to control his breathing, reminding Lana of her mother having one of her heart wobbles. He snorted, 'Svetlana?'

She scolded herself. This wasn't her dispute; she should have left the bag where she found it. Why had she allowed past loyalty to Emily to cloud her judgement, especially as it was Mr Ellis she really needed to keep on side now?

'Who delivered this bag, and when?' he shouted.

She decided to be – *reasonably* – honest. 'It was on the doorstep when I got back from walking the dogs.'

'So, when I was out jogging,' Mr Ellis said, running his hands down his face. 'Which I do at the same time every morning.'

She didn't reply.

'This had better not be EFFING PAUL.'

On Monday morning, Lana took a photo of her meters and plodded up the stairs to work. She let herself in. Noticing that the dogs didn't rush to meet her, she concluded that Emily must have returned over the weekend. She printed out the meter photos and put both in Mr Ellis's in-tray, the less offensive gas one on top of the electricity. Downstairs, she went to fetch a clean housecoat.

There was a sheet of Smythson paper anchored to the top apron with a clothes peg. She recognized the writing.

*Dear Svetlana,*

*I presume Mark destroyed the note I left you before I went to Devon.* There followed a list of chores, and then a PS.

*I need your help. Master bedroom at 10 a.m., please. I will make sure Mark knows where you are.*

She felt a stab of irritation – she couldn't do two full time jobs – but the feeling was soon replaced by relief; at least she wouldn't be in the office when Mr Ellis saw those meter readings.

The bedroom looked like the backstage for London Fashion Week. Ball gowns were festooned across the bed like party streamers, sequins glinting in the late-February winter sun. Shoes and handbags littered the floor, boots were being used as makeshift mannequins wearing hats and Hermès scarves. Lana folded over a bin bag and trod gently on the outside, then reopened it, and laid a beige Ralph Lauren jacket on the top. Her mother was going to be happy this evening. Janet always got first dibs, and the balance of Emily's cast-offs went to a charity shop. Lana picked up a heavy silk blouse, the sales ticket still attached.

'Emily, you haven't worn this,' she scolded.

Her employer laughed; she was laughing a lot this morning, the Devon air seemed to have brought her sparkle back. 'Too big, makes my boobs look like they've drooped.'

Lana stroked the caramel-silk blouse; too big was a magic phrase. Janet would be disappointed, she loved silk. She felt her phone vibrating against her leg and pulled it from her trouser pocket. Mr Ellis. Her stomach clenched; he'd obviously seen the meter readings.

'How much longer?' he demanded.

Lana's eyes flickered to the wall-to-wall wardrobe. She arched her eyebrows at Emily, and said, 'We're nearly done.'

Emily shook her head. 'Sorry, we've been chatting. It's taking much longer than I anticipated, but we can't stop now. Another hour will do it.'

The phone went dead. Lana folded another jacket, lovingly laying it on top of the beige one, as if putting a puppy to sleep in its basket. She heard footsteps thumping up the stairs reminding her of the bag incident on Friday. The door sprang open. Mr Ellis stormed in, his face red as a ripe strawberry, breathing heavily.

'Emily!' he yelled. 'You asked for half an hour of her time. I've tried to be understanding, but either she works for me, or I get a dedicated assistant. I can't run this business on my own while you two mess around up here playing with clothes.'

'Oh, pipe down, you monster,' said Emily, scrambling upright. 'Nothing can be that time sensitive.'

Mr Ellis craned his neck towards his wife, and Lana saw the vein throbbing at the base of his throat. 'How do you know? Tell me, on what basis do you make that claim? You've no idea what I'm doing.'

'Pretending you're still at the bank?' snipped Emily.

Lana's insides squirmed. She was transported back to the thumb sucking child sitting on the top step, staring at the swirly patterned carpet, and felt a rush of sympathy for Mr Ellis. Emily's last comment was downright nasty.

'Svetlana, which would you rather be doing,' asked Emily, 'helping me or working for Mr Angry?'

Oh no, she wasn't going to be caught out like this. She may be employed as a housekeeper, but Mr Ellis held the cheque book.

'I can't do both jobs simultaneously,' she said. 'You decide what you want, while I take these downstairs.'

'A few hours, that's all I wanted! Your mother should have taught you to share your toys with other children.' Emily sneered at her husband.

*Ouch!*

'This isn't a game, Emily. GROW UP.'

Lana dragged the bags to the lift, listening to the squabbling pair swapping insults. She felt like the proverbial carpet being haggled over in a Turkish bazaar, Mr Ellis trying to buy her, Emily reluctant to part with someone over whom she used to have sole charge. Lana had checked with Clare – she didn't have to accept the changes to her role, but she wasn't about to point this out, not until she had a new employer.

Inside the lift, she pushed her glasses – which had slipped down her nose when she was doubled over the bags – back into position; the doors hissed shut, and she descended, breathing in the silence as the lift jerked downwards. She walked backwards down the entrance hall, sliding the bags to the door. Two floors down, she could still hear faint sounds of the battle being waged. It would only take five minutes to dump this lot in the flat.

She opened the front door. Barry was outside, his finger poised over the doorbell, an impish smile on his face.

'Is Mr Ellis expecting you?' said Lana. 'It's not in his diary.'

'Ha. I was in the area and fancied a slice of cake. Need a hand?' he offered.

'Please,' she said. 'Just down those stairs. I'll open the door.'

She left the front door ajar, unlocked her gate, and ran down the steps, Barry jogging behind her, a bin bag in each hand, his brogues clicking on the stone steps. Lana unlocked her flat. 'Anywhere will do,' she said, trying to ignore the pungent aroma of incense.

'What's that smell?' asked Barry, sniffing.

Lana slammed her door shut. 'Let's get back. It's a flat white, one sugar, isn't it?'

'Was that a joss stick?' he asked, grinning.

She shook her head. 'No. My mother likes to burn incense.'

He pursed his lips. 'You still live at home?'

'Kind of. The flat comes with the job, and my mother's not well, so she lives with me.'

'A boomerang parent!' he said, chuckling.

Climbing the stairs, she said, 'I'll get that coffee. What shall I say to Mr Ellis?'

'Tell him I've popped in with another tip.'

In the kitchen, she found her boss fetching himself a bottle of water and told him that Bazza was in the dining room. 'I'll make him a coffee, then I must get back upstairs.'

He grunted. 'How have you managed to use so much electricity in two months? You're way over your allowance.'

She looked defiantly at her boss. 'I'll pay you back.'

'I think you've had this conversation with Emily,' he said, turning towards the stairs, 'You can't.'

Watching his back, she asked herself how he could he be so heartless. He was literally trying to freeze them out of the flat to manipulate her into resigning; by Lana's calculation her redundancy pay would be less than his wife spent on dog food.

Across the street, Mary was unloading the washing machine. Rain spattered against her windows. She'd have to empty those buckets. Again.

*Brring*. There was a soft woof from near the Aga followed by Helen, her housekeeper, calling out, 'I've got it.' Mary hung the last shirt on the rack and tugged the rope; the washing shot upwards. She trotted to the stairs, trying to place the voice she could hear faintly above her, hoping it was the Aga man. Mary rushed into the entrance hall to find Tom's slight frame in her doorway. What was he doing here? She hadn't heard from him since he sent that weird text last week. Why didn't he ask Charles for help? He could introduce him to loads of City people.

'Will you take pity on a starving journalist?' asked Tom, grinning.

She managed a thin smile. 'I can fix you a sandwich. Come downstairs, it's marginally warmer.'

In the kitchen, Biscuit's tail wagged a greeting. Tom dropped to his knees, fondling the dog's ears.

'Cheese and pickle do you?' offered Mary.

It didn't take him long to steer the conversation onto the City.

'Why not speak to Charles?' suggested Mary; it was Charles's friends Tom was after.

Tom got up and walked to the table. He picked up the quote

the decorator had sent her for the work in the hallway. 'Come on, Mary, cut me some slack.'

'No.' She spread the pickle, added a slice of cheese, and pressed the sandwich together.

'Pretty please?' he coaxed. 'This is a serious article – I can pay you, and it could help with this,' he said, flapping the quote at her.

She hesitated. Outside, the rain was still streaking down her windows, filling her mind with an image of metal buckets. 'Tell me what it's about, your article.'

'It's an investigative piece about dodgy practices, like insider dealing.'

Mary felt her stomach churn. She hated references to dodgy City practices. After the "Big Bang" and deregulation of the City, those regular dollops of money which financed the upkeep of the Standerwick house mysteriously dried up. Mary suspected it wasn't a coincidence. Barry had told her that when he worked for her father, he used to boast about making money "the old way". Were people still trading on inside knowledge, even though it was now illegal?

'You should speak to someone on a trading floor.'

Tom smiled. 'See! I knew you'd be able to help. Five hundred quid for each contact.'

She nibbled at a fingernail. 'OK,' she said. 'His name's Barry.'

It was six o'clock on Friday evening, and in the basement flat there was no sign of Janet. Lana made herself tea and toast, cleared away and wrote a note for her mother. Just as she was putting on her jacket, she heard a key in the door, and Janet shuffled in.

'I'm just off out,' said Lana.

Janet yawned. 'Already?'

'Yes, I told you last night. I'm meeting Anne.'

'Umm,' mumbled Janet. 'Just give me a hand taking my blood pressure.'

Lana's jaw clenched. 'Can I do it when I get back?'

'If I'm still here.'

'Oh, Mum!'

'I can't help it if my heart plays up when it's inconvenient for you.' She stopped, put a hand on her chest, and squeezed her eyes shut.

'Right. Sit down, slow breaths,' said Lana firmly. 'In, then out. In . . . and out.' She demonstrated with elaborately long slow breaths. She sat her mother down and fetched the blood pressure monitor, ripped open the velcro and pulled the band tight around her mother's arm. 'You should wear that Fitbit I bought you.' She pumped up the monitor. 'You can check your heart whenever you want. It'll even do an echocardiogram if you ask it to, and it will give you – and me – peace of mind.'

She let the monitor exhale, checking the reading as it hissed.

'False alarm,' she said, feeling her own heart rate normalize. 'I'll take it again when I get home. Go to bed.'

She fussed over her mother for another ten minutes before bolting out the door, texting Anne:

On my way!

Lana panted her way into the brightly lit cinema foyer, puffing out an apology for being late and trying to recall the last time she'd been to the movies. 'Chill, the earlier performance isn't over yet,' said Anne.

Anne bought a beer and a family-sized pack of chocolates, Lana just a ticket. She'd been to the dentist at lunchtime to have her back left molar crowned. The numbness had worn off, but it would take longer for her bank balance to recover.

Anne ripped open her bag of chocolates; the smell made Lana's mouth water. She should've had more than toast for supper. She distracted herself by asking Anne if her rocket had germinated.

Anne's eyes twinkled. 'I swear there wasn't anything last night, but when I went to fill the kettle this morning, there was this green fuzz.'

'Why do you think it's called rocket!'

'I'm so excited. Can I put it outside now it's up?'

Lana laughed. 'Definitely not. And don't kill it. Test the soil with a finger – if it's moist don't water. Oh, and feed it in four weeks' time.'

'Feed?' asked Anne, a puzzled expression on her face.

'I'll give you some. Now, I've got a question: is anyone doing Mr Ellis's old job?'

'Nah,' Anne said, popping a chocolate in her mouth. 'No one can replace Mark.'

Lana screwed up her face. 'So, no one is doing his old job.'

'No one can, and it shows. The juniors are a bit jumpy; they can see we're losing pitches to other banks. There's a big one coming up, and Paul's leading it himself.'

'Paul!' exclaimed Lana. '. . . Williams?' Was Anne working for Effing Paul?

'You know him?' asked Anne, waving the bag of chocolates at Lana. 'Want one?'

'Never met him.' And she wasn't keen to change that. 'I've just heard about him.' Lana opened her hand and Anne shook several chocolates onto her palm. She slid one into her mouth, letting it melt on her tongue as she absorbed what she'd learned. Anne was working for Paul, and Mark's redundancy wasn't a sham. The odds on her earning that commission had just shrunk so low, winning the lottery looked more attainable. She picked up another chocolate, which was now slightly gooey.

'Yes, well, I suppose working for Mark and Emily, one way or another you would hear about Paul,' said Anne. 'Is Mark flat out? Has he got any free time? He used to mentor some juniors, and they keep asking to see him.'

In front of them, the door opened. A stream of people stepped out, blinking, chattering and laughing, pulling on jackets, and crushing empty popcorn cartons in their hands.

'Come on, let's get in and see the trailers,' said Anne.

Lana followed her new friend. Inside, the lights were dimmed, and there was the fetid smell of a recently crowded room. Anne led the way to their seats and flopped into hers. 'Tom has given me a date for dinner,' she said.

'Tom?' asked Lana. Was Anne cheating on Kenny?

'The journalist, you know, time management skills. Didn't I mention his name?'

'No.' Lana's mind wandered back to her recent call with Mr Ellis's mother. She'd been complaining about someone called Tom – or was it a Tim?

'I thought about what you said,' Anne continued, 'and I've said I'll only meet him if you can come too. He says that's fine. What do you think?'

On Sunday night, Lana was restless. She slithered around in bed, trying to ignore her Fitbit flashing like a miniature torch, glowing orange each time she wriggled her arm. She told herself that once she was comfortable, she'd drift off. She fiddled with the pillow and tugged the duvet up over her head. That's lovely, she thought, trying to settle her mind. Ten minutes later she got up, telling herself not to look at the clock; knowing how long she'd been battling to get to sleep would be like a dose of caffeine. She got up, yanked open a drawer and added an extra blanket, then scooted under the pile, and lay back exhausted. But her mind kept homing in on the same topic: in the morning she would have to tell Mr Ellis that Project Revenge was on the rocks. The bank was going to win before the battle had even begun. He didn't have a claim for discrimination, and he didn't have one for unfair or wrongful dismissal.

Lana sat up and flung off the blanket. She had a lot invested in Project Revenge; it wasn't that she wanted Mr Ellis to win, but if it was floundering, she would be out on her ear, with a commission of zero. The agency had been emailing her with housekeeper positions, but they were all in the country. Janet was going to have to compromise or rely on the council for housing. She rolled onto her side and peeked at the time – 2 a.m. Her head started to spin; she MUST get to sleep.

A few hours later, Lana woke up and glanced at her wrist. It had just gone six; she groaned and shut her eyes. Her head was muggy, her limbs felt too heavy to lift, she craved sleep the way her potted plants yearned for water on a hot summer's day. She got up, made a pot of tea, and pulled back the curtains. It was still dark, but the streetlamp illuminated the courtyard, the tiny greenhouse and her pots. At least in the countryside she would have a proper garden. Her plants would be happy even if her mother wasn't. She put her mug of tea down next to the figure of the Madonna, lifted the lid off the heated propagator, sprayed a fine mist of water over the seedlings, and sat down on a chair so her face was level with the seed trays. Yes! There were tiny strips of green, looking like strands of wool pulled loose in a jumper – her tomato seeds were germinating. She popped the lid back and sat on the bed with her planting plan on her lap. She liked to think she was operating on a grander scale, that crop rotation was what she was doing, not just pot rotation. If she shunted the potato tub up under the stairs, she could probably fit in a container of runner beans. Lana put down the plan. Her fuzzy brain made it impossible for her to think straight. Anyway, who was she kidding? By the time it was warm enough to put runner beans outside, she wouldn't be living here. The flat would be rented, or maybe Alex would call it home.

Lana pulled on her work clothes, then undressed again, kicking the elasticated trousers and sweatshirt aside. There was a stark contrast between Mr Ellis's hand-cut suits and her dingy outfits. She chose the heavy silk blouse she'd taken from Emily's decluttering bags – might as well go out with a bang. The fabric slid over her skin, giving her little goosebumps.

Mr Ellis's cup of coffee was early, and he didn't grunt when she put it down, instead muttering, 'Good morning, Svetlana. You look very smart today.'

'Mr Ellis, I need to update you.'

'Topic?'

'Project Revenge.'

'Yup,' he said, snapping his laptop shut. 'Take a seat.'

There was a rustling sound as she checked her notes, then, pleased to hear her voice wasn't trembling, she explained the different types of claim he could theoretically make. His elbows were resting on the table, his hands clasped as if praying. He didn't interrupt, just stared over her shoulder at the door.

'So that's it,' she said. 'And you haven't been discriminated against. Brick wall.' She shuffled her notes together. He inhaled a long slow breath, then exhaled noisily, and shook his head. 'No, this is wrong. There's got to be a way . . . we just need to find it.' He stared at her, unblinking. 'Let me tell you exactly what happened that day.'

Lana put down her notes. She tried to imagine what it would've been like for her boss, casting her mind back to January when she thought she was about to lose her own job. Strangely, she felt no fear now, not in the way she had last night. She didn't think he was about to fire her. Occasionally, she'd wanted to ask Anne why she thought Mr Ellis had been on the redundancy list; was she about to find out? She folded her hands in her lap as Janet had taught her to do at Mass.

Her boss tipped his head back, stared at the ceiling for several moments, then clicked his tongue and lowered his head, settling his eyes on her. 'The bank made a bunch of us redundant,' he said. 'They do it every year – it's quality control, weeding out under performers. I didn't expect they'd fucked up, missed one of the statutory hoops. But after I was dismissed, I was shown into a meeting room.' He paused, shook his head, as if dismissing the unpleasant memory, then continued. 'Someone else was already in that room,' said Mr Ellis. 'Until a few minutes earlier, he had been my boss.' He swallowed, then blinked.

She could see the pain in his eyes. No wonder he wanted revenge.

'He made it crystal clear,' Mr Ellis continued, 'and took great pleasure in telling me that the reason I was on the hit list was because I was married to the woman with whom he had been having an affair for the past year.'

Lana gasped. Emily had been having an affair with Effing Paul, who was still sending flowers and leaving presents on the Ellis doorstep. And to top it off, Anne now worked for him! Lana wasn't about to forget what her boss did to Janet, but she did feel a stab of compassion for him.

'I'm not telling you this for the sympathy vote, but to explain why I'm fighting. I wasn't dismissed as part of quality control. I was singled out because Paul assumed that if I wasn't pulling in a fat package, Emily would choose him. She hasn't – well, not yet anyway. There must be a law which protects people from that, and you and Clare need to find it.'

'We do!' Lana said, wondering why she felt so reinvigorated by this speech. She'd been given a reprieve, more time to earn her commission, but that wasn't why she felt elated. Was this what Anne and the juniors at the bank missed? She used to dislike Mr Ellis, labelling him unapproachable, rude and arrogant. That assessment was wrong; he was just wrapped up in his own powerful world, and he didn't abuse his power. He used it to motivate people.

The door burst open. Emily, clad in a silk dressing gown, wafted in, sighing. 'I don't think the dogs have been fed.'

Lana couldn't look at Emily. This woman had not only tipped her own world upside down, but she'd dragged her husband, Lana and even Janet with her. She rose, telling herself not to judge; she'd never had a serious relationship, had no idea what being married for twenty years was like, let alone to someone you rarely saw. 'I'll do it,' she said.

'Stay where you are,' said Mr Ellis. He locked eyes with Emily. 'How inconvenient for you, darling. I suspect the dogs have survived their ordeal, but please assume they are your responsibility from now on.'

Emily stared at him wide-eyed, her mouth opening and closing, then the door slammed behind her, leaving Lana alone with her boss.

'Better go and help, just this once,' said Mr Ellis. 'I could use another coffee. Bring one for yourself, and we'll call Clare together.'

Downstairs, there was no sign of Emily. Lana scooped out the kibble, two snouts nudging her calves. Puccini started playing. Lana dumped the bowls on the floor and headed upstairs.

She heard muffled voices coming from the dining room. Emily must've slipped back in to make peace with her husband. The soprano was singing loudly in Italian – Lana had researched the aria and discovered it was from the opera *Tosca*; the protagonist was asking why God was making her suffer. God wasn't exactly smiling on anyone in this household either, neither upstairs nor downstairs, despite her mother's religious devotion.

Walking past the office, she heard Emily's voice, a note of desperation in it. 'I must get that, Mark.'

'I'm on it,' Lana called out, striding towards the high-pitched noise.

Emily backed out of the dining room, shooting Lana a frazzled look. Her eyes were wide. 'Let me get that . . .'

'No need, the dogs are eating, and the coffee is on the go.'

Lana opened the front door. It was a man. His overcoat was undone, giving her a glimpse of a pinstripe suit and scarlet braces. He stepped forward, and she smelled his scent, citrusy and sharp. He was swinging a Fortnum & Mason bag, fastened with an orange ribbon.

'Could you make sure Emily gets this, please?'

Lana squirmed; was Emily watching her? She snatched the bag and slammed the door shut. She heard footsteps behind her. 'Who was it?' asked Mr Ellis.

Hiding the bag behind her, Lana muttered, 'It's for Emily . . .'

Mr Ellis had his hand outstretched. 'I'll take it to her. She's gone upstairs for a shower. Oh, and Clare's off sick, not expected back all week.'

Lana held out the bag.

He inhaled sharply. 'A man?'

She shrugged.

'Wearing braces and a bow tie?'

She nodded.

Mr Ellis's nostrils flared, and Lana knew she had just met the effing bastard who had upturned her life.

# *Seven*

**A month later**

For once, Anne didn't want to meet for a drink; she was on a diet. Lana suggested a walk. They met at Pimlico Tube station where commuters were scurrying out, discarding evening papers and buttoning up coats, and the pair walked along the Embankment towards the distant lights of Albert Bridge. Despite the moon being hidden behind a blanket of clouds, their path was well lit by the headlights of stationary traffic. 'What's up at work?' she asked.

'The boss is happy. We won a new fintech mandate – I had to organize a celebratory team lunch.'

Anne went on to tell Lana she had set up three meetings to discuss what Paul referred to as "Project Rear-guard". The first meeting was with all the departmental MDs, the second with a Magic Circle law firm, and the third was also with the MDs, because no one turned up for the first.

'They didn't go?' said Lana, with a little snigger.

'They all had amazing excuses. One told me he was recovering at home from jet lag after catching the red eye back from New York. Paul waited upstairs in the meeting room for twenty minutes, and each time I called him with another apology, he barked at me. So, I messaged him with the ninth. I could hear him marching back from the conference room from the other end of the office. He didn't look at me, just snarled, "Reschedule it, Anne, and warn them to make it this time, or else I'll set the third one up for 5 a.m. on a Saturday morning." Then he slammed his office door so hard I swear I saw the wood vibrating!'

Mr Ellis would enjoy this story, thought Lana.

A few hundred yards before Albert Bridge, a man walked into the road, twisting his body sideways to squeeze between two cars, emerging beside the two women, and scurrying off, leaving behind the greasy smell of a burger.

Anne let out a little moan. 'I could murder a burger.'

'Take your mind off food. Tell me what happened at the second MD meeting.'

Apparently, everyone went, but it only lasted twenty minutes, not the full hour Paul had allocated. Anne had typed the agenda and poured the drinks. Her new boss read out item one in a barrack room voice. 'Examples of non-collegiate behaviour. Who wants to start?'

Anne said she'd struggled to keep a straight face, watching Bazza, one of the few non-M&A people invited, who'd rolled his eyes at her.

'They were all suddenly fascinated with their agendas. Well, everyone except Bazza – he was fascinated with the biscuits. The silly clot repeated the question, as if they hadn't heard him the first time. It was Barry who piped up in the end.'

In her mind, Lana had a picture of Barry shovelling biscuits into his mouth. It was a while since he'd given Mr Ellis any investment tips, but she'd already invested half of her nest egg in two of his recommendations. 'What did Barry say?'

Anne laughed. 'Just that Paul could force everyone to attend a meeting, but he couldn't force them to lie; and that, in Barry's experience, Mark was one of the best team players the bank had ever employed. That in his opinion, even if Paul reconvened the meeting for noon on Christmas day, no one would say anything Paul wanted to hear.'

'Wow,' said Lana. 'What a story.'

The pair walked on. Lana stuffed her hands in her pockets, enjoying the image of Mr Pinstripe being lectured by Bazza. They reached Albert Bridge, which looked like it was gilded: the pillars, the suspension cables, the sides, all glowing with lights that reflected on the water's surface, painting a golden picture across the Thames. Lana gazed across the river at Battersea Park. On the path by the water's edge a trickle of evening joggers was moving in both directions. She would never choose to run, but she envied those people, able to decide how to spend their leisure time.

A truck drew up beside them, brakes hissing. Anne jabbed Lana in the ribs. 'Let's nip down to the King's Road, have a pizza and a glass of wine.'

'Diet, Anne? Better idea: let's go over the bridge, follow the joggers down to Chelsea Bridge – no temptation that route. So, what happened at the legal meeting?'

'Not sure. They didn't say anything interesting while I was in the room. There was a team of six lawyers! I had a squint at the agenda they'd brought when I handed round the teas, and there was something about considering appointing a barrister.'

Six lawyers! Paul was assembling an army to fight Mr Ellis. Were those terse replies to Clare's persistent letters a bluff? Was Project Revenge rattling Paul? Might Lana yet earn her commission?

There were only three numbers in Gwen's new iPhone: her son's mobile – which she'd copied from the emergency pad beside her own telephone – Deidre's, and Mark's assistant Svetlana. Having a mobile meant Mark couldn't dodge her calls anymore, and each time they spoke was an opportunity for her to ferret around for what was bothering him.

'How's the new bank going?' she asked.

'Boutique, Mum.'

'Boutique. There, you see, I'm learning!'

Mark laughed, but it wasn't a happy sound. 'Are you enjoying it, boyo?' she asked. In the background, she thought she heard Emily's voice calling Tosca. What was Emily or a dog doing at the bank? 'When you coming to see your old mum, then?' she coaxed.

'I can't get away at the weekends,' said Mark. 'I can't leave Emily on her own.'

Why ever not? Not that he had to. 'She can come too. I'd like that.'

'Mum don't nag. I must stay in London just now.'

'I miss you.'

She heard him inhaling. 'But you're well? There's nothing wrong?' he asked.

Should she tell him? She didn't want to make him unhappy, but maybe if he knew the truth, he'd make more of an effort. 'The doctor wants me to see someone about my heart.'

The line fell silent; she could almost hear him worrying. She shouldn't have told him.

'Your *heart*!' he said. 'I thought you just had a dodgy hip. Have you got an appointment to see a cardiologist?'

'I'll be seen when it's my turn.'

'No,' said Mark firmly. 'Come to London, I'll sort this. When can you get here?'

'There's my hip.'

'When's that op taking place?'

She felt a stab of pain in her chest, dropped the phone to her side and winced, before lifting it to her mouth again. 'They won't give me a date for the hip until they know if my heart's strong enough.' There, she'd said it now.

Opposite her boss, Lana was researching Barry's new tip, a London-listed company. She told herself most offices were open plan, forcing people to listen to personal calls, but this was the first she'd worked in, and Lana didn't understand the protocol. Mr Ellis put the phone down – should she pretend she hadn't heard anything? The printer hummed into action with an article comparing Bazza's tip with an American rival.

She glanced up. Her boss had his fingers pressed deep into his eye sockets. 'My mother's got a weak heart,' she said, collecting the printed page. 'Damaged it when I was born.'

He moved his hands sideways to cup his face. 'Is that why she lives with you?' She nodded. 'Does it affect her life much?'

Lana clipped the news article to the rest of the pack, wondering how honest she should be; was this her opportunity to explain why she needed the heating on longer in winter? 'Research for you on Bazza's latest idea. Ask him about the American company mentioned in the article I've printed; the journalist prefers their strategy.' She dropped the pack in front of him. 'My mother needs to avoid stress. She can't work, can only do gentle exercise, light housework, she can't walk too far. On the bright side, it hasn't got worse. She sees a cardiologist for check-ups and swears by him. I can ask her for his name.'

'Thank you.'

Lana had a sudden thought. 'Your mother could speak to mine?'

He shot her a grateful look. 'If your mother wouldn't mind . . .' The high-pitched sound of the soprano interrupted his speech.

'I'll go,' Lana offered. 'And I'll get rid of this cold tea.'

'I'm going to add another task to your list,' he said, grimacing. 'That bloody opera singer is beginning to get on my tits. Let's get someone in to change the ringtone.'

She was still chuckling when she opened the door. Her laughter caught in her throat. This time, the braces were purple and white stripes, and he wore a matching bow tie, and carried a turquoise bag large enough for Lana's weekly shop, the orange ribbon tied in a bow. Her hand clenched around her mug.

'For Emily,' said Paul.

Lana heard Mr Ellis's voice behind her. 'Who is it?'

'Go. Now!' she hissed, reaching out to claim the bag. A hand shoved her back against the open door. Her shoulder jarred against the wood, and she cried out, dropping the mug. It smashed onto the doorstep, shattering, and splashing tea over her blouse, Effing Paul's polished brogues, and the turquoise bag.

'How dare you keep coming round, you bastard! Leave my wife alone.'

Lana felt herself being pushed aside, then the door crashed shut, with Mr Ellis and Lana inside. His nostrils were flared, and she could hear him breathing as heavily as when he returned from his morning jog. Without looking her way, he charged up the stairs, yelling, 'Emily!'

Being a remora fish was fabulous, thought Lana. For a few moments, she stared transfixed at her screen: she'd earned a month's salary for doing nothing! The share prices of both of the companies she'd invested in had shot up by over 20 per cent. Lana snapped her computer shut. She had to pack. Tomorrow, Ovington Advisory, the dogs and Emily were all decamping to Croyde for a "bit of fresh air".

She pulled out her overnight bags, tussling with her conscience. Should she share any of her profit with the Church? Her mother had no idea, and Lana thought God was considerate enough to recognize she was already paying a decent whack – he could cut her some slack. She considered each bag in turn, viewing them as her employers might. The bright orange Sainsbury's one was larger, but the hessian bag didn't have a supermarket logo on the side. The largest, and by far the classiest, was the Fortnum & Mason bag her boss had told her to keep – together with the most amazing silk dressing gown – but she wouldn't be popular if she took that bag to Devon.

Her mother was standing by the hob, warming milk. 'How long will you be away?' she asked.

'I don't know . . .'

'Milk. What if I run short of milk?'

'Look in the fridge,' Lana said, wrapping newspaper around her gardening boots and shoving them in the bottom of the hessian bag. If it rained, Emily wouldn't walk the dogs. Surely her mother could manage to reach the local Sainsbury's on Sloane Avenue if she ran low on groceries? 'Mr Ellis's mother isn't well,' said Lana.

'Is that why you're going to Devon?'

'No, she lives in Essex.' Lana took a small bag with her into the bathroom and tossed in toiletries. She leaned around the bathroom door. 'She's got something wrong with her heart. I suggested she should talk to you.'

Her mother spun her wedding ring around her finger. 'I'm not sure that's a good idea.'

'Why not?'

'Well, I wouldn't want to alarm her. And she might not be as unfortunate as me.' The ring stopped spinning, and Janet said firmly, 'I don't even know this woman, she might be sensitive. Best leave it to the professionals. Ready for cocoa?'

'I said I'd ask you for the name of your cardiologist.'

'Whatever did you do that for? She's better off seeing someone local.'

'I was trying to be helpful.'

'You're meddling in my life,' moaned Janet.

In the morning, Lana sat in the back of the Bentley, the hessian bag at her feet, trying to ignore the frosty atmosphere in the car. For the first thirty minutes, Emily had chattered brightly, turning to speak over her shoulder at her housekeeper, but even she ran out of small talk by Heathrow. Mark didn't utter a word.

Lana knew the real reason she was going to Croyde. Mr Shiny Shoes. She didn't believe this story about Emily needing help because the Devon housekeeper only worked Fridays. Nor that Emily wanted company; if she did, Mary would be going. Mr Ellis wanted Emily away from Paul, and where her boss went, Lana followed.

They reached Somerset, and names that conjured memories of Lana's childhood. Weston-Super-Mare. Wasn't there a sweeping circular terrace of buildings, as elegant as that Georgian one in Bath they always used in period dramas? And she thought she remembered a pier where her father had bought her ice creams and candy floss. Either side of the car, fields stretched for miles, backstopped by the sweeping expanse of the Blackdown Hills. Sheep, cattle and horses were snatching mouthfuls of early spring grass. Lana imagined herself working as a housekeeper for someone who farmed, helping with the animals, cooking vegetables grown on the farm. If Project Revenge didn't pay up, Janet would have to compromise, or start relying on the state, rather than her daughter.

That first evening in Croyde, Svetlana served a fish pie. It was her mother's recipe and included capers and chopped gherkins. Alex – still wrapped in his surfing dry robe, making him look the size of a bear – took two plates, one for him, the other for a man he referred to as Ginge, and slunk away. Lana carried her food onto the terrace. She didn't blame Alex for eating with Ginge – Mr Ellis had been less than welcoming. Earlier, when they were unpacking the car, Alex and Ginge had appeared, looking like giant seal pups in their wetsuits. Alex gave his mother a hug, said a cheery "Howzit" to Lana, and fussed over the dogs. Mr Ellis had snorted at his son. 'I'm working while I'm here, so you and your mate can find somewhere else to play.'

'Dad, we're not playing,' Alex said. 'We're working too.'

'In wetsuits? You're surfing!'

'We just haven't changed yet. We're working.'

'Right. Fine. Well . . . it's fine provided it doesn't interrupt the real work.'

'Great to see you too!' yelled Alex, dumping the dog crate. 'Come on, Ginge, let's get out of Mr Angry's way.'

'Mark,' said Emily. 'Please try. You two haven't seen each other since Christmas . . .'

Lana bit her lip and slid into the house, clutching her hessian bag.

Now, sitting on the terrace wrapped in her waterproof dog walking jacket, the stiff sea breeze whipping her hair round her face, she listened to the waves crashing on the rocks of Croyde Bay. A gust of wind blew the peas off her plate. The door slid open. It was Alex.

'You look frozen.'

'I can't eat with your parents.'

'Nor can I. Why is he being so vile? Come and eat with me and Ginge.'

She followed him downstairs, wondering why Alex and his father always argued. Was it a clash of male pride? Ginge was sitting with a plate on his lap, staring at a computer. When she got closer, Lana saw the screen was filled with numbers – how could that be so absorbing? Alex sat down next to his friend. 'Ginge, this is Svetlana. She cooked dinner.'

Without looking up, Ginge muttered, 'Great food. Think I've found the gremlin, Alex. It was in J1044.'

'Sorted?'

'No, but it will be soon. Did you ask him?'

Alex shook his head. 'Not tonight, he's still shooting me dirty looks. The man's in a foul mood – he'd say no without even asking to see the business plan.'

The pair sat side by side, forking in food, jabbing fingers at the screen.

Lana watched Alex's furrowed brow. The men were oblivious to her presence. What was so interesting? She offered to fetch dessert. Neither responded, so she added their dirty plates to her own and left.

Upstairs, her employers had lit the wood-burning stove and were sat in armchairs facing the fire, their backs to her. The reception area was one large open-plan space, sectioned off by the stairwell, but there were no doors; she could hear every word. Lana was no marriage counsellor, but it sounded like they were having the sort of conversation they should've had two months ago. She didn't like listening, but she had to clear the dishes. Using a damp cloth, she wiped over the dirty plates then stacked them in the dishwasher.

'We never met at the house,' said Emily.

'Then why does he keep showing up now?'

'He doesn't have to be Hercule Poirot to get your address . . . You worked for the same bank!'

Holding a sponge under the tap to dampen the sound, Lana ran a sink of water.

'Are you still in touch with him?'

'I told him it was over before Christmas.'

'Well, he clearly doesn't believe you, and I'm not surprised with the way you acted at Charles's birthday party.'

'I was drunk, and you'd been behaving like a pig all day, then demanded I leave with you as if I were a child.'

Lana dunked the saucepans in the water and fished around for the sponge.

'Have you blocked his number?' asked Mr Ellis.

'It won't make any difference.'

'I'll take that as a no.'

'He was in love with me,' said Emily. There was a pause. Lana turned the tap a notch, drizzling out water, and rinsed off a saucepan as Emily continued mournfully, 'Worse, he was in love with the whole idea of me. You always told me how lonely the other MDs are. All divorced, any excuse to be in the office at weekends because they've nothing better to do, and you used to join them, to fit in. None of your work chums date, because they can't afford a second divorce.'

Beneath the soapsuds, Lana's hands were motionless, her mind clawing through the bits of employment law she could recall. What had Clare said about discrimination, that employers couldn't sack you because of your marital status? Was there a case for discrimination after all?

# Eight

Sitting at the furthest corner of the balcony, spreading her own homemade marmalade onto toast, Lana could just about blank out the sound of Alex screeching at his father. She hadn't heard one of these scraps since Christmas. She gazed out at the sea, tracking a little dinghy skimming over the water, its sail taut. There was only one person in the boat and, nibbling on her toast, Lana tried to imagine it was her – how would it feel to be so free, harnessing the wind, thinking only of yourself? The sun went behind a cloud and Lana shivered. She balanced the knife on her crumb-strewn plate and got up. Halfway along the balcony, she heard Alex shouting, '. . . Not everyone who works wears a shirt and tie.'

'Most people with decent jobs wear shoes,' yelled Mr Ellis. 'You and your mate may be great at playing computer games, but that, son, is not work.'

She shivered, her hand jolted and the knife fell onto the decking. She knelt to pick it up, her eyes straying inside – Alex was pounding the kitchen table with his bunched fist as if kneading a slab of dough.

'Thanks for your support and interest, *Dad*.' He stood up and his chair tipped backwards, landing with a jarring thud.

'I'm sure your father is interested, aren't you, Mark?' said Emily in a wavering voice.

'Forget it. I'm going to catch a few waves. Could you let my play date in when he gets here, Mum?' said Alex, storming off.

Lana rapped her knuckles on the door and slid it open. 'It's too cold out here.'

'Come in, Svetlana,' said Emily. 'Mark, *must* you be so dismissive?'

'I didn't have the same chances he's been given. He's had the best education money can buy and he's wasting his life playing computer games.'

'There's a very good career in gaming,' said Emily. 'Some players make a fortune.'

'Alex isn't one of them.'

Lana carried her plate through to the sitting room. The wood-burning stove was out, but the room was still warm.

'How do you know?' demanded Emily. 'You haven't shown the slightest interest in what he and Ginge are doing.'

'Don't be taken in, Emily. They're not cracking quantum computing.'

'I'm not claiming it's a real business, but couldn't you try? He's your only child.'

'I can't play act. When I see him doing something sensible, I promise you I will be the first to congratulate him.'

Her employers went out for the day, and Lana telephoned to see if Clare was back from sick leave. She was put through and recounted the conversation she'd overheard the night before about Paul firing her boss because he was married to Emily. 'Isn't that discrimination?'

Clare was skeptical. 'The legislation is designed to protect people who might be seeking flexibility because of their commitments to their spouse – wanting to get away promptly, not wanting to do antisocial shifts, spending time with their kids, that sort of thing.'

'But Emily said he used to go to the office at the weekend to fit in. Isn't that a good example?'

Clare explained that to succeed, she must provide evidence of discrimination linked to her boss being married: department meetings scheduled at inconvenient times, requests for flexible working hours refused, and weekend bonding sessions that clashed with his personal life.

Mr Ellis was a workaholic; the last thing he craved was time with his family.

'But the man defending this case told him he was being fired because he was married. Paul can't deny that.'

The lawyer clicked her tongue, and Lana imagined Clare fiddling with her glasses.

'Well, he could, but yes, I see where you're going. Paul is unlikely to perjure himself, and it might make him amenable to negotiating. Let me think about it. I need a bit more detail, could you get Mark to call me? What we really need is counsel's opinion.'

'What do you mean?'

'An expert who can tell us how strong a case we would have if we ended up in court.'

'I thought that was you?'

'I don't argue cases in court. Only barristers do that. We need someone to tell us how these facts are likely to be interpreted by a judge.'

'Is that expensive?'

'More expensive than me, and don't get your hopes up,' she warned before ending the call.

On her doctor's advice, Gwen – and Romeo – were taking longer walks. Today's walk was along the wide sandy pathways of Chalkwell Park. The flower borders were coming to life, daffodils swaying in the breeze like a colour chart for yellow paints, ranging from bright banana-yellow to almost white, interspersed with tiny double-headed narcissi. Gwen was enveloped with the smell of lily of the valley from a nearby bush, its massed bead-like flower buds pulsating with scent. The scents lightened her spirits and she relaxed her grip on the stretch lead, allowing Romeo the maximum range.

'I've lost two pounds this week,' announced Gwen. She felt a finger prod her side and became conscious of her tummy wobbling as she walked.

'Well done. How d'ya do that then, eh?' asked Deidre.

'Not eating biscuits. I don't have anyone to bake for.' Why wasn't Mark visiting? He was still insisting he had to be in London, but she knew he was in Devon because Alex had told her. Had she done something to upset him? 'But I need to lose two stone, not two pounds.'

The lead jerked, and Gwen stumbled; a stab of pain shot through her hip and she yelped, digging her stick into the sandy path. 'Give that dog here, Gwen,' said Deidre, taking the lead. 'Let's have a sit down.'

Deidre wound the lead around the leg of a bench and the women sat, Gwen with her legs straight in front, Deidre with one knee crossed over the other. 'Two stone – is that your target, or have you got to lose it before they'll do the op? Is that why you're still waiting for a new hip?'

Gwen watched Romeo chasing a dragonfly, jumping and snapping, his jaws closing on air each time.

'Gwen Ellis,' her friend said sternly. 'Tell me the truth.'

'It's more to do with my heart.'

'Have you told Mark this?'

'He wants to pay for me to see a cardiologist privately.'

'Let him. He's got the money.'

'But it's not right.'

'What's not right is having to wait. Don't feel guilty. Everyone would jump the queue if they could; you holding back won't make a jot of difference to anyone but you.'

'Ooh,' she groaned, feeling the fluttering start in her chest. Maybe Mark was right, and she should go to London and see a specialist.

Deidre turned and placed her arms around Gwen's shoulders, giving her a little hug and a waft of lily of the valley, reminding her Mark wasn't the only person who cared. 'You all right, girl?'

Gwen patted her chest; just thinking about Mark made her anxious. What was he hiding?

'Gone now,' she said, trying to sound calm.

'You gave me a fright there.' Deidre stood up and shook her head vigorously, her ponytail wagging from side to side like Romeo's tail. 'You have to go to London!'

On the first Monday in April, Ovington Advisory returned to London. They'd been away for over two weeks. Janet had been forced to take care of herself, although Lana had arranged a food delivery. Lana dumped her bag in the flat and rifled through her mail, fishing out two large white envelopes. She was disappointed. Inside were similar documents, one for each of the companies she'd bought shares in. She flicked through the first.

Dear shareholder . . . blah blah blah . . .

Lots of tiny dull words, a standard "thank you for becoming a shareholder" missive. What a waste of money. She tossed both in the recycling bin. She had more important things to consider – today the electricity tariff was changing, prices shooting up by more than 50 per cent. She photographed her meters and went straight upstairs. Lana didn't want to risk annoying Mr Ellis.

There was no one in the office. She opened the post and hid her meter readings under a pile of bills.

*

On Tuesday morning, Lana woke early, spritzed her propagator, planted a tray of orange pepper seeds and checked the share prices of her portfolio. All positive. Checking her nest egg had become a quasi-coping mechanism, a part of her life headed in the right direction.

Upstairs, she made toast and coffee and took it into the dining room. In Devon, Ovington Advisory had settled into a routine of discussing Mr Ellis's diary over breakfast, but today his coffee was cooling and Lana chomped her way through her share of the toast without him. She heard the front door slam and, seconds later, her boss poked his head into the room.

'Sorry, overslept . . .' he panted. 'Tried to run faster . . .' He paused, gulping to catch his breath. 'Can you postpone Clare by half an hour? I'll nip upstairs and shower, then we'll do the diary.'

His head disappeared; she heard the stairs creaking as he ran up them. She messaged the lawyer. Although Clare had been unenthusiastic about accusing the bank of discrimination, when Lana mentioned the idea to Mr Ellis, he'd instructed the lawyer to pursue it, and now, apparently, the bank had responded to their allegation.

Lana went to make fresh toast, feeding the cold slices to the dogs. Fifteen minutes later, her boss was back in the office, his hair wet from the shower.

'I'm only settling if the bank pays up – I was due a blowout bonus,' he said, biting into a slice of toast. 'After meeting Clare, I'm going to have to go straight on to that client lunch. Can you follow up with Bazza about that article you printed on his new tip? I forgot to do it before we went to Devon, and you're right, best to check he's sure I'd be backing the right horse.'

The soloist started singing.

Lana froze, her mug in mid-air – *not again*! Mr Ellis stood up, frowning. Lana reached the corridor ahead of him. Emily was at the front door in a pale blue, silk dressing gown, and above Emily's head Lana could see Paul. His hands were on Emily's shoulders, and his head was dipped. Had they been kissing? How could she be so brazen? Or did Emily think she was alone in the house? Had she checked her husband's diary? If Mr Ellis hadn't overslept, he and Lana would've left for the meeting with Clare half an hour ago.

Mr Ellis pushed past Lana, blocking her view. Emily screamed, and then a man yelped.

'Now fuck off!' cried Mr Ellis.

The door slammed shut. Lana's boss had his back against it, as if wedging it in place. 'Emily,' he said, 'you're encouraging him.'

Emily was shaking. Lana stood aside and in a swirl of silk Emily swished past and slunk up the stairs. Lana's insides were churning – this farce shouldn't be played out in front of her.

'Right, grab your stuff,' said Mr Ellis, yanking open the front door. 'We need to leave.'

Lana collected her bag, tore her coat off the rack, and jogged down the steps behind him.

There was a cab waiting, its door open; she got in and he clambered in behind her without looking her way. The cab sped off and up to Hyde Park Corner, past Buckingham Palace and onto the Mall, then around Trafalgar Square. In the strained silence, Lana waited for the topic of yesterday's meter reading to be broached, but the only sound was the gentle thrumming of the taxi's engine. On the Strand, Lana gawped at the theatres, then the Ritz, wondering how much the bank might offer to settle. She couldn't ask and had no idea what a blowout bonus meant; was it £100,000 or £500,000?

'I'm sorry you witnessed that, Svetlana,' said her boss, staring out of his own window. 'Yet again.'

'I've seen my own share of marital disputes,' she replied.

He was massaging his right hand.

'You didn't hit him, did you?' she asked, thinking she hadn't witnessed any disputes that ended in fisticuffs.

He turned and grinned. 'Glanced off his jaw. I wish I'd got his pompous nose.'

She gave a short laugh. 'I know it's not funny, but he does look so stuck-up. He won't report you, will he?'

'Nah. But we might have seen the last of those Fortnum bags.'

At the solicitors' they were shown into a plain room with no pictures and stark white walls. There was a large glass table with ten chairs squashed around it, each one abutting its neighbours. With no space to push the spares into a corner, Lana and Mr Ellis pulled one out opposite each other and scrambled in, like pilots into a fighter jet. Clare sat at the head, her elbows resting on the table.

There were three items on the agenda – response from bank, next steps and AOB.

'You've heard from them? What did they say?' asked Mark.

'In a word. No,' said Clare.

Mr Ellis tutted. His face was expressionless. 'Are they disputing my account of events, or claiming it doesn't constitute discrimination?'

Clare tapped a pen on her notebook. 'It's a craftily worded response. Here, take a look,' she offered, sliding a piece of paper down the table. 'That's a copy for you. There's no reference to your meeting with Paul in January, just a reminder that the time to accept their offer has expired, but they are still willing to pay.'

Damn, thought Lana, the bank was stonewalling, refusing to take Project Revenge seriously. Why had she allowed her hopes to rise, imagining that claiming discrimination would intimidate the other side? This was like using a peashooter to breach a castle wall bristling with archers, their bows pulled back, itching to shoot. She was never going to earn her commission. Her boss read the letter and pushed it towards Lana, chuckling. How could he laugh when the opposition were dismissing them as a minor inconvenience?

'Doesn't surprise me,' he said. 'What's your advice?'

'Well, it does surprise me. You were an MD. They know you won't be intimidated by losing what's on offer. So where do they think this is going? Is the bank prepared to go to court? Most employers don't want the drag on senior management time, and the legal fees preparing for the case will cost far more than I think you would settle for.'

'I doubt it. They have a better idea of how much I want than you do.'

'Want to share?' asked Clare, angling her head to one side.

'It's not the right time. What do you think their game is?'

Clare sat up straight and said, 'I'm wondering if they think you may be bluffing. That you won't want your wife's affair played out in court.'

'They should know me better than that.'

Lana stifled a gasp. Wouldn't her boss be embarrassed having Emily's infidelity discussed in public?

'I just have a hunch that's not the way the other side sees things,' said Clare. 'They don't think you will take them to court.'

'Disabuse them of that,' snipped Mr Ellis. 'Emily was unfaithful, but she chose me, not him.'

'Which brings us neatly on to next steps.' Clare tapped her pen on the agenda again. 'I suggest we write and propose arbitration.'

'What, like the trade unions?' asked Lana.

Clare glanced her way. 'Not quite as grand as that, but yes. It always plays out well if we do end up in court; demonstrates we tried our best to settle but were left with no alternative, because the other side wouldn't negotiate.'

Mark's phone rang. He glanced at the screen. 'Back shortly,' he said, clambering out.

While he was out of the room, Lana raised the topic of her own employment contract.

'I can't advise you, but if it's a general question . . .' said Clare.

'It's about my flat. It comes with the job,' said Lana.

'Is it a service occupancy?' asked Clare.

'Yes.'

'You understand that means that if you stop working there, you must vacate the flat.'

'I do. And I don't mind. The flat goes with the job, I get that.'

'The Ellises pay all the bills? You don't pay your own Council Tax for example?'

'They pay for everything. That's the problem. The thing is my mother lives with me. She's got a weak heart. I just want her to be warm but they limit my electricity, and restrict when the heating goes on.'

'Hmm,' said Clare. 'Sounds like a proper service occupancy. It's perfectly reasonable for them to restrict utility usage – after all you're supposed to be at work most days.'

'I understand, and I know utility prices have shot up. I've offered to pay for the extra cost of keeping the heating on during the day, but he won't let me. Can I insist?'

'Quite the contrary. It's his responsibility and I entirely understand why he won't let you contribute. If he did, it would give you tenancy rights, the right to stay if the job ended. He's also looking after you; if you didn't have a serviced occupancy, the value of your accommodation and all the bills he pays would be treated as a benefit in kind, and you'd have to pay tax on it.'

Clare arched her eyebrows. 'Imagine what your package is worth: a flat in Knightsbridge . . .'

Lana mumbled thank you. Why hadn't Emily explained this? She should never have blamed her boss for what happened to Janet last March. She'd assumed his motivation was selfish, but he had been protecting her; if he'd allowed her to pay a portion of her heating bill, she could have landed herself with a fat tax bill. She wished she hadn't made her resentment so obvious. The door opened, and Mr Ellis walked back in. Lana watched him with grudging respect.

'Anything else?' he asked.

Lana revealed what she'd learned from Anne, when they'd been walking on the Embankment nearly three weeks ago, finishing with the news that the opposition was considering appointing a barrister.

'Looks like they *are* expecting this to end up in court. I think I know who they'll be appointing,' said Clare.

'Who?' asked Mr Ellis.

'There's one standout KC in my field.'

'You'd better get some quotes. No rush, we've got to cycle through the arbitration dance first, but the next serious act is in the courtroom, isn't it?'

In Hyde Park, the soporific sound of grass being mown accompanied by birds serenading spring made Mary want to spread a picnic blanket and doze in the sun with a book. For the first time that year, she and Emily were being passed by joggers wearing shorts and T-shirts instead of baggy sweatpants and hoodies. The balmy backdrop contrasted with Mary's mood; Emily was complaining – again – about Paul's attention. Mary tipped her thermos cup, dribbling in peppermint tea, trying to swallow down her irritation. Was Emily secretly enjoying the drama? Was she bored? Mary didn't have time to be bored; she'd squeezed this walk into her afternoon schedule packed with tutorials, and she still had the ironing to do. She tried not to sound critical. 'It sounds like you're hedging your bets. Paul wouldn't risk a bloody nose from Mark if he didn't think he was in with a chance.'

Biscuit skidded to a halt, a muddy tennis ball in his jaws. 'Drop,' Mary instructed, holding out her hand. When was Emily going to admit what Mary already knew? Last night's dinner conversation with Charles wasn't chiming with Emily's version of her non-relationship with Paul. Charles had met Paul for a drink. 'He's so happy, it's like he's twenty years younger!'

'Why's he so happy?' Mary had asked.

'He's about to propose. Wants me to be his best man.'

Recalling her husband's words, Mary hurled the toy, watching the dogs scamper after it. 'Are you giving off vibes that might make Paul think you still care?'

'I don't think I am.' Emily crossed her arms over her chest.

Gripping her friend's arm, Mary said, 'Emily, this isn't fair. You're not telling anyone the truth, not even me. Mark's pride is crushed, and he's still working his butt off to maintain the lifestyle you crave. Meanwhile, Paul is telling Charles that someone – and we both know who – is about to leave her husband. Make up your mind and then spell it out. To both of them.'

Emily sighed. 'You may be right.'

'I KNOW I'm right. Paul's already asked Charles to be his best man.'

Emily groaned and hid her face behind her hands, 'I'm so torn.'

Mary inhaled deeply. It was tough being friends with someone this selfish. Did she really want to spend her precious free time here, soaking up Emily's "spoilt little rich girl" act?

Emily spoke softly. 'I wanted to give my marriage another chance, so I ended it with Paul. Then, when Paul fired Mark, I felt like I'd done the right thing . . . But it's been three months since he found out, and Mark still hasn't forgiven me, in fact, I think he's punishing me. He never makes any time for me, for us, and . . . well, I'm not sure I gave the right man his marching orders. Please don't judge me too harshly.'

At least *now* her friend was being honest.

'It's your life, but I think you're being cruel to both men. If you want my advice, try explaining how you feel to Mark, and give him a chance to change.'

# Nine

Gwen wasn't pleased to see the skinny journalist on her doorstep again. This time, Romeo barked. Good judge of character, that dog, thought Gwen, taking tentative steps towards the man.

'Mrs Ellis,' he said. 'I've come to invite you to dinner.'

'Why's that now?' she asked. 'Sit, boy.' She peered down at the dog. 'I said sit, Romeo.' Romeo remained standing.

'We'll be discussing the City, and I thought you'd be interested.'

'I'm not interested in the City. You should invite Mark.'

'No. This is about him . . . that's why I'm inviting you.'

Gwen looked down. Romeo was sniffing Tom's shoes, his whiskers twitching. Romeo's snout shifted to the bottom of the man's trousers, and Gwen bent and pushed him away. 'Why not ask Emily?' she suggested.

'She's not coming. But I'm going to invite her friend Mary. Look, I'm picking up some rumours about dodgy—'

She cut in. 'Dodgy what? Is someone saying nasty things about my Mark?'

'This is why I want you at the dinner. Someone who knows him well, who can stick up for him.'

She didn't like the sound of this. Who could be spreading rumours about her son, and why? Should she tell Mark?

Romeo cocked his leg, squirting at Tom's ankles. 'Charming!' said Tom, leaping back and shaking his trouser leg.

'You'd better come in and let me hose that off,' Gwen said, opening the door. 'I'm not coming to any dinner, but I'll give you my phone number – you can call me if you have any questions.'

'I don't believe the rumours. I think Mark may be the victim of a smear campaign,' said Tom.

Gwen frowned. Who would want to smear Mark?

Mary was grateful Charles didn't ask why they were walking Biscuit around Lennox Gardens rather than Hyde Park. She promised herself this was the last time she'd allow her name to be used as an alibi. She resented walking the streets to avoid bumping into Mark on his morning jog when she was theoretically in Paris with Emily, their return flight due in later this morning.

'The decorator is still chasing me about the quote,' said Mary wistfully.

Charles dropped her hand and tutted. 'And if we pay for that, what's next on the never-ending list?'

Mary gaped at her husband. That was a snap. She was saved from replying by the sound of a phone ringing.

'I think that's yours,' said Charles softly.

Mary dug into her handbag, pulled out the phone and flipped open its protective cover. *Tom!* She couldn't explain why he was calling. 'You go on ahead and I'll catch you up. This is work,' she said, trying to sound indifferent. 'Morning, how can I help?'

She watched Charles stride off, Biscuit's tail wagging slowly.

'You can help by saying you got my text and are coming to dinner.'

Mary visualized Tom's breakfast message. She had a nasty feeling about it.

Making great progress on my article. I'm hosting dinner tonight for my contacts. Please come.

She had to go. Barry would be there – he had a habit of talking freely when he'd had a drink; she didn't want him sharing tales of making money "the old way" and dropping her father's name into the conversation.

'Yes,' she said, her reluctance obvious. 'I may be late. I've a pupil at 5 p.m.'

'Why?'

'It's what I do.'

'But why? You don't need money.'

'Have you any idea how much it costs to run that house?'

'You've a roof over your head. The pipes are lagged. Stop worrying. I don't.'

And soon we will have a roof that doesn't leak, thought Mary, remembering that the scaffolding was being erected around their house next week. Was that why Charles was moody, because he didn't want the summer spoiled by scaffolding in the garden?

'Well, I do worry,' she said, ending the call.

She felt a tight sensation in her chest. Tom was clearly pleased with his progress. Why had she given Barry's contact details to a journalist?

The coach departed Colchester bus station promptly. Deidre told her it would be faster by train, but Gwen was firm. 'I know where I am with a bus, Deidre, and I'm not exactly in a rush.'

Fanning herself with a copy of the coach timetable, dressed in her special-occasion, belted raincoat and the stylish cloche hat which Deidre said made Gwen's face look friendly, she told herself it was the right decision. She'd allowed Mark to book an appointment with the cardiologist for Monday. 'Come down Saturday,' he'd suggested, 'make a weekend of it.' She hadn't told him she was coming a day early; she would surprise him.

As the coach trundled down the A12, she drank her way through a flask of tea, peering out at the Essex countryside. It was a pleasant journey, but Gwen couldn't dispel a sense of foreboding. There was another reason why Gwen was travelling to London. This was not a trip she wanted to make; it was one she felt compelled to make. Tom had sent her a message:

I can't find anyone to speak up for Mark, please come to my dinner.

Something was very wrong. This journalist was on to something, and if no one else would do it, she must defend her lad.

By the time Gwen reached her son's house, she was sweating in her outfit. She sniffed at the air; it smelled dusty, as if it needed a spring clean. She hadn't been to London since Steve drove her up to see *The Mousetrap* to celebrate their first wedding anniversary. She pushed the bell. Someone inside was singing in a peculiar high-pitched voice; she almost sounded in pain . . . was it Emily? The singing stopped; the door opened. A smartly dressed middle-aged woman stood in the entrance hall, one hand gripping a dog by the collar.

'Hello, luv. Is Emily in?' Gwen asked. She leaned over and fondled the dog's ears. 'Are you Tosca or Floria?' she asked, dragging her trolley into the hallway just as Mark rushed out of a side door.

'Mum!' He froze. 'Why didn't you tell me you were coming early?'

She opened her mouth, then shut it. What was he doing at home in the middle of the day?

'I'll just finish in the office, and then I'll be right with you,' he said, beaming at her and disappearing again.

The office? Her heart was racing, she felt dizzy and then she collapsed against the wall. The office was at home. He wasn't starting a new bank, this was a "kitchen table" business. That journalist was right: he'd been fired. Oh, this was terribly wrong. Gwen breathed slowly, her heart racing. She put her hand on her chest and looked up at Emily on the half-landing.

Emily spoke in a slightly clipped tone. 'Gwen? Why didn't Mark tell me you were coming today?'

The hallway fell silent. Gwen rubbed her chest, trying to ease the pain. This was a bad idea; she wished she hadn't come.

For the second time that day, Gwen was sitting in the back of a London taxi wearing her hat and raincoat, the belt secured and neatly tucked into the buckle. This time, she was fidgeting with her walking stick, tapping it on the floor, then resting it flat across her legs. What was she going to hear tonight? Tom claimed someone was spreading rumours about her son; he'd been right about Mark losing his job, he might also be right about the smearing.

Her second taxi was prepaid; she'd given Mark the address, and he'd scowled at the slip of paper. 'Why are you going to South London?'

'I'm meeting someone.'

'Who?'

'Don't be nosy.'

'Mum, this is London.' He wagged a finger at her. 'Is this someone you've met online?'

'I'm not daft. And there's no need to worry, I won't be alone.'

When the taxi arrived, Mark ushered her into the back, doing up her seatbelt and tucking a fifty pound note and a front door key into her hand.

'I wish you'd tell me what you're up to,' he said, as if she were the child. 'Now you've got your mobile, haven't you? Call me if you get nervous, and I'll come and fetch you.'

'But you're out with your client.'

He pulled a quizzical face. 'He's a client, not the king. He won't mind if I take a call from my mum.'

The taxi stopped in the middle of a steep street of terraced houses, reminding Gwen of her parents' house in Bargoed. In snowy winters, she and her friends had taken turns to slide down that street, sitting on top of a homemade toboggan fashioned out of part of an old hen house. Unlike that street, this one was lined either side by parked cars.

'Number 19, luv,' called out the cabby from the front. 'On the left, blue door.'

Using the grab handle to pull herself upright, and with the aid of her walking cane, Gwen shuffled off the seat and out of the taxi. She leaned onto the stick and plodded to the blue door, eyes searching for the correct bell: Flat 1. There was a scratchy sound, and she heard Tom's voice through a speaker to the side of the door, 'Come in, I'm straight in front of you.' Then a sharp buzzing noise.

Gwen pushed the door and found herself looking down a short corridor to another door propped open with a pile of books. Breathing heavily, she hobbled towards the sound of voices, one of them recognizable as Tom's. A burst of laughter rang out, then a loud female voice, also familiar somehow, said, 'And just like that, the diet was over. I can't say no to Prosecco!'

Gwen walked into a small room that looked like it was the hub of the flat. In front of her was a large, black leather sofa facing the biggest flatscreen television she'd ever seen. At the far end was the kitchen, with a central island. She eyed the shiny chrome stools at the counter suspiciously – how was she going to climb onto one of those?

Three other women were present – she recognized Mark's housekeeper. What was she doing here? The Prosecco lady crossed the room, removed Gwen's stick, and hung it from the edge of the breakfast bar. 'So you don't forget it!' she said in the sort of carefree voice adopted by those who don't appreciate there isn't any danger of you forgetting your walking stick.

*

Listening to a Prosecco-fuelled gabbling Anne, Lana picked at her food asking herself why she'd agreed to come; she would have nothing to add to the discussion about time-management skills. She should be at home snipping off the side shoots of her tomato plants. But she had to be here, not to support Anne – the woman had more confidence than a market trader hawking knock-off Louis Vuitton bags – but because Kenny didn't want his wife here alone.

Lana found herself positioned between her boss's mother and Emily's friend Mary – what were they doing here? Mary was a teacher, which must necessitate time-management skills, but Mrs Ellis senior was unlikely to have anything more to add than Lana.

'Sounds like they're lucky to have you, Anne,' said Tom. 'What are they like to work for?'

'They're a bit of a dull lot. Workaholics . . .'

Lana thought of her boss; work was his life!

'Bet you livened things up a bit when you arrived,' said Tom.

'I was a tasty prospect for those young bankers,' Anne continued. 'I knew what was on offer, could have had my pick, on my terms. But I was never really tempted.'

'So, you didn't fancy life as a trophy wife?' asked Tom, leaning over to top-up Anne's empty glass.

'You sound like my mate, Raquel,' Anne said, picking up her full glass. 'Trade up, she used to tell me. Kenny for the money!' She laughed and snatched another gulp of Prosecco. '"Tell me, Anne," she'd say. "What's not to like? All that money and the freedom to spend it any way you want while he's stuck at work."'

Anne was talking loudly. Lana had counted three glasses of Prosecco before Tom carved the chicken, and her friend was holding her glass at an odd angle.

'But Raquel never met any of them,' said Anne, shaking her head. 'All they ever talk about is work.' What was going on, wondered Lana. They weren't talking about time-management skills. Anne was laughing, stroking the side of her glass. 'Do you know what else she used to say?' She held out her glass towards Lana, as if toasting her. '"Who even cares? You won't see anything of them, will you?" And she was right there.' A thoughtful look spread across Anne's face. She put down her glass.

Tom refilled it, and asked, 'What did Raquel mean?'

'She had no idea what life as a banker's wife is like. I know the trade-off. A big house, staff, privately educated children, wardrobes bulging with Christian Louboutin and Jimmy Choo. But the wife never sees their husband cos they're always working, and when she does, *poor her*, they're so boring they make a train timetable look interesting.'

Lana glanced sideways at Mrs Ellis whose face had drained of colour. She could hear the older woman breathing hard. Did she think her son was like the bankers Anne was describing? She must know he wasn't. Mr Ellis may have sold his soul to the City, but Lana had been working for him for four months now, and her boss was neither nerdy nor dull.

Watching Anne's glass hover on its way up to her mouth, Lana tried to decide if Anne had just sat back on her stool or slumped. 'I'm glad I didn't make the trade.' said Anne. 'Better off just working there. Money traps them. They use the bonus to placate the wife, cos she's alone, and so the cycle continues.'

Tom's eyes wavered towards Mrs Ellis as if assessing her, then he asked, 'Is that what Mark does? Placate a bored wife with money?'

Lana's fork dug into her plate, making a screeching noise. She eyed the journalist over her water glass. 'That's a mean suggestion,' she said.

Anne pointed her knife at Mrs Ellis. 'Mark is different.'

'How so?' asked Tom.

Anne gave him a penetrating stare. 'He still has a wife.'

'For how much longer?' asked Tom.

Beside her, Lana noticed Mrs Ellis stiffen.

'Marriages don't always recover from an affair . . .' said Tom with a smug look on his face.

A spluttering noise came from Mrs Ellis. Lana patted the older woman's back and leaned across, saying, 'Don't listen to him – they're working things through.'

'Your new boss and your old one don't get on,' Tom said to Anne as he collected the dirty plates. 'Is that because they have the same taste in women?'

Lana had a mental picture of Effing Paul at the front door with one of those turquoise bags.

'Cut that out NOW, Tom!' shouted Mary.

Tom smiled the lazy smile of someone who has got exactly what he wanted. Lana shot her friend a beseeching look. 'Anne, change the subject,' she pleaded. 'Now!' She was relieved to spot a worried expression cross Anne's face.

Her friend leaned towards Mary and said, her words slurring, 'There's a bit of a flap on . . .' Anne took a swig of Prosecco and lowered her voice. 'My friend in compliance says someone's in hot water on the trading floor . . .'

'ANNE!' cried Lana, her heart racing.

'Who's in trouble and why?' asked Tom, latching onto the suggestion.

'It's nothing to tempt you with, Tom,' said Mary firmly.

'You'd be surprised what tempts me!' quipped Tom.

Anne picked up her wine glass. 'Someone in the department mentioned trading irregularities,' she said.

Lana glared at Anne and mimed to her friend to zip her

mouth shut. At last, Anne clammed up, reverting to explanations of how she managed to fit in running Kenny's life for him around her busy day job, but Lana sensed the women either side of her shared her own goal to scarper before Anne revealed any more secrets.

The four women shared a taxi home, three of them sitting silently, while Anne, strapped onto one of the drop-down seats, kept up a monologue eulogizing about the evening. Wasn't the chicken delicious? She must ask for the recipe for that chocolate cake, and hadn't Tom been generous with the wine? Trying not to look at Mrs Ellis or Mary, Lana clutched the sides of her own drop-down seat, willing her friend to stop burbling. Didn't she realize she was the only one who'd enjoyed herself?

The first stop was Rawlings Street. The cab pulled up under a streetlamp, and Mrs Ellis and Mary pressed themselves against the back of the bench seat, moving their legs sideways as if worried that an inebriated Anne might dump an unwelcome gift in their laps. Lana got out, skirted around the back of the taxi, and opened the door for Anne. Her friend was struggling with her seatbelt, giggling. 'Tricky little monster, aren't you?' she said. Lana leaned in, batting away Anne's scrabbling hands, and released the belt. Her friend fell forward against Mary's legs, and Mary huffed. 'Oopsy daisy,' said Anne, pushing herself upright.

Lana grasped her friend under the armpits. 'Sorry, Mary,' she said. 'Come on, girl, let's get you upstairs to Kenny.'

'Lovely evening, nice to meet you both,' said Anne, falling out of the cab.

Lana stumbled backwards, wrestling to keep herself upright under the extra weight. 'Mind the kerb there, Anne,' she said. Checking the traffic, she led Anne across the road, whispering, 'I don't think Mrs Ellis knew about Emily's affair.'

Anne stopped in the middle of the road, a hand clamped over her mouth. 'NOOO,' she cried out. 'What have I done?' She struggled like a squirming puppy, but Lana clung on.

'Anne, stop it!'

'I've got to go back and apologize.'

Lana shook her head. 'An apology won't help.'

Mrs Ellis was discovering her son's innermost secrets; Lana only hoped her heart was up to the strain.

Waiting in the taxi beside Gwen, Mary was conscious of an uncomfortable silence. Mary had been surprised to discover who the elderly lady was when Svetlana introduced them. How had Tom managed to find Mark's mother? Why had he even bothered . . . and where was Barry?

She watched the two younger women standing in the middle of the street, the sober one remonstrating with the tipsy one, who seemed to want to return to the taxi. Mary hoped not; she wanted to get to bed, she had a packed morning. Saturdays were always popular for tutorials, and there was Pilates with Emily.

Mary couldn't think of anything to say to Mark's mother; she'd seen the look of horror on the older woman's face when Tom mentioned the affair. And now Gwen was breathing strenuously, avoiding Mary's eye. Did she suspect Mary had helped hide Emily's affair from her son? Did she want to jab her walking stick into Mary's foot or whack her with it? Would Gwen tackle Emily tomorrow morning? Should Mary message her friend? She reached for her handbag, and then realized she couldn't warn Emily: she would want to know how her mother-in-law had discovered the secret, and Mary didn't want to confess to the dinner with Tom. She had a nervous feeling about it all; was Tom really writing an investigative piece about the City? She didn't like that smirk on his face when he had said goodnight.

# Ten

From somewhere above her, Lana could hear voices. Someone laughed. She watered the base of the seedlings she'd planted over the weekend, then tilted her face to the sun, letting it warm her skin. There was a crowd standing on the pavement in front of the Ellis house. What were they doing there? Lana turned away and opened her greenhouse. She hoped this fine weather would hold – it was Chelsea Flower Show week, not that she'd ever been with tickets costing £40 each, but she enjoyed watching the highlights on TV. She heard a guffaw of laughter and glanced upward. A man leaned over the railings, a flashbulb went off, and Lana raised a hand to cover her face. The photographer called down, 'Mrs Ellis?'

'No,' she said, sliding shut her greenhouse and dashing to her front door. The overnight infestation of aphids would have to wait.

Inside, she pulled the curtains shut and switched on the lights. Someone was hammering on the door – they must have vaulted her gate! What was going on? Janet appeared from her bedroom, doing up her silk dressing gown, a pair of kitten-heel mules on her feet. She yawned. 'What time is it? Who's banging on the door, luv?'

'Don't know, Mum,' Lana said, reaching for her jacket, 'but I'm going to have to find out. I must get upstairs; Mondays are always hectic.'

'Any water in that kettle?' asked Janet, giving it a shake.

Lana picked up her keys. A boom came from the corridor, as though someone was trying to kick in the front door, and her hand tightened, forcing the keys into her palm. She hoped the reason these people were clustered round her employers' house wasn't connected to Tom. Should she warn them? There was a rat-a-tat at the front bay window, and a muffled voice said, 'Mrs Ellis.'

Lana stuffed her keys in her pocket. If people had climbed over the gate to get down here, imagine what was going on above – Emily and her boss wouldn't need warning. She opened her front door. A stampede pushed forward, cameras flashed, microphones were waved. For a bizarre moment, she had a mental image of the scene in *Notting Hill* when Julia Roberts is tracked down to her new boyfriend's house and Rhys Ifans opens the door in his underpants. She did a quick scan of her torso.

'Mrs Ellis, this way. Look this way,' called a man.

There was so much shouting; everyone was talking over everyone else, and she couldn't separate the voices, or decipher specific questions, but the crowd seemed to think she was Emily.

'I'm not Mrs Ellis,' she said firmly, elbowing a man aside. 'Let me through. I've got to get to work.'

'But you know her, right? You must do. Could you comment on what she's done?' shouted a female voice.

'What's she like?' yelled someone else.

Heart pounding, head lowered like a rugby player making the final push for the opponent's touchline, Lana forged a path through to her gate. She left it ajar – she didn't want someone breaking the lock. On the pavement, someone gripped her arm. 'Is she glamorous?' asked a man. Lana shook him off and, using her elbows, forced her way to the Ellises' front door, people crushing and pushing all around her, like football fans eager to pass through the stadium turnstiles. How could they do this job? She turned around and said in a steady voice, 'Leave me alone. I'm not going to say anything to any of you.'

There was another rumble of voices, and business cards were thrown at her amid shouts of '*We'll pay for your story.*' She leaned back against the front door, breathing as if she'd been chasing the two terriers around Hyde Park. If she unlocked the door, would some of these monsters try to push in behind her? Suddenly, the door opened, a hand gripped her shoulder, she tottered, and then was pulled in backwards. The door crashed shut. Lana turned around and put a hand to her chest, feeling her heart hammering.

'You OK?' asked Mr Ellis, peering down at her.

'I've had better Mondays,' she spluttered. 'What's going on out there?'

Peering past Mr Ellis, she spied Emily sitting on the bottom step, looking like a child in her silk dressing gown, her hair askew. Next to her, with her legs out straight, was her mother-in-law, rubbing Emily's back as if trying to dispel a bout of hiccups. 'There, there, now,' said Mrs Ellis kindly. 'Nothing can be that bad. No one's died.' It was as if she were comforting a toddler after a bad dream. She really is a remarkable woman, thought Lana, she'd only discovered Emily had been having an affair two days ago.

Behind her, Lana heard the crashing sound of fists on the door; the dogs were barking, and above the noise, the soprano was singing – it was like being at the opera with a very rowdy audience. Lana was sick of listening to Puccini. Tosca had nothing to complain about compared to what was going on in this household.

'Fetch me a screwdriver so I can disable that, please, Svetlana,' said her boss. 'I doubt we'll be answering the front door today.'

'Yes, Mr Ellis.'

His eyes sparkled, his mouth stretched wide, then he was laughing. 'If there was ever a more appropriate moment for you to start calling me Mark, surely it's now?'

She managed a smile. 'Yes Mr . . . Mark.'

With the doorbell disconnected, Lana and the Ellis family took refuge in the kitchen. Lana donned a housecoat, and soon the grinding and gurgling of the coffee machine eclipsed the noise from the street. Mrs Ellis and Emily were sitting at the kitchen table; Floria was on Mrs Ellis's lap, Tosca on Emily's. At the breakfast counter, Mark had his phone in his hand. 'Well, that explains why we're being door-stopped. The question is: who spilled the story, and why?'

Lana's eyes met Mrs Ellis's – she wondered if her own face had the same panicked expression as the older woman's. Emily pushed Tosca off her lap and got up. She peered over at Mark's screen and let out a howl which Lana suspected Janet could probably hear.

Mark glared at his wife. 'Who have you spoken to?'

Emily was shaking. 'Only Mary, and she wouldn't say a word.' Emily snatched the phone off her husband. 'There's reams of it . . . and photos . . . Oh, Mark, I can't even read it,' she sobbed, dropping the phone.

'Mark! Don't be so cruel,' scolded Mrs Ellis. 'You'll make her cry.'

Mark picked up his phone, then glowered at Lana. She met his eyes, and her heart sank as they burned into her.

Across the square in the Standerwick kitchen, Mary could hear the comforting sound of Biscuit's bowl scraping across the floor tiles as he nosed down the last remnants of food. The television was on, the presenter giving an update on the Russian invasion, and Mary was half-listening while scribbling a shopping list. Charles walked in and muted the TV.

'I was listening to that, Charles,' said Mary.

'Something far more important needs your attention,' he said, placing his phone flat on the kitchen table.

Had something happened to one of the girls? She swallowed, searching Charles's face for clues. His lips were pressed tight together, but he wasn't flustered or distressed. Mary crossed the room and bent to pick up the dog bowl.

She heard Charles tutting behind her. 'Mary . . . Mary, not now . . . You've got something urgent to sort out.'

She turned her head. 'What is it, Charles?'

He picked up his phone and tapped the screen. 'It's an email from Tom.'

Mary gulped. Had Tom told Charles she'd sold him Barry's phone number? Slowly, she walked towards the table, panic bubbling up inside her. 'What does he want?'

'He doesn't *want* anything,' said Charles, shaking his thatch of brown hair. 'He's sent us a copy of an article he's published today.'

'About . . . what . . .?' she asked, her voice trembling.

'I think you know what it's about.' Charles's eyes settled on hers. 'If you're this "close friend of the couple", you've got a lot of fence mending to do.'

Mary let the dog bowl clatter onto the kitchen table and scooped up the phone. She turned her back on Charles, the phone wobbling in her shaky hands, dipped her head and read.

Top notch banker and his lover hatched plan to shaft the husband.

She felt dizzy. This wasn't an investigative piece. 'How could Tom do this?' she whined. 'He's one of your oldest chums. He's ex-army, he shouldn't be shooting at friends.'

Charles removed the phone and took both her hands in his. 'He's just doing his job. And he was a gunner, the drop-shorts were never much good at aiming.'

She wrenched her hands free. 'But he *knows* she's my best friend!'

'He doesn't care.' Charles's eyes swept over her. 'Darling, he *can't* care, he wouldn't have got to where he is today if he cared what people thought of him. He's got a hide that would make a rhinoceros look thin-skinned. He probably thinks he's doing you a favour forwarding the article.'

She groaned. Did Tom really think he was being kind? She picked up the phone and forced herself to read. There were three pictures. The first was of Paul; it looked a few years old and must have been taken in Canary Wharf, she recognized the HSBC Tower. The next was of Emily leaving her house, dressed in body-hugging pale blue Lycra; it was the outfit her friend had worn to Pilates two days ago. Tom must have arranged the photographer for the morning after the dinner. Beneath that photo was the comment:

Sexy Emily torn between two lovers.

What was Emily going to say? She closed her eyes, muttering 'Oh, shit . . .' The last photo also featured the Ellis house and showed Mark in jogging shorts and a damp T-shirt. He was unshaven and his hair dishevelled, which was, no doubt, the photographer's brief.

Mary lowered her hands, gripping the phone tightly as if she could squeeze away the story. She let out a strangled moan. 'Oh my God . . . the filthy little rat. I went to that dinner to protect her, to try to stop—'

Charles raised his hands. 'Woah . . . Dinner . . .? Is that where you were on Friday? What have you done? Who else was there?' He had adopted his parental tone.

'I didn't think he had a story. He cooked delicious food, served lovely wine, he couldn't have been more attentive.'

'Mary, I didn't ask what was on the menu,' Charles said in a brittle voice. He repeated his previous question drawing out the words: 'Who . . . else . . . was . . . there?'

She swallowed. 'Mark's mother—'

'Mark's mother!'

'—Svetlana.'

'Why? What was *she* doing there?'

'She was giving Anne moral support.'

'Who the bloody hell is Anne?' he asked, his kind eyes suddenly looking poisonous.

'Mark's former PA. She works for Paul now.'

'Oh my God, he rounded you up like a bunch of kids, fizzed you up with sugar, and let you wreak havoc. You never stood a chance.'

She looked down at the screen, not wanting to read the words. 'How bad is it?'

'It's bad. You'd better read it, then call Emily.'

She sat down, scanning the article, hoping he was exaggerating. He wasn't. Tom painted a picture of a raunchy affair with "*sizzling sex*" – how could he possibly know that? Emily was reported to be "*trapped in a loveless marriage*". Mark was the cuckolded husband fired when he demanded the affair stop. This was all her fault. Tom had met Paul and Mark in her house. She should've realized his journalist antennae would pick up on the love triangle.

She read on.

A source close to the bank confirmed that Mr Ellis lost his job four months ago but declined to comment on rumours that the reason behind this could be traced to insider dealing allegations.

And there was a lengthy explanation about the crime of

insider dealing. Where had that information come from? But she didn't need to ask. Barry. The trader would know all about insider dealing, not that she thought he would suggest Mark was guilty of it. But Bazza might have confirmed Tom's suspicion that Paul had fired Mark, and with two of the best ingredients for selling newspapers – sex and money – Tom had sauced up the story by linking the two. The only thing missing was that none of the parties involved were household names. Well, they weren't yesterday, but they certainly would be now.

What if Emily found out about the dinner? What would she say if she knew Tom had paid Mary for her contacts? She didn't want to speak to Emily, but Charles told her she would regret it if she didn't. 'Better to own up than be outed. It will be much worse if she calls you,' he said, putting his arms around her. She let out a strangled sob. 'I'm sorry, darling,' he murmured into her hair. 'I'm sure you thought you were doing the right thing, going to the dinner.' He kissed her forehead, cupped her face in his hands and said gently, 'I must fly. Full day. Make peace with Emily. You'll feel better once you've told her.'

And he was gone, leaving Mary wondering who to call first: Tom, to get the truth; Paul, to check if he'd dipped his spoon into the mess for a stir; or Emily to shore up their friendship.

Across the Square, Lana's cleaning caddy was on the breakfast bar and she was French-polishing the hob: dabbing pea-sized dollops of polish and working the mixture in tiny precise circles with one finger. Mark's mother was mopping the floor. Emily was leaning against Mark, who was still glaring at Lana.

'I'm going upstairs to work. If I can concentrate,' he said, leaving.

Lana looked up at Mark's mother, whose face had a peculiar grey tinge, like a dull winter's day.

Emily's phone rang. She took it with her into the pantry, saying, 'It's Mary.'

'Do you think Mary knows what's happened?' asked Lana.

'Depends how early she reads the papers,' Mark's mother replied.

'I wish I hadn't gone,' moaned Lana, dabbing more polish onto the hob and picking up her cloth.

Emily walked into the kitchen. 'I know about the dinner,' she spat, her eyes darting between the two women.

Lana shut her eyes and puffed out a sigh; why had she gone? The first time she could remember going to a dinner unconnected to the church, and it turns out she'd been supping with the devil.

'Are you going to tell him or am I?' asked Emily.

It looked like Lana wouldn't be calling her boss Mark for very long. He would never forgive her, and looking at Emily's taut face, she didn't think there was any sympathy there either. She was going to lose her job.

Gwen slid the mop under the kitchen table. 'Come on then,' she said to the housekeeper. 'Let's face the music together.' She hadn't liked listening to the conversation on Friday, especially when Tom mentioned her son's affair – was that what this article was about, his office dalliance? Poor Emily.

She carried the mop and bucket into the pantry, taking a moment to steady herself, swallowing away a lump in her throat and dabbing at the corners of her eyes with her sleeves. She'd been right. Mark was unhappy, so unhappy that he'd cheated on Emily. It was someone he worked with, that much was obvious at Tom's dinner. The classic affair at the office, and now all their friends would read about it. After draining the mop in its bucket, she tore off a piece of kitchen towel and blew her nose. Gwen knew what it was like to be cheated on.

Her son's actions left her deeply disappointed, but she placed the blame squarely on herself. And tucking the kitchen towel inside her sleeve, Gwen placed the mop and bucket in the broom cupboard and returned to the kitchen. Emily was gone. The housekeeper looked like Lot's wife turned into a pillar of salt, holding a bottle of polish in one hand and a microfibre cloth in the other.

Gwen unwound the housekeeper's hands. 'Give those to me. Let's get this over with. It makes no difference if we were there or not. That man had his story, and he was going to write something no matter what we said.'

Gwen plodded up the stairs, wishing the lift didn't bypass the kitchen; she could hear weary footsteps following behind her. She leaned on her stick and knocked on the dining room door.

'Come in,' said a gruff voice.

She gave the housekeeper a tight nod. 'Wait here.' As she let herself in, her son got up, mussing his hair with his hand.

'Mum, I'm sorry, I didn't want to worry you,' he said, pursing his lips. 'I'm sorting it out.'

She gripped the back of a chair. 'I thought you had the perfect life. I had no idea you were so unhappy.'

'I did.' He paused. 'I will again – have the perfect life. Right now, it's a mess, but . . . Emily and I will get through this.' He walked towards her, his arms wide. 'Come and give me a hug, I need one.'

'Not so fast, boyo,' she said, pointing her stick at him. 'How could you do this to your wife? I've never seen a woman so upset.'

He frowned. He looked so like his father; had he inherited that wastrel's wild streak? The streak she initially found attractive, the one she assumed she'd tame once they married.

'You haven't read the article, have you, Mum?'

'No. And out of consideration for Emily, I won't . . . I thought I was protecting you, but I should've explained why I kicked your father out.'

Her son was staring at her, his mouth open. For a few moments Gwen watched him, then he said, 'Kicked him out . . .? I thought Dad left . . .'

'It wasn't your father's choice. He was a womanizer. I packed his bags for him.'

'Wow!' Mark slumped into a chair.

'I'm sorry, it was selfish not to tell you, and now I've let you ruin Emily's life.'

He barked a laugh. 'No, Mum. You've got this all wrong. *I* didn't have the affair, *Emily* did.'

Gwen collapsed into the chair opposite Mark. She felt light-headed, and that uncomfortable stabbing had started again in her chest. '*Emily* . . . had an affair?' she gasped.

'Yes,' Mark replied, his tone resigned. Gwen pushed her chair backwards and doubled over. *Emily!* She squeezed her eyes shut as waves of pain pulsed through her chest. She felt Mark's arms on her back. 'Mum, what's wrong?'

She groaned.

'MUM!'

She waved him away and sat up, trying to regulate her breathing. 'It's passing . . .'

He was kneeling beside her chair, his hands stroking her arm. 'Better yet?'

'Getting there, love. If it's any comfort, I've been there. I know how it feels to be betrayed.' She shook her head. 'I'm sorry, but I'm about to add to that misery.'

She told him about the dinner, who'd been there. 'Don't get angry with any of us, boyo. He already had his story. He was always going to write something.'

For several minutes, neither spoke. Gwen listened to a siren, the sound rising and falling, fading into the distance. London was so noisy! Mark stood up with his hands covering his face – she had to give him time to process this news.

'I feel betrayed,' he whispered, shaking his head slowly.

She stood up and wrapped her arms around her son, squeezing him tight, feeling his warm breath on her forehead. How had she not seen through her son's thin veneer of happiness? How long had he been struggling alone? She knew something was wrong that Sunday back in January, but she'd never guessed it was this bad. Poor Mark. He'd been like a canoeist confidently paddling along, then suddenly finding himself upside down in a whirlpool battling the currents, fighting to right themselves. She had to help him work out what was important, separate the parts of his life to cherish from those to discard, just as she had done forty years ago, weeding her own family by packing her husband's bags.

Outside the office, Lana pressed an ear against the door, surprised not to hear shouting. The minutes ticked by, and she rehearsed her apology, running through possible explanations that all sounded lame. *I went because Anne didn't want to go alone, or, it was a free night out, and I don't have much of a social life*. Her boss would know Anne didn't need a chaperone, and he didn't have much of a social life either. Mark had trusted her, given her responsibility for Project Revenge . . . What a way to reward him. She had been naive and irresponsible with that trust. She couldn't expect him to brush this aside.

The door opened. Mark was holding out his phone towards her. 'You'd better read this.'

'I don't want to.'

'You're quoted.'

'What!' She hadn't said anything newsworthy.

Mark read from his screen:

Mark's live-in housekeeper, Svetlana Smith, confirmed that since he was sacked, Mark has been working from his house in Ovington Square.

'I never said that,' she muttered, shaking her head. No one had said that.

'Here, you'd better read the rest.'

She took the phone from him; unsurprisingly there was no mention of time management skills. It was mostly about Paul's affair with Emily, which was bad enough, and the photos were horrid, but it also suggested Mark had been sacked because he was being investigated for insider dealing. Where had that come from? Lana recalled Anne burbling something about trading irregularities, but she didn't name anyone.

'I am so, so sorry,' said Lana.

'It's a bit late for that,' he snapped.

'I never said any of this . . .'

'But you went to dinner with this journalist.'

Her throat constricted, and her voice came out in a squeak, 'Yes.'

'And talked about our private affairs, which is a clear breach of the confidentiality undertaking in your contract. You know what this means, Svetlana.'

Gwen's voice was sharp, 'Mark!'

Her boss shook his head. 'You're right, Mum,' he huffed, and Lana swallowed. 'You didn't tell the bastard anything he didn't know already. But learn from this, Svetlana. My affairs are confidential. Keep it that way.'

'Thank you,' she said, letting out a deep sigh. 'I made a mistake, but I won't make it twice, and I will find a way to make this up to you, I promise.'

*

On Tuesday afternoon, Gwen and Mark battled through the pack of journalists to a waiting taxi. Mark had delayed the cardiologist's appointment by twenty-four hours. Gwen didn't think her heart was in any condition to be assessed, but he insisted they go.

Afterwards, they taxied back to Ovington Square where she stepped out gingerly with Mark's keys in her hands. A wave of journalists pushed past her, rushing towards her son.

Using her stick, swinging her left leg wide, Gwen dragged herself up the steps. Behind her she heard shouting. Poor Mark. When would this lot move on? She fumbled the key into the lock as the door opened. Alex.

'Hi, Gran.' He folded her into a hug.

'Hello, love, what a smashing surprise!'

'There's another one waiting for you in the sitting room. Give me those,' he said, snatching at her coat and hat. 'You must be roasting wearing that lot!'

She grinned at him. He moved to one side, and she tapped her way to the sitting room. The door was ajar, she stepped inside and fainted.

The journalists camped outside the house overnight, forcing Lana to fight her way home on Monday evening, and back again on Tuesday. For the second day running, Emily huddled upstairs like a jilted teenager, weeping her way through boxes of tissues and refusing food. Lana concentrated on her old job. In the afternoon, she tried to take the dogs for a walk in Hyde Park but the journalists swarmed after her, and she didn't get further than the Brompton Road.

Walking back, pursued by her new fan club, Tosca and Floria trotted in front of Lana, joined by a stick clenched in their jaws, both trying to wrest control of the prize from the other. Lana bent over, tugged the stick free and tossed it into the Square's communal garden, trying to avoid deadheading a hydrangea bush. The leads jerked in her hands, and the dogs lunged towards the stick as it accelerated out of reach.

'No!' she scolded. 'You can have a treat when we get home.'

Back at the house, the journalists stood aside as the dogs skipped up the front steps and stopped with their snouts wedged between the railings. Tosca gave a low growl. Lana peered over at her courtyard. A man was sitting halfway down the steps. He didn't look up; his head was slumped forwards, showing a bald plate with a ring of grey hair below it – probably a journalist exhausted in the heat and taking time out. He wasn't doing any harm. Janet was on a church day trip to Buckland Abbey in Devon, and not due back until five.

Later, closing the front door on her day, she noticed the man still sitting on her steps. Unlocking her gate, she felt a rush of sympathy; she would not do anything stupid like invite him in, but she would offer him a glass of water. The gate clicked when she opened it, and the man looked up. If asked, she would've judged him to be mid-sixties, but she didn't need to guess, she knew exactly how old he was.

She fell back against the gate, jarring her elbow. Pain pulsed along her arm.

'Hello, Lana,' he said, eyes twinkling as if he'd been away for a week instead of thirty years.

'What do you want?' she asked, stomping past him, keys in hand.

'Can I come in?'

'No.' She stabbed the key at her front door, missing the lock. She glanced down at her hands; they were quivering.

He was behind her, close enough for her to smell his after-shave, the same spicy scent of her childhood.

'Nice to see you too,' he said.

She spun around. 'You can't come in because Mum lives with me, and the shock of seeing you back from your business trip after thirty years wouldn't be good for her heart.'

The colour drained from his face; he looked as if he was about to faint. 'Please tell me you didn't fall for that one,' he whispered.

Lana jiggled the keys in her hands. 'What do you mean?'

'There's nothing wrong with your mother's heart, Lana. She's just lazy.'

Lana stared at him, eyes wide. 'N-nothing . . .' she stammered. 'Nothing wrong with her heart?' He was lying. He must be. She'd heard her mother wheezing with the effort of walking to church sometimes; she took all those pills, went for regular check-ups and scans; you couldn't fake a heart problem.

# Eleven

By Tuesday morning, Mary had accepted that Tom wasn't going to answer his phone. She left a two word message, "*Call me*", then hit redial, and with shaking hands, added another three: "*You little shit*". Was Tom indifferent to the fallout from his story? She would never talk to him again. He was a coward, going to ground.

She threw the phone onto the sofa and picked up her class schedule, trying to hold it upright, but the page was trembling as if it had come to life. Feeling guilty – yesterday she'd cancelled all of her classes – Mary stared at the paper, not registering the pupils' names. She scrunched up the page. She couldn't teach today.

How had she got herself into this mess? What if Barry told Charles or Mark that she had put Tom in touch with him? What if Tom told someone he'd paid her for that introduction? She unscrewed the page, reached down the crack in the sofa and retrieved her phone. She must get hold of Tom, beg him not to rat on her, and then fight to shore up her friendship with Emily.

That evening, waiting for the kettle to boil, Mary heard the kitchen door grate open.

'Hello, darling, feeling any better?' asked Charles.

'Why does the door make that noise?' moaned Mary, dropping teabags into a pot.

'Yes, quite a good day at the office, thanks,' Charles jibed. 'It's fallen a fraction over the years. I've looked, but it's held up on eighteenth-century screws. If I take it off and file a bit from the bottom, I'm not convinced I'd be able to rehang it.'

She shook her head at him. 'Well, buy new screws. They're not expensive.'

'Not supposed to do that with a listed building, and it's not as simple as that: new screws won't fit in the old fixings and . . .'

Mary didn't want a DIY lesson. 'Then hire an expert.'

'He'd be in a long queue wouldn't he, all waiting to gobble-up our money.'

She detected exasperation in her husband's voice and changed the subject. 'What news from the City?'

'I had lunch with Paul. All hell has broken loose over this article of Tom's. He's got compliance officers and in-house lawyers raking through Mark's old files, probing the insider dealing allegation. It's nonsense, of course, but they've got to take it seriously, and Paul's got his hands full managing morale. Mark was very popular with the juniors.'

'No one likes seeing their hero face-down in the mud,' she said. 'I can't feel sorry for the bank. They've treated Mark abominably, and it's easier for them to ride out this story than him.'

'He's not my best mate, but I agree, the bank's acted very shabbily.' Charles gestured at the teapot. 'Speaking of which, have we time for tea? Aren't we due across the square at Mark's council of war?'

'I . . . I'm a bit nervous,' stammered Mary, 'It's the first time I'll have seen Emily since the article.'

He walked towards her, his arms open, and she cuddled in, breathing in his comforting presence, her fears subsiding. 'Darling, you and Emily go back a long way. She's not going to blame you for what Tom's done. You went to that dinner to try to prevent something like this, you didn't do anything to help him . . .' He paused, then pushed her away from him and looked down, meeting her eyes. 'What's wrong, darling? Why did you just go tense?'

She lowered her face, burrowing it into his shirtfront. She wasn't going to lie, but she wasn't ready to confess, not even to Charles.

Gwen felt something nuzzling her neck; she smelled dog breath, and a rough tongue licked her face. She moved her hands, her fingers raking over stiff wool. She was lying on a carpet . . . Why? And how did she get here? She moaned, and arms tightened around her shoulders. Gwen blinked, catching glimpses of Alex, Emily and a ginger-haired young man badly in need of a trip to the barber.

She felt warm breath on her face and looked up into her son's face as he said, 'Give her some air. Mum, are you OK? Should I call an ambulance?'

Another male voice spoke. It was an Essex accent, and Gwen felt two knots form at the base of her throat as she remembered why she'd fainted. She hadn't heard that voice for nearly forty years and she didn't like hearing it now. What was he doing here? Had Mark found him, or had Steve found his son?

'I think it's me,' said Steve. 'The shock of seeing me.'

A face peered down at Gwen. It was etched with lines that weren't there forty years ago. The once dark curly hair was now wispy and white, but there was still that roguish look in his eyes, the promise of excitement that had lured Gwen, tempting her with a life of opportunities unavailable in the Welsh mining valleys of the early seventies.

'Pass me my stick please, Alex,' Gwen said.

With the familiar solidity of her stick in her grasp, and Alex's helping hands under her armpits, she heaved herself upright. Her eyes met Mark's.

'I think I should go for a walk,' said Steve. 'Give Gwen some space.'

'I think that's a good idea,' said Mark.

Gwen fixed her gaze on her shoes, willing Steve to leave, listening for the sound of the door clicking shut. Instead, she heard an opera singer.

Mark tutted. 'Wish I hadn't reconnected that bell. Oh, shit, that'll be Mary and Charles for the council of war.'

'I'll go . . . Suggest they come back tomorrow,' said Emily.

'No,' said Gwen firmly. 'I'm fine, let them in. Let's get on.'

The Ellis door opened, and Mary's hand shot up, cupping her mouth. Emily was so pale, she looked haggard, thinner, and there were fine lines around her eyes that Mary was sure hadn't been there at Pilates on Saturday. Worryingly, she wouldn't meet Mary's eyes; Emily's were darting about as if tracking the path of a fly. *Does she blame me? Has she found out?* 'Emily . . . I—' she stopped, noticing a stranger, an elderly man, standing behind her friend.

Emily stood aside. The man spoke in an Essex accent, 'Can I squeeze past please?' Mary and Charles moved sideways, and the man walked outside and down the steps, whistling cheerfully.

As they entered the house, Mary gripped Charles's hand. She was hoping no one would ask too many questions about Tom and praying that Mark's famed expertise at extricating clients from scrapes would disentangle her from this mess.

In the sitting room, Mark was standing with his back to the fireplace, his hands on his hips. He spoke with an authority in his voice which Mary assumed he used when addressing clients. She imagined him sitting at the head of a long table packed with City grandees dressed in sombre suits, assembled for a briefing on the tactics of bidding for a rival company. There weren't many women in her mental picture.

'Everyone, grab a seat. Mum, I don't think you know Mary's husband, Charles. None of us want to be here. No one asked to be the latest hot gossip, but we are, and we need to handle it. Let's talk this through without the crutch of alcohol, agree on a way forward, then we can all have a drink.'

Mary followed Mark's gaze as he cast it around the room. His mother was sitting on the sofa opposite her, looking a bit bemused, as if she didn't understand a word her son was saying. At the other end of that sofa, Emily was huddled in the corner, staring transfixed at Mark like a child waiting for a magician to produce the proverbial rabbit out of his hat. In the far corner of the room, Alex stood with a sullen expression on his face. Poor Alex, he'd been dropped into this mess face first. Mary wondered if he knew about his father losing his job, or if he'd been fed the cover story of Mark wanting to set up on his own.

'You've probably all got three questions,' Mark continued. 'How, why, and what next?'

Beside Mary, Charles squeezed her hand. 'Is "how" that important?' he asked.

Mary liked that question. She didn't want anyone delving too deeply into how Tom got his story.

'Not to me,' Mark shot back. 'That just leads to rooting out someone to blame, and we need to stick together. We are where we are. I've spoken to several PR agents, and they've all said it looks like the story hasn't got any legs. The journos will be gone by tomorrow. They reckon the bank has come down hard to kill off the insider dealing line, pulled in a few favours, and shut down that angle. No one knows who I, Emily . . . or . . .' He paused. 'Who any of us are. Our names just conveniently spiced up the story, which sold because of the supposed scoop about insider dealing. I hate to give bloody Tom any credit, but he's researched the piece thoroughly and writes infuriatingly well about insider dealing. Must have good contacts in the City.'

Mary sat up and crossed her arms, feeling her heart pounding against her wrist. Were they about to speculate on who those contacts were? Was she going to be asked if she knew who "a source familiar with the City", or "a trusted senior banker" was, and how Tom had got hold of their contact details?

'Look, you all know he's a mate of mine,' said Charles, 'but I promise you, Mark, I never spoke to Tom.'

Mary stifled a gasp. Was that what Emily and Mark thought, that *Charles* was Tom's source? She couldn't let him take the blame.

Beside her, Charles gave a gentle laugh. 'I didn't even know about the affair. Mary doesn't gossip, not even with me.' Mary felt a simultaneous rush of relief and guilt. Charles was throwing a protective blanket round her, but she didn't deserve it. She reached for his hand. 'The "why" is easy enough to answer,' said Charles, giving her hand a reassuring squeeze. 'Money.'

Mary gave an involuntary shudder. They were still on dangerous territory; she wanted to race onto the action plan, not linger on the topic of money. She was pretty sure she knew what Mark would do. If he was prepared to take on the bank, he'd be up for a court battle with Tom.

'Yup, Emily and I are just collateral damage – Tom didn't care who got hurt as long as he got paid.'

Across from Mary, Emily gave a little whimper, like a dog having a bad dream. Mary looked at her friend's gaunt face, the eyes shut tight. Was that to prevent tears? In the last thirty-six hours, she suspected there had been a lot of weeping on the Ellis side of Ovington Square.

'So, what do we do? Action is the best cure for fear, and that's what I smell in this room right now. Fear. Anyone got any ideas . . .? Charles?' asked Mark.

Waiting for her husband to speak, Mary decided on her own

action plan. She bitterly regretted taking Tom's money and would do whatever Mark suggested. She must be honest, tell Emily the truth, all of it, and rebuild her trust. It had looked like easy money, and she never thought anyone would get hurt. She had to stop chasing ways to generate cash.

Gwen sat on the edge of the sofa in a daze, not taking in what anyone said. Why was she still in London? She should be on a train to Essex, but after seeing the cardiologist, Mark had asked her to stay and join his war council. Had that been a ruse to force a reconciliation with Steve? Had Mark paid a detective to track down his father? She didn't know when had Steve arrived or if he'd spent any time alone with Mark.

'Mum . . .' She gave a start and looked across at her son. 'Mum, this is important. Everyone needs to know this.' He crossed the room, passing her, and stopped in front of Emily, who was curled up in the sofa's corner, cuddling a cushion to her chest. Since Gwen discovered the truth about the affair, Emily had locked herself upstairs. Gwen couldn't look at her. Mark slaved all hours so his wife could lead a charmed, pampered life. Her son deserved better than an unfaithful wife.

'This is not Emily's fault,' said Mark, his gaze was flicking between Gwen and Alex, standing in the corner.

No one spoke.

Gwen glanced over at her grandson slouched against the wall, his lower lip rolled out like a child. He'd always kept his mother on a pedestal. Who was looking out for the boy? Everyone's attention seemed to be focused on Emily, and it was all very well, Mark making grand gestures about this not being Emily's fault, but the Ellis family wouldn't be newsworthy if Emily had kept her lacy knickers on.

'The person at fault here,' said Mark firmly, 'is Tom.'

Gwen took in Alex's sulky expression. Mark was floundering. She suspected he'd never played the role of family peacemaker before, normally being cast as the villain, and despite her own views on what her daughter-in-law had done, she had to help her son. 'I know, love,' she said. 'All the blame lies with that Tom.'

'Thank you, Mum.'

'Will you go legal?' asked Mary's husband.

He looked like a sensible sort of man, thought Gwen, and that sounded like a good idea. Get the paper to apologize.

Mark shook his head. 'There's no point. The affair did happen. He spiced it up, but I've spoken to a defamation lawyer and, to quote her words, "mere vitriolic abuse" isn't an offence.'

'But surely the insider dealing allegation is an attack on your professional standing?' said Mary's husband.

'The story is very carefully worded. Tom didn't accuse me, just alleged that sources claim I'm being investigated. There may be an angle against the source, but we don't know who he or she is.'

'So, you can't even demand a retraction?' said Mary.

'No,' said Mark, wearily. 'We've got to face facts. This story is permanently available. Unless we change our names . . .' He glanced Gwen's way, and she sat upright. 'Which, for the avoidance of doubt, I have no intention of doing. So, anyone who searches on the net will be fed this article.' He shrugged and raised his voice slightly. 'We've just got to learn to live with it.'

Gwen's heart surged with pride. Mark had them all spellbound. No one had challenged anything he said. He may not be living the classic happily married life she'd always assumed he was, but he was leading it the way he wanted to. She must let Mark deal with his own affairs and concentrate on sorting out her own. What was she going to do about Steve? Why hadn't she put that demon to bed properly? Divorce wasn't the end of it. She should have told Mark the truth.

'So, we do nothing? Just suck it up?' spat Alex.

'No,' said Mark. 'We ignore the tittle-tattle. Personally, I think Emily should go away for a few days.' He turned towards Mary. 'I was hoping you might offer to drive her down to Devon.'

'Of course,' said Mary brightly, looking towards Emily. 'The sea air and walks on Exmoor, where no one knows you . . . it will help get things into perspective. I'll hire a car and drive, so Mark and Charles both still have wheels.'

Gwen saw Mary glance at Alex, glowering in the corner. 'I'll take you and Ginge back down too, if you like, Alex?' offered Mary.

'Thank you,' said Emily. 'I think I'd like to get away.' She smiled at her son. 'You'd like to get back to the surf too, wouldn't you, Alex?'

Alex addressed his father. 'When I'm ready, I'll catch the train.'

Gwen watched Emily shrink back into the corner of the sofa as if someone was pressing against her.

'Is that it?' asked Alex testily. 'Powwow over?'

'That's it, son. I wanted to make sure we all stick together. No one must speak to the press.' Mark replied. 'Who'd like a drink?'

Alex grunted. He pushed past the sofa without looking at his mother, and stomped out.

The Standerwicks only stayed for one glass of wine. Shortly after they left, Emily brought a relaxed-looking Steve into the sitting room.

Emily spoke gently, 'I'll make a pot of tea. Mark wanted you to be alone. He and Alex are next door in the dining room.'

Steve apologized for keeping Gwen waiting, claiming he had been too absorbed in a snooker game to notice the time. No change there, thought Gwen, although she suspected it might have been a woman, not snooker that detained her ex-husband.

She studied her vacant ring finger, the pictures on the walls, her eyes circling, refusing to look at the person so close to her she could hear him breathing. He smelled of limes – she didn't recall that scent. For a few minutes, neither spoke. Gwen asked her first question politely: 'Did Mark invite you?'

The creased face puckered into that smile which used to send her heart fluttering. 'No. I found him.' She thought about her son – unable to think of him as *theirs*. So, this was a shock for Mark and Alex too. No wonder the pair were holed up in the dining room. Would Steve's reappearance unite her son and grandson? 'How?' she asked.

'That story in the paper.'

Gwen looked at her ex-husband slouched in his chair. Didn't it occur to Steve that Mark's hands were full, coping with that article and his wife's affair? The last thing Mark needed was more emotional turmoil.

'He's the spit of me at that age, isn't he?'

'I wouldn't know. You'd been gone over twenty years by then.'

He ignored her jibe. 'When I read his name, I knew he was my son. He always had drive, that boy. I knew he would get to the top of whatever game he chose.'

She tracked Steve's eyes circling the room, seeing the elegant curtains, the polished floorboards, the furniture and art, a room as tastefully decorated as any interior photographed for *Hello* magazine. 'He's done well for himself, hasn't he!' said Steve smugly, as if he was the one who'd furnished the room. 'He's in hot water, but I reckon he'll right his ship again.'

No thanks to you, thought Gwen. Was Steve here to tap Mark for cash? Surely not. He'd never been motivated by money when she knew him. 'Why now?'

Steve gave a soft laugh and sat upright. 'You always were a stickler for detail. I could never fob you off.'

She smiled, despite her inner turmoil. His reasons didn't matter – he was sitting opposite her, and she had to deal with it. 'What makes you think you're welcome here?'

He puffed out a long sigh. 'I haven't spoken to him yet, just briefly to Emily and Alex. He was with you when I arrived. He might want nothing to do with me.'

Her brow wrinkled. She tried to recall the happier parts of their romance but struggled to remember beyond Mark's primary school days, and her marriage had floundered long before her son started school. Her mind was trapped. She felt like a weary athlete halfway through a marathon. Her moral compass could see the finishing line, and that part of her wanted to get past the pain barrier – the memory of the slow decay of her marriage, the lies, the rows, the hurt, the shame, the desperate attempts to shield Mark from the chaos – and reach the reason why she'd married this man. But she didn't have the mental energy. Had she been selfish, throwing him out, thinking of herself and not her child? Would Mark have grown into a different man if he'd retained a connection with his father? Should she have put up with the deceit, the mistresses, the part time husband docking with his family when it suited him?

She stared at her ex-husband, with his white hair, now wiry and shaggy where once it had been curly and inky black, just like Mark's. She had a sudden image of lying beside him, fingering the nape of his neck, where his hair used to coil into tiny curls. She shook it away, reminding herself that this was the man who'd forced her into the hand-to-mouth existence of Mark's childhood. Would Mark forgive him? It wasn't right to deny her son the chance to rekindle a relationship with his father. The decision should be Mark's, and Alex too would have to make up his own mind if he wanted to know his grandfather.

She heard a soft tap on the door, then Emily's voice asking to come in.

'You're all right, luv,' said Gwen.

'I brought you some biscuits. Something sweet after the shock.'

'I think I might need a brandy with that biscuit,' said Gwen.

Later, Mark brought her dinner on a tray and sat on the end of Gwen's bed. She dipped her fork into a cottage pie, listening to him talk about the weather, expecting a flurry of questions about Steve. She took a mouthful; it burned her tongue, reminding her to be careful. To avoid Steve's reappearance affecting her relationship with Mark, she needed to watch her step. She pushed the mashed potato aside and stirred the meat, watching the steam rise.

Mark cleared his throat. Here we go, thought Gwen, blowing on a forkful of food. Her son had every right to be curious. 'Mum, I've got something important to say.'

She lowered the fork; this sounded serious. Was he going to tell her he wanted his father to be part of his life? Already?

'I didn't really keep you here to take part in that gathering earlier on.'

'I didn't make a major contribution, did I?' she said, forcing a laugh. 'So why am I here?'

'You're here because I love you, and I want to keep an eye on you for a night or two. The cardiologist is concerned, and . . . why is my father here? Did he tell you what he wants?'

She didn't want to be reminded that Steve was downstairs. Gwen didn't think he would be uncomfortable, as a stranger in the house. He was a chameleon, able to project an image that appealed to whoever he found himself with, especially if it was a woman. He'd soon be cosy with Emily.

She shrugged. 'You'd better ask him yourself.'

'He's a stranger!' Mark said, shaking his head. 'Emily's asking me if she should lock her jewellery in the safe.'

Just like Emily to make herself the centre of every drama, thought Gwen. 'He's not a bad man.'

'The cardiologist wants to see you again.'

She'd take care of herself like she always had. Unlike Steve, she wouldn't add to Mark's burden. 'All in good time. The doctor said he'll refer me.'

'You can't mess around with your heart, Mum. I'll come with you again.'

She waved her hands at him as if flapping a duster. 'Don't fuss, boyo. I'll be seen when it's my turn.'

He stood up and leaned over, brushing his lips against her cheek. 'That wasn't a suggestion, Mum. That was an order. You're staying here until the end of the week. Svetlana will look after you. Now, eat your dinner and get some sleep.' He shook his head, then spluttered, 'I've got to go and see what my father wants.'

# Twelve

The arrangement was to meet in The Enterprise at 7 p.m. Lana pulled the brass handle and the swing door opened, revealing the usual smartly dressed customers mingling round the bar. Tonight, the laughter jarred – the sound of cheerful people was an inappropriate backdrop for this meeting. She spotted her father, sitting at a table for two at the back, close to the kitchen and serving counter. With his balding head and T-shirt, he was an incongruous figure. There was a bottle of beer in front of him and two menu cards. She fiddled with the strap of her handbag. He waved but didn't get up.

'You going in or what?' snapped a woman, pushing up against Lana.

She sidled past the crowded bar, scanning the customers, hoping Anne hadn't popped in for a midweek swift one. She reached her father. The smell of cooked meat and hot fat drifting out from the nearby serving hatch was making her feel queasy. Lana pulled out a chair but didn't sit. Should she have come?

'I was getting worried you were a no-show,' her father said. 'That your mother had changed your mind.'

She chewed her bottom lip. As Lana was locking up, her mother had messaged to say the coach was stuck in a tailback on the M5, hadn't even reached the M4. Lana had hours to hear her father's story; she still suspected he was lying but couldn't work out his motive.

'What would you like to drink?' he asked.

She stared vacantly at him. What was she doing in a pub with a man she hadn't seen for thirty years? What did he want, and why now? He hadn't bothered to keep in touch and had never tried to track her down before. Was he ill? Was she about to learn he was dying and wanted forgiveness for abandoning her? He stood up, reached across the table, and took hold of her arms.

'Sit. For God's sake, sit.' He waited until she sat, then ran a hand around his circle of hair, as if brushing a halo. 'Look, can we start again? I think a drink might do us good, relax us both a little. I'm sorry, this must be such a shock.'

She managed a thin smile. 'Glass of white wine.'

He signalled to a waitress and ordered a bottle. 'Have you eaten?'

She shook her head. Lana had done plenty of thinking since she'd agreed to meet him, but not about food. She'd flopped onto the sofa, muttering '*Oh my God*' to herself, and replaying their five minute doorstep conversation. Could he be telling the truth? If her father was to be believed, Janet had been hamming up a non-existent heart condition. She had hitched a free ride from Lana, dictated what her daughter did for a living, where she did it, and even how much of her salary she could keep. She made Mark's pack of remora fish freewheeling on whales look like a swarm of worker bees. How could anyone be so selfish? It couldn't be true. But why would her father lie?

Lana's stomach rumbled. 'You order for me.'

'We'll both have the sausages. Extra chips,' he said, handing the menus to the hovering waitress, who had brought over the bottle of wine. He settled himself against the button-backed banquette. 'You used to love sausages,' he said, pouring her a large slug of wine. 'I won't ask what your mother's told you. I'm just going to tell you the truth.'

Lana picked up her glass and drank. She would listen to what he said, then leave. After a few mouthfuls she stopped, telling herself it was wine not water. Her father finished his beer, poured himself a glass of wine, and started speaking. I'm sure you've been told often enough how your mother and I were forced to marry by our Catholic parents.'

Countless times she'd listened to her mother complaining about being forced to marry someone she didn't love, but unlike her mother's recollections, her father claimed that at first he and Janet were very happy, as they prepared for the birth and celebrated her arrival. Lana felt her throat constrict; her heart started beating faster – could he be telling the truth?

Her father's story resonated with her childhood memories, and she asked herself why she'd never questioned Janet's version.

'Yours was a difficult birth. Your mother is tiny. I wasn't allowed into the delivery room, and a few months after you both came home, they ran a series of tests on her heart. She told me she'd been advised not to fall pregnant again. I was gutted, but we had you, and we both doted on you. We couldn't have asked for a sweeter, more compliant child.'

Lana screwed up her face; compliant or gullible?

'Still the same Lana,' he said, smiling at her reaction. 'You never were any good at receiving compliments. Janet stayed at home with you, and the three of us couldn't have been happier. It was the seventies, and lots of women didn't work until their child started school. I used to love those evenings. We'd bath you and put you to bed, then Janet and I would eat and, while she cleared away, I'd open my books and study for my accountancy exams.'

A waitress brought their food. Lana ground salt over her chips and picked one up, nibbling up towards her fingers, letting the warm, crisp fatty taste soothe her.

'I waited until you were nearly six before I said anything. But we needed extra money. Rent was going up; everything was going up.' He gave a wry laugh. 'Just like it is now. That's when things started to go wrong. I suggested your mother work part time, just mornings, so she could still pick you up from school.' He poured more wine. 'But Janet told me she couldn't work. That the cardiologist had advised her not to, because her heart was severely weakened and she needed to avoid stress.'

'To lead a gentle life,' mimicked Lana. How many times had she heard that phrase?

Her father cut his sausages into bite-sized pieces as if for a child, speared one, then wagged the loaded fork at her. 'Janet told me she blamed us both in equal proportion. I couldn't let her take her spite out on you, so I told her I would stop studying and work extra hours to earn enough to look after the three of us. Do you know, I remember having that conversation, and it was as if a switch had been flicked. Your mother went power-mad, started dictating minute details of my life, and whenever I pushed back her health was thrown back at me.

Lana had been there so often herself. She imagined her mother's voice: '*If you knew what it was like to suffer with a weak heart, you wouldn't want to . . .*' Fill in the blank with whatever Janet wanted to avoid. For the last thirty years, that phrase had hovered on the edge of Lana's life, like an over-attentive milk monitor, sweeping away any resistance to Janet's plans. It had prevented Lana becoming a PA. It was this phrase which siphoned off 20 per cent of her pre-tax salary, so her mother wouldn't be anxious about contributing to church funds. It locked Lana to the Ellises, to avoid the stress of a move and the loss of the Church family that supported Janet.

A rumble of laughter from a nearby table interrupted Lana's thoughts. When it died down, her father continued. 'For the next ten years, I worked my butt off. I shelved my plans to qualify as an accountant. I did everything that woman asked me to do. Lana, look at me.' She raised her eyes, locked onto her father's, the same gentle eyes from her childhood. He shook his head. 'It isn't true. There's nothing wrong with her heart. There wasn't then, and there probably isn't now. It sounds like she's been idle for the last thirty years.'

Lana huffed, chewing her lip for a moment. Was it true? Had that weapon been loaded with blanks? Was her mother capable of fending for herself? It might explain why her father left, but it could be an elaborate cover-up. This was his word against Janet's, there was no proof.

'She sees a cardiologist for check-ups,' Lana said defiantly.

'You go with her, do you?' Lana shook her head. 'Didn't think so. I know people with proper dicky hearts . . . goes with getting older. She wouldn't be seen by a cardiologist for a check-up every year for thirty years. The nursing team would do that.'

Lana thought about this. She remembered that night in the A&E cubicle when Janet insisted on privacy with the doctor, asking Lana to wait in reception. Was that a ruse to prevent Lana hearing the results of the echocardiogram she'd insisted was taken?

'How can you be so sure?'

He popped a piece of sausage into his mouth and chewed. Lana watched him, recalling family meals from her childhood. The tension between her parents, her father's attempts to shield Lana from the atmosphere, complying with Janet's petty demands to grind his salt carefully so it didn't fall onto the table, to stop scraping his fork against the plate, to not chew so loudly.

He put down his cutlery and spoke again. 'One day, I headed home early because I wasn't feeling well. I was following a bus through Bristol – it stopped, and I saw your mother leap off it and run down the street. I couldn't believe what I was seeing. I followed her as she ran all the way home. When I let myself in, she had her feet up, watching some silly afternoon show – she must have run so she didn't miss it. In those days, we didn't have catch-up TV.'

'Did you confront her?'

'Not then. I was steaming mad, but I wanted proof. I laid a trap. I asked her to come with me to the doctor to discuss me having the snip. Not that we had much of a sex life, but she'd been on at me to have it done, said I was being selfish risking her falling pregnant.'

Lana squirmed. Her own love life had been snuffed out before it started. She'd had boyfriends, but nothing serious. After her father left, she started working full time, several evenings and even some weekends. There was no time to keep up friendships, let alone forge new ones. Her father refilled her wine glass and she sipped, listening to the voice that used to be so familiar, allowing it to conjure a memory of lying cocooned in blankets while he read her a bedtime story.

He told her that he made an appointment with the doctor and managed to steer the conversation onto contraception in general, exploring different methods, enabling the doctor to bring up both sets of medical records, and then he asked for a private moment.

'I told the doctor your mother had expressed a wish to have another child before I had the snip. You were only sixteen, so she would have been . . .' he pursed his lips, calculating,'. . . in her mid-thirties. I claimed I wanted to check she was physically up to bearing another child after the difficult birth and told him a work colleague's wife had been advised not to fall pregnant because her heart was damaged during childbirth. Was there any chance of that in Janet's case? The doctor told me not to worry.

He gave a short laugh. I remember his words so clearly, ironic when you think about it . . . He told me Janet was telling me the truth, she was physically fit. The tests after your birth had shown her heart wasn't damaged at all.'

Lana felt the food clog in her mouth. She tried to swallow, but her mouth was too dry. Her father was watching her, his eyes steady. She coughed, took a sip of wine, then asked why he hadn't told her. 'I was sixteen, old enough to learn my mother was a liar.'

'I wish I had.' He reached across the table for her hand. Unused to the gesture, she snatched it away. 'I can't tell you how sorry I am that I didn't.' He took a gulp of wine, then explained, 'Oldest trick in the book. When I confronted her, she begged me not to say anything, told me she wanted to find the right moment to tell you herself. I was the only one her lies affected. You were at college, I made sure of that. So, I agreed, but I started travelling more. I didn't like being away from you, but I couldn't stand the sight of her. And, well, I knew my marriage was finished, and then . . . I met someone else.' He chewed his bottom lip, and his face softened, seeming to brighten. 'Her name is Eleanor,' he said.

Lana gasped. 'You remarried?'

He shook his head. 'No. I asked for a divorce, but, well, you can imagine what your mother had to say about that! And don't worry, you haven't got a string of illegitimate half-brothers and sisters. But that's why I left. I wanted to start afresh with Eleanor, in Manchester - that's where we live. Force your mother to manage for herself. I never thought she'd cast the same spell on you.' He hung his head and mumbled, 'And I was sure you wouldn't fall for it if she tried. You were always such a smart cookie.'

Lana swallowed another mouthful of wine. She didn't feel

very clever. Her father was watching her, his eyes smiling just as they had on those stairs so long ago, when he promised to look after her. Tonight, the memory of the swirly carpet wasn't unpleasant. He's giving me time to process this, she thought. Was he telling the truth? Unlike her mother, there was no reason for her father to lie. Why had Lana never suspected anything? Probably because, just as Lana had learned the subtle role of the perfect housekeeper, her mother had perfected her own performance of "the lady with a damaged heart". So, why would Lana question her illness?

But one thing still niggled away at her. 'Why didn't you stay in touch?' she asked.

He gave her a puzzled look. 'But I did. Why didn't *you* keep in touch with *me*?'

'No, you didn't,' she spat. His first lie, she didn't like that.

Her father put his head in his hands, pressing his knuckles into his eye sockets and let out a low groan. 'How spiteful.'

Her heart was racing again. 'What . . .?'

He ran his hands down his face and spluttered out a long sigh. 'All these years, did you think I didn't try to keep in touch?' His eyes bored into her. 'Lana, you knew how much I loved you. That's why I put up with her for so long. I left a letter for you, hid it under your pillow.'

'I never got it . . .' she said shaking her head.

'I assumed she might destroy that one. But I wrote to you: every week, for three months, which was when the lease on the house was up. I even got strangers to write the address so Janet wouldn't know the letters were from me. When you never replied, I assumed she'd poisoned you against me. I left it a few years before I tried to make contact. Then I spent a week in Bristol, but everywhere I went, your old college, the café where you worked, your mother's church but no one knew where you'd gone. I tried so hard to find you, I even hired a detective, twice! I thought it would be easy to find a Svetlana Adamczyk. It was only when I read that article in the paper about your employers that I wondered if it was you. Why did you change your surname? Was that to spite me?'

Lana shook her head, recalling it had been Janet's suggestion that she adopt her maiden name of Smith, saying it was less of a mouthful than Adamczyk. No doubt that had been to prevent her father tracing her.

'Eleanor persuaded me to come to London, told me to take a chance on it being you, said I would forever regret it if I didn't. I asked the postman which house it was . . . and, well, here I am.'

He was telling the truth. It was the only way all the pieces of the puzzle fitted together. Janet found the first housekeeping job that moved them to the other side of Bristol; Janet convinced Lana to change her name, and it was Janet's idea to move to London. For thirty years, Lana's life had been dictated by a fictitious medical condition. She felt numb, like the victim of a miscarriage of justice. She had been locked up; her life confined to fitting in with her mother's whims by a wicked lie. The wine tasted sour in her mouth. She pushed her food away, unable to eat another bite.

'What a coldhearted, selfish . . .' Words failed her. She'd been conned by her own mother.

She felt a tap on her shoulder and glanced up into Anne's curious face. 'I thought it was you,' said Anne, her eyes flickering to Lana's father.

'Oh.' Lana mumbled, glancing from Anne to her father.

He smiled at her. 'Up to you,' he said.

Lana noticed a man standing next to Anne. Physically he was like her – a little taller, broad-chested, and he had slightly darker, dirty blonde hair, but then, thought Lana, his colouring probably wasn't artificially enhanced. She guessed it was Kenny.

'You must be Lana. I'm Kenny . . . Ken,' said the stranger, smiling in a way that made Lana believe he was genuinely pleased to meet her. No wonder Anne had chosen this man over money! He pulled his wife aside. 'Anne, come on, don't interrupt, let's leave these good people to it.'

Lana shook her head. 'No, honestly, you're fine. Anne, Kenny, this is my father.'

Her father stood up. 'Can I buy you both a drink? You look a bit shocked. Did you think she'd fallen for a much older man?' She heard, a deep-throated guffaw that took Lana back to her childhood. Memories of being held aloft in those giant hands, looking down at his laughing face as he threw her up into the air, his eyes fixed on hers, arms outstretched to catch her as she squealed and fell into his embrace. She swallowed the memory, wondering how she had ever fallen for her mother's lies. Her father had adored her, spent every free moment with her; he would never have abandoned her, that idea had been sown by her mother. But history is always written by the victors, and it was her father who had surrendered.

Lana slumped onto the bed in Anne's tiny spare room. She felt lightheaded and suspected she had drunk too much wine. Her world had capsized; she couldn't think straight. She and her father had exchanged phone numbers, and when they said goodbye he had hugged her tightly, as if afraid it was the last time he'd see her, dropping a kiss onto her head like he used to when she was a child. 'I love you, Lana,' he mumbled into her hair. 'I can't tell you how happy I am to have found you again.'

The bed creaked. She felt Anne's arm around her shoulders.

'I'd offer to lend you some clothes . . . Do you want me to slip anything in the wash overnight?'

'No, you're all right, thanks, Anne.' Clean clothes were not uppermost in Lana's mind.

'You've got to talk to your mother,' said Anne. 'There must be an explanation. There are always two sides to every story.'

Lana glanced at her friend. In the cramped cloakroom of the pub, she'd given Anne an overview of what she'd learned from her father. Anne didn't comment, just offered her the spare room. She hadn't expected Anne to stick up for Janet less than an hour later.

Lana let out a short laugh. 'No, Anne,' she said. 'There can only be one good person in this story, and it's definitely not Janet. I can't speak to her yet.'

'But she'll be worried.'

Using her sleeves, Lana swiped at the tears threatening to spill, 'I'm not that cruel. I've messaged her – I told her I've gone to Devon with Emily.'

'But she's bound to see Emily, isn't she? And then she really will be worried.'

'No, she won't. Emily messaged earlier to say she's going to Croyde early tomorrow morning. She wants me to look after the dogs. They'll leave before Janet gets up: she likes her lie-ins, does my mother. I'll walk the dogs before she's up.'

'Try to get some sleep,' said Anne. 'I'll probably be gone before you get up. Help yourself to breakfast. Kenny will show you where to find stuff. You'll feel better after a good night's sleep.' Anne patted her arm. 'I'll get you a towel and my travel sponge bag. The bathroom is over there.' She pointed at a white door across the hallway before leaving.

Lana switched the light off at the wall, plunging the room into darkness, and stumbled back to the bed. She lay down, thoughts fizzing around her mind.

What was she going to do about Janet? She felt numb, dazed,

as if someone had knocked her out and she'd woken up in a different century. Her life could've been completely different; for the last thirty years she'd been imprisoned and now, suddenly, she'd been handed the key to freedom. What did she want to do with her newfound emancipation? And how would she react when she saw her jailor?

How could someone do this to another human being, let alone their own daughter? What had driven Janet? The word "*WHY?*" was etched in Lana's mind, in the same way a thirsty person lost in a desert can't dismiss the thought of water. Had Janet been so resentful at the loss of her own freedom, being forced to marry young, that she ruthlessly plotted to live the rest of her life at the expense of everyone else? In her own way, did Janet feel that her parents had dictated her life, and that entitled her to control her own husband and daughter's?

But Lana's father had said they were happy to start with, so why the sudden change? Why did Janet fabricate her heart problem and drive away a husband she'd been happy with? And if her father was the problem, if Janet fell out of love with him and wanted him out of her life, why did she perpetuate the lie when she'd driven him away? What had she achieved? Janet was hardly living the dream, sharing a one bed basement flat and wearing Emily's cast-offs.

In the morning, Gwen was up early. She made her bed, spritzed the bathroom and went in search of a cup of tea. In the kitchen, she found the housekeeper. She offered to help but was shooed to a seat. Gwen sat, inhaling the smell of grilling bacon, itching to do something, and watching the housekeeper scoot from the pantry to the oven to the fridge. And this woman also worked as Mark's assistant? Where was Emily? Why couldn't she look after her own house?

Mark came in. 'Sleep well, Mum?' he asked, shooting her a

concerned look. She heard a gurgle of laughter from outside the kitchen, and then Alex and his friend walked in.

'Dad, Ginge and I need some business advice.'

Mark raised an arm, shook back his sleeve, and glanced at his wrist. 'Tight timings today, maybe this afternoon – ask Svetlana to slot you in.'

When Emily came in, she ruffled Alex's hair. 'Good morning, darling.'

Alex twisted away from her, snipping, 'Don't do that, Mum, I'm not seven.'

Emily sat beside her son. He picked up his mug, shrugged his chair backwards with his legs, seeming to Gwen to rejoice in the nasty scraping noise, and moved to the other side of the table, next to his father.

If it weren't for the presence of Alex's red-haired friend, Gwen thought she might scream. The housekeeper was probably used to this pantomime, but Gwen wasn't. This family had everything – two caring parents, all three of them were in rude health and had no idea what it was like being short of money, yet they were snipping and snarling like a pack of stray dogs fighting over a scrap of food. Gwen had done a better job of raising Mark by herself on a tight budget than her son and Emily – flush with money – were doing with Alex. At least Emily was off to Devon – that should improve the atmosphere.

Steve sidled in like a novice actor making his debut appearance on the stage. 'Morning all,' he said jovially, rubbing his hands together. 'Full English, eh? Just the ticket.'

Gwen didn't acknowledge her ex-husband. She was hoping he'd had his meeting with Mark last night and would clear off after breakfast.

'Do join us, Steve, I hope you slept well,' said Emily politely. 'Why not sit next to Alex? How do you like your eggs?'

Mark stood up. 'Tea or coffee?' he asked in the kind of formal voice Gwen suspected he reserved for clients.

'Tea, Mark, and fried eggs please, Emily,' said Steve.

Gwen was on her third mug of tea when the kitchen emptied so fast that she wondered if there was an unofficial fire practice, leaving her and Steve staring at each other, and Gwen feeling as tongue-tied as if she'd been asked to appear as a panellist on *Question Time*. She sipped her tea, listening to Steve slurp his, one of his peccadillos she'd always disliked. He placed a piece of toast on the table next to his side plate and slathered a thick layer of butter like marzipan on a fruitcake. Next, using his fingers, he dipped his sausage in the egg yolk, and dropped that onto the buttered toast, dripping yolk onto the table. He licked his fingers, folded over the toast, and crammed it into his mouth.

Gwen got up. 'I'll make us a fresh brew,' she muttered.

She heard a belch and gritted her teeth, remembering that it wasn't only the womanizing that had made her kick him out.

Sitting alone in a rental car, Mary was thankful there was no longer a camp of journalists on the pavement waiting to photograph her friend. She had already been there for an hour, listening to the radio, the heater on low, fogging up the windows as if she were chain-smoking cigarettes. It was cold for a May morning, and a heavy dew still clung to the car bonnet like a giant spider's web.

The Ellis front door opened. Emily peeked out, her head darting from left to right as if searching for whoever had rung her doorbell.

Emily slipped out of the house, setting down an Hermès overnight bag; she had a woollen hat in her hands, turning it round and around like a set of rosary beads. Mary got out of the car and raised an arm. Emily plodded towards her. Why so slowly? Didn't she want to run away after the last few days?

Knowing it would be their first time alone since the article dropped, Mary had thought a lot about this meeting. Should she drive like a getaway driver after a bank robbery and just get the hell out of London? She'd chewed over the possibilities with Charles, weighing up different strategies, and concluded that if they were going to get their friendship back to where it belonged, to where Mary desperately wanted it to be, they needed to clear the air and talk through what had happened. If they didn't, it would always be there hovering in the shadows of their friendship, threatening to intrude, like an unpleasant smell temporarily masked by a few squirts of air freshener. She would try not to be defensive. She hoped the conversation would meander naturally like it always had before, only this time with a peculiar topic at its heart: how did it feel to be the centre of a media storm orchestrated by your best friend? Not that Emily knew Mary was responsible, not yet – but Mary intended to confess.

When Emily was in earshot, Mary spoke. 'Jump in, let's get you away.'

Emily gave her a glum look. Her face looked grey and a little puffy. As Mary started the engine, Emily got in and stuffed the hat into her jacket pocket.

'Radio on or off?' asked Mary.

'Off.'

Emily didn't move. Mary leaned over and stabbed at the dial. An eerie silence fell, and Mary busied herself checking the rear-view mirror and reversing the car out of the parking space. It was an odd sensation; the silence wasn't companionable, and Emily wasn't helping, sitting bolt upright, staring out of the front window, like a dog caught digging up the flower border.

She flicked a sideways look at Emily, who taken her hat back out and was toying with it, as though it was a child's comforter. This didn't look like a good time to own up. Why did she take Tom's money?

'Emily. Talk to me!'

'This was a good idea,' said Emily. 'Thank you. I'm not sure I could have driven myself.'

Mary's shoulders dropped back to their normal position, and the tension seeped away. 'That's better,' she said. She glanced sideways and saw Emily lean over, pushing the hat back into her pocket. 'Have you spoken to anyone else?'

Mary stopped at a set of traffic lights and looked at her friend properly. Her face had even more lines than she remembered from last night's council of war; was she sleeping? 'Are you OK? You looked a bit fragile last night. Bloody hell, how did you cope, all cooped up together with the journos stalking you?'

Emily shifted in her seat and turned towards Mary, screwing up her face. 'Let's just do this once. Then don't ever ask me again. *Ever*. Promise?'

Mary's eyes widened. She gave a slow nod. If there was only going to be one discussion, she would have to spot her moment to own up. The lights turned green and she pulled away.

'When I first read the article and saw those photos, I was in shock. You and Mark were the only two outsiders who knew about the affair – or so I thought.'

She winced at her friend's choice of words but accepted that technically Mark was an outsider to his wife's affair.

Emily cleared her throat. 'I realized how much hurt I'd caused, not just to Mark, but also to his mother. Gwen is one of the sweetest, kindest people I've ever met. Don't get me wrong, she's got a steel backbone, that's where Mark gets his from. Do you know, bless her, Gwen had somehow got the wrong end of the stick, and she thought the article was about Mark having an affair.'

Mary concentrated on the road. She didn't want to discuss how Gwen had made that mistake. Thinking back to that night at Tom's, she realized that all Gwen had learned was that one of the Ellises was having an affair with someone from Mark's office, and had automatically assumed it was her son.

They sat in silence for a few moments, the only sound that of the car blasting out heat against the early morning chill. Mary indicated to pull onto the M4 elevated section and asked, 'How *did* you get through it?'

'Not well. That first day I hid upstairs. I couldn't face food and I couldn't face Gwen . . . That woman suffered at the hands of an adulterer herself, and for her to see Mark going through what she had endured. I can't imagine being forced to be in the same room with someone who'd hurt Alex as much as I've hurt Mark.' Emily sighed deeply. 'This article has set Mark and I way back, not that we were making much progress along the road to reconciliation. I do wonder if him packing me off to Devon is another delaying tactic, removing me from Paul's clutches.'

'What about counselling?' suggested Mary.

'What about trying to talk to each other first?'

'Maybe he's not ready. It was a brave speech last night, but it's one thing knowing your wife had an affair, and quite another seeing it emblazoned on tabloid newspapers for everyone who knows you to read about.'

For a few minutes the pair sat silently, Mary ruminating on Emily's plight. Infidelity would be a red line for both her and Charles. Was that why she'd found living through Emily's affair so challenging, because secretly she judged her friend by her own rules? Unlike Emily, Mary never felt lonely, and if she didn't think Charles was devoting sufficient time to her or their daughters, she told him so. But Mary had no right to foist her own values onto her friend.

They were driving west, into the sun, which was streaming through the windscreen. With the heat on her hands and face,

Mary debated adding to her discomfort by confessing, but couldn't work out what to say. She pulled the sun visor down.

'I've thought things through,' said Emily, 'and I'm going to stop all contact with Paul. Someone well-placed in the City helped Tom write that article. It must be Paul. They met at Charles's birthday party, and Tom was pestering him for an interview.'

Mary didn't comment. She suspected Emily was blaming the wrong man. Paul would never risk linking his bank to insider dealing. It must've been loose-tongued Barry.

'I think Paul's hoping that now the affair is out in the open, it will destroy my marriage, but I can't forgive him.'

This was the perfect moment: Mary opened her mouth to confess . . . But then she shut it again. There had been a brittleness to Emily's words. Mary sensed her friend's anger, and she didn't want it projected her way.

'I'll end it nicely,' said Emily. 'Meet him for a coffee, somewhere public. I definitely do not want alcohol involved.'

As they talked their camaraderie shone through, like the summer sun burning through early morning mist, replacing the tension with a lighthearted spirit. Mary sensed her friend had told her all she wanted to, that a curtain had been drawn over the episode. She would have to wait for the right moment to tweak it back open and admit to her role in Tom's story.

At midday, Steve had a beer with the cheese sandwiches that Gwen had made; it was probably what loosened his tongue – that, and her direct question: 'Why didn't you write to Mark, instead of turning up unannounced with an overnight bag?'

'When you've spent thirty-five years regretting your first thirty-five,' he said, 'you seize any opportunity to put things right.'

She looked away. Here we go, she thought, taking a mouthful

of sandwich. Woe is me; I'm misunderstood; give me another chance. She'd lost count of how many times she'd heard this sob story.

'I know what you're thinking, Gwen. I'm not asking to come back.'

She swallowed. 'Good,' she said in a strangled voice. She sipped her water. 'Cos I'm not inviting you.'

'I just want to be part of Mark's life if he'll have me. To get to know him and Alex.' He dipped his head and added, 'And I'd like us to be friends, but I'm not asking for anything else.'

She grunted.

'I'll be off this afternoon,' Steve continued. 'I've made my peace with Mark, and he's asked for some time to think things through.'

Gwen put down her sandwich, realizing that Mark thinking things through would involve her. He would want to quiz his mother about Steve. That must be why she was still in London.

'You've made a fine boy there, Gwen,' Steve said. 'A son to be proud of.'

'He did that all by himself.'

'Children often like to think it's their own work, but it rarely is. There's generally a guiding pair of hands, or better still, two, somewhere in the background.'

She gave a half-laugh. 'Quite profound for you.'

'As I said, I've had thirty-five years to think about it.' He finished his beer. 'I hope you don't mind, but I've added my contact details to your phone. They don't charge you extra if you have more than three names, you know, love.' He winked at her. 'Don't delete it yet. Think about keeping in touch. I'd like to.'

She cleared their plates, thinking about what he'd said. Had she really been instrumental in Mark's success? She'd always thought her son had succeeded despite his background, that he wore his childhood almost like a battle scar. How often had her heart lurched, seeing that haunted look in Mark's eyes when another child was clapped on the back by a father congratulating them for winning a school prize?

Carrying the dirty plates through to the pantry and plunging them into the sink of warm water, she reached for a scouring pad. Had she got it all wrong? Had she really done a decent job of bringing up her child alone? Had she done the right thing for herself and for Mark by turning his father out?

Dodging her mother wasn't difficult. On Wednesday, Lana got to work long before her mother rose – she had breakfast to cook for a houseful – and she was familiar with Janet's diary. She knew when every prayer meeting, Mass, choir practice and Bible reading was scheduled; she'd often stressed over it, questioning if her mother was doing too much.

Lana's day started – and would likely finish – in the pantry. She hardly saw Mark; her office tasks had dwindled to opening the post and answering the phone – but there wasn't much post, and the phone didn't ring. She took her time opening each letter, arranging the correspondence in what she considered a helpful pile – bills at the top, junk mail beneath. There was nothing interesting. No one wanted to be advised by or even seen with someone whose name was linked to insider dealing. Two pieces of junk caught her eye – only because she'd had similar ones herself – boring documents about companies Bazza had recommended; Mark must have bought shares in them too.

Mark's mother was staying until the end of the week. Alex wasn't saying how long he and Ginge would be there, but she was glad of their company. Lana cleaned the fridge, throwing away the out of date jars, trying to marshal her thoughts onto Janet, but each time she tried, her mind danced off at a tangent.

She fretted about her vegetables then wondered if her hosts would mind watching the *Chelsea Flower Show* on TV that evening; she tried to work out when she could slip into the flat unnoticed for a change of clothes. Her mind hopped from topic to topic like a jay bird, landing on anything but Janet, but most frequently questioning why her mother had lied.

She cleaned the skirting boards and vacuumed the biscuit crumbs from the dogs' baskets, but her frenzied bout of cleaning couldn't dispel the anxiety. She kept shaking herself out of a trance, discovering a duster or spray bottle in her hands, trying to recall what she'd been doing. How could her mother have done this?

At a quarter to two, Lana hid behind the sitting room curtain. There was a prayer meeting at two o'clock. She heard the basement flat's door slam followed by a clanging noise, then peeped out, and saw her mother shuffling down the street. Lana snorted. Janet's laboured walking must have become second nature. Lana waited five minutes before dashing out of the front door and down the steps to grab a change of clothes.

Until Mark cleared his name, Ovington Advisory was in hibernation, but there was a meeting with Barry scheduled for 3 p.m. Lana was looking forward to it. She liked the trader, and she also liked the turbo charge he'd given her investments – her reserve fund was entirely composed of Bazza's stock tips. He was a talented man; when she'd quizzed him about the press article praising the American company, he didn't waver, and it was Barry's choice which had outperformed. Today, craving good news, Lana was secretly hoping for another tip.

At three o'clock Puccini rang out. 'That effing noise . . .' said Mr Ellis, 'I wish I'd never reconnected the effing thing.'

Lana cut him off. 'You need a working doorbell. But I've booked someone for next week. You won't be listening to the opera for much longer.'

She let Barry in. He was unshaven, with a short, straggly beard that made him look like a teenager sporting the first facial signs of manhood. His hands were stuffed in his pockets, jangling his change.

'Hello,' he said, without smiling.

'Come in.' Lana held the door wide. 'He's in the office.'

It took Lana longer than normal to make coffee. Alex and Ginge were in the kitchen, pestering her about a meeting with Mark, and while she wasn't looking, helped themselves to the coffee she'd brewed. She made a second batch, promising to check Mark's diary. She knew it was empty, but she also knew he wouldn't want to meet with them.

When Lana walked into the office, neither man looked her way. Mark's eyebrows were lowered, lines creased his forehead, and Barry was slouched in a chair, as if recovering from running a marathon. Something was up; she was reminded of whenever Alex and his father were in the same room. Had they been discussing Tom's article, and Lana's part in it?

While Lana poured coffee, Barry spoke of being made an insider two days before a takeover offer was launched. Apparently, after the offer was announced, a former colleague of Mark's was called by the regulator, the Panel on Takeovers and Mergers, concerned about increased trading activity in the target company's shares during the week prior to the announcement.

'He had to give the names of all the insiders, when we had been made insiders, and why.'

'Chill, Barry,' said Mark. 'That's not unusual. I've been through similar investigations. It never comes to anything; they never match the insiders to any dealing.'

'But what if they do?'

Mark stood up. He put his thumbs in his waistband. 'You don't own any shares in the target, do you?'

'It was a coincidence,' explained Barry, stopping for a mouthful of coffee. 'Someone suggested the company, I thought it looked undervalued, and took a punt.'

'But you cleared it with compliance before you bought?' The straggly beard was being stroked. 'How close to the announcement did you buy?' prompted Mark, his tone switching from reassuring to authoritative. Lana chewed her lip.

'About two weeks?'

*Was that long enough?* Lana wondered.

'So, before you were made an insider?'

'Yes. Way before then.'

'Why didn't you say something when they brought you over the firewall?'

'I trade a lot. I can't remember when I realized I owned shares in the target company, or when I bought them . . . I just thought it was better to keep shtum, that no one would believe it was a coincidence. I didn't think it would ever come out.'

'Relax, then. This will sort itself out. They're following the book by suspending you. Go and enjoy your racehorses. You'll be back at your desk soon enough.'

*Suspended!* That sounded serious. Poor Bazza, no wonder he was unshaven.

'What if they discover I own those shares and they don't believe it was a coincidence?'

'Mate, you don't have to prove your innocence. They need to be convinced you knew about the potential offer, but you didn't. How could you? You were on the other side of the wall. So, they can't.'

That sounded better, and Mark would know. He said he'd been through this sort of drama himself – only not the suspension part.

'You're the first person I've told. I'm being interviewed by compliance this afternoon.'

'Be transparent. Don't hide anything.'

Bazza was nodding furiously. The conversation switched to recruitment; Barry mentioned he thought he'd spotted a pair of very capable hands advising the target company. 'I've known her for a while, and I could tell from the way their team kept gravitating towards her -  she's a winner.'

'You always were good at recruitment,' said Mark. 'Get me her details. I owe you one.'

Lana decided that was a good omen. Mark wouldn't be looking for staff unless he thought the business would soon be back on track.

Later, Lana was standing in Emily's bath, polishing the back mirror, when she heard the tap-tap of a walking stick and Mark's mother shuffled in.

'Need a hand in here, luv?'

'I'm fine thanks, Mrs Ellis.'

'I wish you'd call me Gwen! Mark doesn't know, but I still do a few of my regulars, I know how to do a thorough clean.'

*Mark's mother was a cleaning lady.* Lana looked in the mirror, seeing the lines around Gwen's smiling mouth. A woman the same age as Janet, with a real heart problem and no need to work. She put down her polishing cloth and turned to face Gwen. 'Only if you call me Lana.'

'Well, Lana, let me know if there's ever anything I can do to help.'

Lana's phone rang; Gwen limped out. Lana sat on the edge of the bath. Why was Anne calling? They'd be eating dinner together in just a few hours.

'I had to share the joke,' said Anne, laughing. She lowered her voice and whispered into the phone, 'I just took a message from the lawyer on Project Rear-guard. Paul is in meetings all day, so

I told her I'd get him to call back this evening. She left a very specific message. She said they'll have to appoint their second choice barrister. The first one won't act. She didn't explain. I thought you'd enjoy their little setback.'

Lana heard the front door slam shut downstairs. 'Gotta go, see you later,' she said. She squirted bleach around the inside of the toilet bowl, closed the lid, folded the top sheet of toilet paper into a triangle shape and jogged downstairs to the office.

'I need to brief you,' she said.

Mark smiled and gestured at her seat. 'Only if you take off that ridiculous apron. I can't be briefed by someone wearing daisies.'

She peeled it off and sat down, conscious of the whiff of bleach.

'Come on, out with it. You look like the proverbial cat that got the cream!'

'I just got off the phone with Anne.'

'What news?'

'Project Revenge just scored a direct hit.'

His brow creased. 'I doubt it. I won't be taken seriously until we're at the steps of the High Court.'

'Effing Paul' – she felt a little frisson of pleasure, copying her boss's nickname – 'is about to be given some seriously bad news.'

'What is it?' Mark asked.

'Remember Clare telling us there's one stand-out barrister in employment law?'

'Yes. You left some quotes; I haven't got around to them yet.'

Lana waved a hand, dismissing the comment. 'Well, there's a message waiting for Effing Paul. The top barrister won't act for them.'

'Why not?'

'He's conflicted.' She felt a little surge of pride using that word – five months ago she didn't even understand what it meant!

'How?' Mark narrowed his eyes at her.

'*I* instructed Clare to hire him.' Mark snorted, and Lana rushed on. 'I knew you weren't focused on those quotes, and I did promise after Tom's dinner I'd make it up to you . . .' She chewed at her lip – instructing the barrister was costing £15,000! Should she have cleared it with her boss first?

Mark threw his head back and roared with laughter. 'FANTASTIC! I'd love to be a fly on the wall when Paul reads that message.' He winked at her. 'Well done, Svetlana. This should rev up Project Revenge.'

The next morning, Lana was at work by eight. She borrowed a watering can from the pantry and stealthily crept down to her flat. The curtains were drawn across the bay window. She knew her mother wouldn't be up for another hour, so she pottered around the courtyard, pulling up weeds and pushing in supporting canes for the pepper plants. She worked methodically, wondering if her mother would notice – there was only one person who could, or would, tend to these plants and she was supposed to be two hundred miles away.

At midday, Lana was scrubbing sweat marks off the exercise mat in the gym, when Mark walked in. 'Reckon that can wait. I've organized a meeting - and you're invited.'

She stood up and looked at the bleach stains on the cuffs of her sweatshirt. She was conscious that, beneath the housecoat, her trousers were grubby from moving her runner bean pot. 'I'm not really dressed for a meeting.'

'We're not leaving for half an hour. Pop home and change,' he said, walking away.

That was easy for him to suggest. He didn't know she wasn't living in the basement. She mentally ran through her mother's diary – Thursdays were free. Janet would be in. Lana dropped the scrubbing brush, ran up the two flights of stairs and out the front door. If she jogged all the way to Rawlings Street, she should just make it back in time.

The meeting was with Clare. The other side were still denying Mark was the victim of discrimination. Their story remained the same: Clare's client was made redundant because of a downturn in the market. *If nothing had changed then why convene a meeting?*

'As you predicted,' said Mark.

'Yes, but as I said on the phone, their tone has softened.'

'Has it?' He laughed. 'To me, this looks like the same fuck off.'

'No, read it carefully. I sense a conciliatory note.' Clare used a finger to trace down the page. 'Here,' she said, reading aloud, in a slightly excited voice. 'We are sorry to hear your client hasn't secured an alternative role . . .' She looked up, saying, 'There was none of that in their last letter.'

*So, there was a reason for the meeting.*

'They don't give a damn. I'd have landed another position in a heartbeat if Paul hadn't briefed against me.'

'But they're still saying it. You've got to admit, it's a softer tone.'

'You're dancing on a pinhead. What do you think we should do next?' he asked.

'Keep pushing for arbitration,' said Clare.

'I'm not so sure.' Mark stroked his chin between his thumb and forefinger. 'I think they're toying with us. They still think they're in control; this is a delaying tactic. They reckon once the dust settles on that article, Ovington Advisory will take off, I'll lose interest, and won't have time to fight.'

Lana watched her boss's face. She saw his nose wrinkle, his

brow furrow, and the gap between his eyebrows disappear. Was he right? Was the bank toying with him – were they that cruel? Hadn't they treated him badly enough already?

Mark was still speaking. 'The art of negotiation is to shake things up, suggest the unexpected when the opposition stalls. I think we should start court proceedings. Speak to our barrister, maybe ping over a detailed disclosure list, start wasting their effing time.'

Listening to her boss, Lana sent up a silent cheer. This sounded bold, and Clare was smiling. The lawyer shifted a little in her seat, as if she'd sat down on top of a pen. 'This article—'

'It's not true,' spat Mark.

Clare peered over the rim of her glasses at her client. 'Some of it is. The bits about the affair and you being sacked, and the allegation you were singled out because you were married to your boss's . . .' she paused '. . . paramour. That part's not unhelpful to our case.'

Mark's face was impassive. 'But not the allegation of insider dealing,' he said. 'I would NEVER do that.'

'Good. Because that bit isn't helpful. So, it's completely fabricated?'

Mark gave a loud tut. 'I was tempted to sue the bastard for defamation, but your colleague told me the article was quite cleverly worded. Technically, he didn't slander me. The source might have, but the journalist isn't going to reveal who that was.'

Clare was smiling. 'You look like you've got a hunch who the source is. Who's your money on?'

'Paul.'

# Thirteen

It was a demand not a request.

Running low on food. I need a delivery like last time you went to Devon.

No please, no question mark, just a full stop.

Lana's hands clenched around the phone, seeing the words but hearing her father's voice saying, 'There's nothing wrong with her heart.' She bit her lip and deleted the message, stabbing at the phone as if it was responsible for her mother's lies. There was another message underneath Janet's, from her father, asking if she had time for a chat.

They met for breakfast the next morning at a café on the King's Road. Her father was dressed in chinos and a T-shirt. Lana had scrubbed the dirt off her trousers and rolled up her sleeves to hide the bleach stains, but she still felt scruffy. They chose a rickety metal table outside on the pavement, barely big enough for their mugs and plates. Her father wedged a napkin under one of the table legs and they sat side by side. The sun was already strong, making the exhaust fumes from the stationary traffic in front of them hazy, and giving Lana anxious pangs about her plants. 'How's your mother?'

Lana scowled into her mug, and tore off a piece of croissant, pushing it into her mouth and waiting for the buttery pastry to sooth her temper. 'Wrong question. I haven't seen her. I'm staying with Anne.' He gulped a mouthful of coffee as if swallowing what he'd been planning to say, and she regretted her outburst. 'I'm not ready yet.'

'The problem won't go away.'

He laid a gentle hand over one of hers, stroking her skin with his fingers, and Lana's throat constricted; she couldn't recall the last time anyone had touched her so tenderly. She didn't want to stop it, and she didn't want to taint the episode by talking about Janet.

'Change the topic, please.'

Her father released her hand. She lifted it to her face, smelling the spicy remnants of his cologne, filing away the memory. 'Got anything planned for tomorrow?' he asked.

'I normally work until midday on Saturday.'

'Could you take a half-day as holiday?'

'Why?'

'I thought we might go to the Chelsea Flower Show.'

She swallowed, then feeling her eyes well up, bit the insides of her cheeks. On the other side of the King's Road, she saw a tide of pedestrians wearing sensible flat shoes flowing towards the Thames; they would be headed for the Flower Show. 'Can you get tickets this late?' she asked.

He stacked their two empty plates, picked up her mug and balanced it on top. Then, he took something out of his jacket pocket and dropped it onto the table. 'I'm a member – where do you think you got your love of gardening? Eleanor and I go every year, but this year she'd like you to have her ticket instead.'

Lana picked up the envelope, slipped out the tickets, taking in the Royal Horticultural Society's dark green logo with its tiny caricature of a tree. She'd never questioned why she enjoyed gardening, just knew she did, and that Janet didn't. Her mother was so disinterested in her daughter's hobby, she couldn't even be relied upon to distinguish flat leaf parsley from coriander.

Could she get Saturday morning off? Emily was still away. Alex and Ginge were around, but they were planning to spend the weekend at some tech show. She didn't think Mark would mind. She knew she'd have the most amazing time and be out of Anne and Kenny's hair.

'Yes,' she said, nodding so vigorously her glasses slipped down her nose. 'I mean, yes please. I've never been.' She looked sideways at him. 'And please say thank you to Eleanor. This is very kind of her, and it means the world to me.'

'She's a very kind woman. When you're ready, I'd like you to meet her. She certainly wants to meet you. For now, she wants to give us space to get to know each other again. Let's meet early tomorrow, beat the crush.'

In the morning, Lana woke early, her insides squirming with excitement. It was an unusual sensation, but she was convinced she'd experienced it before. While she made herself a cup of tea, did the washing up, and then slipped onto the balcony to water her hosts' pots before the sun became too strong, she tried to recall when she'd last felt this way. Tracking through her memories, she finally pinned it down: childhood Sundays, "special time with daddy".

They arranged to meet outside the main entrance at 7.45 a.m. Lana walked there, passing a few early-morning runners and a street cleaner trundling his cart down the road, diligently stopping to sweep up litter discarded by yesterday's careless show guests. The gates didn't open for another fifteen minutes, but already the queue stretched back to Royal Hospital Road. Security was efficient, and within ten minutes, they were part of a crowd shuffling down a road lined either side with stalls each with a different slant on Lana's hobby – from the obvious wet weather gear, sturdy footwear, and seeds, to the obscure: specialist pruning saws, garden designers, and a nursery supplying fully mature trees.

Her father steered her towards a stand selling jackets, boots and belts. Lana pulled out the sleeve of a brown velvet jacket and stroked the soft fabric upwards, creating a darker streak. She flipped over the price tag and recoiled.

'This isn't gardening kit,' she exclaimed.

'It's Eleanor's idea,' he replied. 'Last night, she pointed out that I owe you thirty birthday and Christmas presents. She likes the Moloh brand – British designed and manufactured. Go on, choose something.' He snatched her hand away, adding with a brief laugh, 'Stop looking at the prices.'

She smiled, then realized she had slipped into the role of pampered daughter as easily as an otter sliding into a river. Did he have enough money for these treats – dinner at The Enterprise must have cost £80. She didn't want him feeling responsible for what Janet had done, paying for luxuries that he couldn't afford to assuage a misplaced guilt. But she wouldn't think about Janet. She didn't want to spoil today.

'Do you still work?' she asked.

'I do,' he replied, smiling at her. 'When I left Bristol, I went back to my dream and retrained as an accountant. I do the books and tax returns for a few local businesses. Go on, try that one on.'

She slipped a powder blue military style jacket off its hanger, checked the size, sneaked a glance at the price tag and cringed, but allowed her father to help her into it.

'Bit late for my dreams,' Lana replied. She walked the length of the stall to a mirror propped against the far wall.

Her father was standing behind her, looking at her reflection. He put his hands on her shoulders. 'That colour suits you . . . It's never too late to follow your dreams, Lana.' He glanced across at the assistant. 'I think we'll take this, please.'

He insisted on carrying her new jacket in its smart suit carrier bag. Linking his other arm through hers, he suggested they get to the show gardens before the crowds.

She laughed. 'There's no chance of that, is there? This place is one big crowd!'

He stopped and dropped a kiss on her head. 'That was a happy sound. Come on, this way.'

As they walked, he chattered about his life. Lana learned how much he and Eleanor enjoyed gardening, and that a decade ago the couple had moved to a cottage with a half-acre plot near a village on the southern edge of Manchester. Eleanor had designed their garden, but they'd chosen the plants together and spent most weekends tending it. 'You know the saying, it's never the wrong weather for gardening provided you're wearing the right clothes. Now this is an interesting plant design,' he said, pointing to one of the smaller show gardens.

'What's so special about this one, Dad?'

He turned to reply, his face glowing, but Lana didn't hear what he said, her mind stuck on the single word that had elicited his joy: she'd just slipped back thirty years and called him Dad.

Over a sausage bap lunch, sitting on the grass beneath a plane tree, he became serious. 'Remind me, where does Janet think you've gone?' he asked, biting into his roll.

Lana swallowed. 'Devon. My employers have a house there. I've been down with them before.'

'And how long is this mystical trip to Devon going to last? This won't go away, Lana. You must face up to life's dramas. Ignoring them only makes the inevitable confrontation worse. What if she sees you?'

She finished her food, rubbing the grease off her fingers with a paper napkin. Her gaze dropped to the alstroemeria plant she'd bought for Anne and Kenny, wondering if they'd be able to keep it alive. If it died, it wouldn't be for lack of effort. That couple had more kindness in one of their little fingers than her mother had ever shown her. 'I don't really have much compassion for her at the moment,' she said.

Her father narrowed his eyes, reminding her of when she'd disappointed him as a child. 'Stop hiding. Confront her and get it over with: you'll feel much better when it's done.'

Although Gwen only left London on Friday morning, Mark invited himself to Essex for Sunday lunch. She walked Romeo, tidied the house, made toad-in-the-hole with onion gravy, and warned Deidre not to pop in; they needed privacy. Was Steve's reappearance about to alter her relationship with Mark? If it did, she only had herself to blame. She shouldn't have been so selfish; she should have told Mark the truth as soon as he was old enough to understand.

He was at the door by noon, carrying a bunch of flowers. She let him in and limped off down the corridor, the corgi trotting in her footsteps like her four-legged shadow. The kitchen smelled of caramelized onions. It was a homely smell that reminded her Mark was staying for lunch, something he hadn't done since January. She dropped her head into the blooms and sniffed in the scent, then ran water into the sink and pushed in the stems.

'I've arranged that follow-up appointment with the cardiologist for you,' Mark said, slipping her a Post-it note. 'Here. I've written down the details.'

She picked it up, fingering the sticky underside. 'Already? I only saw him on Tuesday. I'll make tea, then we can go into the front room and have a natter. You are staying for lunch, aren't you?'

'Yup. Emily's in Devon. I think she's waiting for Alex, but he's dodging her. Last night he told me he's off to Croyde when she returns.'

Gwen had a flashback to her grandson at the council of war,

skulking in the corner, refusing to make eye contact with his mother, and then giving her the cold shoulder at breakfast.

'Has your relationship with Alex thawed?' she asked.

'Not really. He's out a lot or keeps to his room with Ginge.'

'What about meal times?'

He laughed. 'I eat at my desk.'

*Well, there was a missed opportunity*, thought Gwen. How was anyone going to help Alex if Mark wouldn't talk to him, and the boy refused to be in the same room as his mother. The kettle whistled. 'Right, let's get the tea made,' she said, wrapping a tea towel around the handle.

'Mum, why didn't you tell me the truth about Dad?'

And we're off, she thought, reminding herself she owed Mark the truth, even if it was decades late.

In the early years after Steve left his name was never mentioned; Gwen wanted to forget him and she suspected, out of consideration for his mother, Mark never spoke about his father either. He tried to hide his emotions, but she saw the anxious look in his eyes at birthdays, furtively flicking through the post. Now, he must have so many questions. She took baby steps to the tea tray and set the kettle down, leaning her weight on the back of a chair.

'I should never have married him. But it was what folk did in those days. Got married, so you didn't have a child out of wedlock.'

'Why?' asked Mark, wrinkling his nose. 'I wouldn't have minded.'

'You would have,' she scoffed, taking the lid off the teapot and filling it with boiling water. 'Back then, not many kids were born to single mothers, and those that were got bullied. Children are just as tribal as adults. They pick on anyone slightly different.'

'But I was born in the Seventies. There must've been scores of single mums after the Sixties.'

She poked at the teabags with a spoon, steam warming her hand, then replaced the lid. 'To those who didn't live through them, the Sixties might seem liberated, but back then, we were not as free to make our own decisions as youngsters are now. Even by the Seventies, neither of our families wanted the stigma. We were put under a lot of pressure.'

'Was it a disaster from the get-go?'

In the last few days, Gwen had asked herself that question numerous times, and concluded she'd probably been a bit star-struck by Steve – he was a few years older than she was, and different from anyone she'd ever met in Bargoed. 'I didn't stop to ask if we were suited,' she said. 'I just got caught up in the excitement of getting married, moving to England, setting up a home, and having a baby.' She sighed softly. 'Your father was never cut out to be a husband.'

'So, it wasn't a love match that went sour?'

She picked up the tea tray, then put it back down again. 'I did try.' She had a flashback to her wedding day at Colchester Registry Office, dressed in a pale blue mini dress. 'Marriage is like a fire. It needs nurturing, because if it goes out, it's difficult to rekindle.'

'But why did your fire go out?'

'Both parties have to try if a relationship is going to work.' She took Mark's hand in hers. 'Do you and Emily want to make a go of things? The affair . . . There must have been something wrong before that started. Be honest with yourselves. Your father never was, but I worked out it wasn't about me or you. Steve didn't want to be married to anyone. He's a free spirit. I was only ever intended to be another fling.'

Mark looked a bit shocked. Had she been too honest? Did he think she was warning him not to have a relationship with his father?

'I'm not trying to put you off. He's not a bad man, Mark. He just wasn't a good husband. He was a womanizer, couldn't resist temptation, and he was good looking, just like you.' She reached over and ruffled his hair. 'I thought he'd change, settle down when you were born, but he didn't. He talked about it often enough, promised me he'd change, but some people can't.'

'But you told me he'd left. Why didn't you tell me the truth?'

'You were just a nipper. It wasn't right to burden you with my problems. He was away often enough, shacked up with someone else. You hardly saw him. And then one day, I thought, I've had enough of being a part-time wife. I thought I'd do a better job bringing you up alone without dragging his dead weight along with us.'

'Are you going to see him again?' asked Mark.

'This isn't about me and Steve. He wasn't trying to find me. I was as much of a shock to him as he was to me.'

'What do you think I should do?'

She scrutinized his face, recognizing the expression from his childhood, when he would ask permission to stay up late to watch something unsuitable on TV. Did he need her to sanction seeing his own father? That was a step too far for Gwen. 'Whatever you think best,' she said. 'Now let's have that tea before it gets cold.'

It hadn't rained all weekend, and the forecast for Monday was another hot, sunny day. When Lana arrived for work, she looked over the railings at her drooping plants, itching to revive them – would it hurt Janet to spend ten minutes outside with a watering can? She let herself in and trooped downstairs to the kitchen. There was a single dirty cereal bowl discarded on the marble island. Alex and Ginge must have left, which meant that Emily would be coming home. Lana would be able to apologize to her for going to Tom's dinner.

Later that morning, Lana walked into the dining room with a plate of chocolate muffins. Mark was on speaker phone. She recognized Clare's voice.

'Progress,' reported the lawyer.

Mark gestured to Lana to sit. She dumped the plate and pulled up a chair next to his, feeling a frisson of excitement. What had happened?

'Finally, *they* are suggesting we try arbitration,' announced Clare.

'No. Keep pushing them towards court.'

For a man who earned a living selling advice, he was remarkably reluctant to follow any, thought Lana. Project Revenge was treading water. It couldn't move forward if the two sides didn't meet to thrash out a deal. Was Lana ever going to earn that commission?

'I would advise you to reconsider,' said Clare. 'You must be seen to consider every avenue and demonstrate that you had no option but to take them to court.'

Lana crossed her fingers. Mark tutted loudly.

Clare gave a final push. 'I share your suspicion that they won't negotiate in good faith, but my strong advice is to show willing. Don't eliminate this route without exploring it. You've nothing to lose. I can insist Paul isn't part of their negotiating team.'

'OK then,' said Mark, his reluctance obvious. 'Let's go through the charade. That's all it will be, though.'

Clare swooped on the opportunity. 'Right, I'll talk to my opposite number and agree on an arbitrator who has experience with City packages. Then let's meet to discuss tactics.'

Mark ended the call. 'Don't expect anything to come from this, Svetlana,' he warned.

*

A week after Tom's article dropped, Mary and Emily drove back from Devon. Mary returned the hire car, then joined her friend at the gym. The weightlifting session only lasted thirty minutes. Emily left Mary with a complicated set of core exercises on the orange fit-ball – which reminded Mary of her childhood space hopper – while she went for a shower.

Mary planked, jackknifed and reverse-crunched her way through the routine, then stretched, wondering what Emily was doing; she didn't need to shower, she was the trainer. In the changing rooms, Mary found Emily sitting in front of the mirror, applying lipstick slowly and carefully. She stepped behind her, and was hit by a wave of Chanel Noir – had Emily showered in the scent?

'Thought I'd do a spot of shopping,' said Emily in a cheerful voice.

Briefly, Mary caught Emily's eyes in the mirror and widened her own. Emily averted hers. Mary didn't believe Emily was on her way to the shops. The summer sales were on. Emily always waited for the new ranges, and she certainly wouldn't go shopping at 1 p.m. Was she meeting Paul? Was she going to tell him it was over?

On Tuesday, Lana arrived early to walk the dogs. She hadn't seen Emily the day before, but had her mother? Returning from the park, she let herself back in and bumped into Emily, who fell to her knees to unhook the terriers.

'Morning, Svetlana. I hate to ask, but would you mind coming in early again tomorrow? Mark tells me Ginge and Alex are coming to London for a meeting, and you know how young men adore a cooked breakfast.'

*But they only left yesterday!*

'I'll be in by eight o'clock,' she promised.

'Thank you. Gwen's coming too. Mark says she's got a follow-up with the cardiologist. Just put everyone in the same rooms they used last time,' said Emily, shooting Lana a grateful look. 'And, Svetlana, thanks for, you know . . . thanks for being so supportive. You've been a rock, looking after the dogs for me while I was away, and Mark and Alex too.'

Lana felt herself blush. She pushed the leads into Emily's hands, mumbling, 'You're welcome.' Emily's little speech was impressive. She was facing her demons head on. Why couldn't Lana do the same? It was a week since she'd seen her mother, yet whenever she thought about her, Lana's stomach cramped. She thought about her mother's latest text:

Emily is being selfish. You have other responsibilities. I hope she didn't make you work on the Sabbath.

Was Lana ready to speak to Janet? She'd certainly like to put a stop to those bleating messages.

She apologized to Emily for going to Tom's dinner.

'Thank you, but don't worry about it. We all make mistakes,' said Emily. 'If I hadn't had an affair, there would never have been a story to print.'

At noon, with her next pupil not due for two hours, Mary decided to stretch her legs. She collected a suit carrier she'd left by the front door and stepped outside. It was a warm day – the trees in the communal garden were rustling in a gentle breeze and she could smell the lavender in the mock-lead tub on her doorstep. She stood for a few moments, imagining what it would be like on such a fine day in Devon.

With the suit carrier slung over one shoulder like a mail sack, she turned right onto Walton Street and crossed the road opposite La Picena, the local delicatessen. The bag was heavy, and outside San Lorenzo, she stopped to adjust it to a more comfortable position. Mary had a soft spot for the restaurant; Charles often took her there to celebrate their wedding anniversary.

She glanced at their regular table, but her eyes were drawn to a corner. *Emily!* Her companion had his back to her, but she saw his stripy braces and the ice bucket beside him. Mary tutted and walked on. Was Paul the explanation for Emily's perfume yesterday?

There was a queue at the dry cleaners – it was lunch hour, the busiest period of the day – and it was twenty minutes before Mary took another sneaky peek through the restaurant window. Emily's eyes were shut, and Paul's right arm was stretched across the white linen tablecloth, clawing for one of her hands. Maybe this *was* adieu time.

The couple were absorbed in themselves, allowing Mary to watch unobserved. Emily shook her head, Paul leaned towards her, his head inclined to one side. Suddenly Emily stood up, flung her napkin onto the table, and ran to the restaurant door, yanking it open. Paul rushed after her, reaching the entrance seconds after Emily. Mary dashed aside, turning to stare into the next-door shop window. Heart pounding, she listened.

'Emily darling, please.'

'Don't *Emily darling* me,' cried Emily. 'It's over.'

Mary glanced over her shoulder. Paul had his back to her and was holding Emily by the arm. 'But it's not, is it? That's not what you want, you're just feeling guilty. You shouldn't. I hated seeing those photos in the paper, but it's better now it's out in the open. You and I are made for each other.'

Emily let out a sob, her shoulders shaking. She stared down at the pavement and spoke slowly, 'I am begging you to stop interfering in my life.'

Paul put his hand under Emily's chin and slowly tilted it upright. He looked straight into her eyes and said, 'Leave him. He doesn't cherish you like I do. He doesn't deserve you. Come and live with me, you know I want to marry you.'

Emily burst into tears, shook herself free, and ran straight into the road.

A horn hooted. Mary heard a screech of tyres, and gasped. Her hand shot up to cover her mouth. A white car was stationary in the middle of Walton Street, the driver hunched over the steering wheel, her friend stood inches from its bonnet. That was close, thought Mary.

'EMILY!' cried Paul.

Emily ran off, reached the other side of the street and disappeared into Ovington Square.

In front of Mary, Paul seemed to collapse. 'Thank God,' he gasped. Straightening, his head darted both ways, checking the traffic in preparation for running after Emily.

Mary grabbed Paul by the arm. 'No,' she said firmly. 'Leave her be.'

He peered at Mary, at her hand on his arm, a sullen look on his face. 'Are you spying on us? Was it your idea she should end our relationship?'

'I feel responsible,' Mary said crisply. 'I introduced you to Emily, and to Tom. Now look what's happened.'

Mary noticed two men behind Paul, standing with their backs to the restaurant; the expressions on their faces made it obvious they wished they could beam themselves elsewhere. She pulled Paul to one side and waited until the men passed before turning back to him. 'Paul, did you speak to Tom – did he interview you?'

The reply was snapped. 'He asked to interview me dozens of times, but I didn't let him. That weekend, he ran the gist of the article past me – never mentioned the part that covered the affair. I corrected a few facts. That's all.'

'And planted ideas. Like Mark being investigated for insider dealing. Was that you?'

'I'd never link the bank to something like that.'

'But you didn't think you were linking the bank's name, did you? I bet Tom told you he wouldn't mention the bank. It *was* you . . . You planted that idea.'

'The whole piece was supposed to be about insider dealing. He was remarkably well informed. He must have a source who understands how investment banks are structured, how information might leak from one department to another.'

She took a deep breath. That would be Barry. She'd often heard him joke about how he could retire if he could plant a camera in the M&A department. Why had she given a journalist Barry's contact details? Mary swallowed.

'Was that you?' Paul studied her with a curious expression on his face. 'Mary . . .? Were you Tom's source?'

'Of course I wasn't!' she said dismissively. 'What would I know about insider dealing?'

'Look at me, Mary.' She raised her face, her cheeks burning with shame, praying he wouldn't notice. 'You look a bit shifty to me.'

# *Fourteen*

'You're late,' huffed Janet, getting up from the sofa. 'You know I go to prayer meetings on Tuesday nights.'

Lana gritted her teeth. Her trip to Devon may have been mythical, but Janet didn't know that; where was the '*welcome home*' or '*how was your trip?*' Janet rambled on. '. . . I don't know. You gallivant off to Devon without so much as a by-your-leave, then you come home a week later, don't even pop in to say hello, or bring me a pint of milk. Didn't you get my texts? You can be a bit selfish sometimes, Lana.'

'Stop right there,' said Lana, digging her fingernails into her palms. Her lower lip trembled, and she bit it, counted to three, then let rip. '*I* can be selfish. I wonder where I inherited that streak from?' She glowered at her mother, who froze, one arm inside a pastel-pink Chanel jacket.

Searching for the sleeve, Janet's arm started flailing around like a bird trapped in a net. 'Where's your luggage?' she asked.

Lana gave her mother a black look. Hadn't she heard what she'd just said?

'I must get on,' muttered Janet.

'Yes,' said Lana, drawing out the word, letting it rumble on, her anger bubbling up. 'We can't have you rushing, straining that weak heart of yours, can we?'

The arm stopped flailing. Janet's elbow was stuck in the armhole, straining the fabric, and making her look comical. Hesitantly she asked, 'What's wrong?'

'I know.'

There was a pause. 'Know what?'

To Lana, her mother's voice sounded tremulous, and she swooped in like a seagull spotting a shoal of mackerel. 'Cut it out. Stop the play acting. There's nothing wrong with your heart, and never has been.'

Janet sagged onto the sofa.

'What?' Lana snapped. 'Not going to the prayer meeting? You could run there if you wanted to, couldn't you? You've got a whole lot of explaining to do.' Lana lowered her voice to a hiss. 'And let's start with *why*. Why did you lie to me, *Mum*? Wasn't ruining Dad's life enough for you, that you had to ruin mine too after he bolted?'

The flat fell silent, an uncomfortable silence that seemed to speak volumes for Lana's lost dreams. Lana wanted answers, she had to make sense of the lie – why had her mother done it? She glared at Janet who was sitting in a crumpled heap, shoulders hunched, her head in her hands.

'I'm going for a shower,' Lana said. 'Then I'm spending some quality time with my plants because they look a bit parched. Too much effort for you to stagger outside and give them a sprinkling of water, was it? By then, I should be calm enough to listen to you.' She stalked to the bathroom door. 'Don't even think about going to that prayer meeting. But you might want to say a few of your own. And you can cancel any plans you have for tomorrow. You're working upstairs. Make sure you're ready by eight o'clock sharp.'

In the shower, Lana stood shaking, letting the hot water cascade over her skin. Her brain felt water-logged and she needed to get her thoughts straight. She picked up a nail brush and pressed hard, oblivious to the pain, rubbing it up and down her arms, as if trying to remove a stain, trying to scrub away the implications of her mother's lie. She turned off the water, but remained standing in the steam, crying. Tears washed down her face with almost the same force as the water from the shower. Would her mother tell her the truth, or was she about to be fobbed off?

Lana wrapped herself in a towel. She took another and fashioned it into a turban around her hair, then rubbed steam off a patch of the mirror and examined her face. Her eyes were red, her skin blotchy. Anger replaced her sorrow, frothing up like an unattended jam pan. She didn't care how she looked. She wanted answers!

The door squeaked as Lana opened it, and Janet turned around. Her mother had taken off her jacket and her eyes were swollen, red and puffy. Lana looked away, wondering briefly if the tears were from shame, guilt, or self-pity. She padded in, the carpet feeling scratchy beneath her bare feet, reminding her of the uncomfortable path she'd been forced to tread these past thirty years.

Lana sat beside Janet. Her plants had suffered long enough, they'd survive another hour. 'I'm listening,' she said calmly.

Her mother claimed she'd initially invented the story to avoid having another child with a man she didn't love. It had been a difficult birth, and her mother did have a series of tests to check her heart. But Lana's father was right: those tests proved her heart wasn't damaged. When her mother was given the all-clear, the nurse told her she was lucky, not everyone was so fortunate, and that's when the idea hit her.

'Once I'd started, there was no way back. It snowballed to the point where I started to believe it myself. Taking things easy, all those tablets—'

'What *are* those pills?'

'Multivitamins, cod liver oil . . . whatever was on special offer. I just put them in prescription bottles. The thing is, I got used to being a housewife. And I kept a good home, all the meals were cooked from scratch, the house was immaculate. We argued a lot, but most couples do. We seemed to be muddling through. I thought he'd go when you left home, that we'd come to some sort of arrangement.' Janet blew her nose, gave a long sniff, and then said sarcastically, 'I knew about his fancy woman, but I didn't see it coming. When he didn't come back from that business trip, I knew he'd gone for good. I knew he wouldn't support me unless I gave him a divorce, and I wasn't doing that. I panicked. You took charge - I shouldn't have let you, but I didn't have any money. Your father had given notice on the house and stopped the direct debits. I'd never worked, Lana. No one would've employed me.'

'You didn't even try!' scoffed Lana. 'When things started to sort themselves out, that first job with the flat, or when we moved to London. Why didn't you come clean then? Start putting your own life together, instead of paralyzing mine?'

'Would this conversation have been any easier a decade ago? It takes courage to own up to something like this.'

'Oh, come on! One thing you are not is weak willed.' Lana unwound her turban and started combing her tangled hair. Each painful tug reminded her of the needless sacrifices she had been forced to make.

'I have thought about it often, and I've prayed for guidance.' Janet's gaze flickered towards the Madonna statue, and she gave a little laugh. 'I've said so many Hail Mary's for my sin. But you seemed content with life.'

Yes, thought Lana, good choice of word; content implied acceptance, it wasn't something people aspired to, like happiness or fulfilment. She would prefer to be discontent, but responsible for her own life choices, even if she regretted them. 'God may have forgiven your sin, but no amount of Hail Marys will buy you my forgiveness.'

'You never complained,' said Janet softly.

Why *had* she never complained? Because she believed her mother and accepted Janet's Christian desire not to be a burden on the state – a phrase easier to understand now that Lana recognized Janet's cover would've been blown had she tried to claim disability allowance. Lana had processed her mother's incapacity as her own personal cross to bear. What was the point of complaining about something she couldn't change?

'It doesn't mean I didn't want to lead my life differently! I had dreams, like most eighteen-year-olds . . . And they didn't involve looking after someone who didn't need taking care of.' Did she still have dreams, wondered Lana. She certainly used to. Was her father right that it was never too late?

'I know the words are a bit late,' said Janet. 'I'm sorry. I really am sorry. In a strange way, it's a relief that you know.'

'Saves you a few more Hail Marys, does it?' spat Lana.

A troubled look appeared on Janet's face. 'How did you find out?'

'Dad tracked me down.'

Janet's jaw dropped. 'Your father . . .?' She shuffled in her seat.

'Yes. He read that nasty article about the Ellises. Saw my name and their address, and he took a punt it was me.'

Janet puffed out her chest. 'Well, I hope he doesn't think he's going to gatecrash our lives after thirty years.'

'He doesn't want to gatecrash yours, and he shouldn't have to be elbowing himself into mine after a thirty year gap. Why did you destroy his letters?'

Janet was nervously twirling her wedding ring around her finger.

'At least you're not denying you did,' said Lana. 'I suppose the explanation is obvious: you didn't want him to tell me. He assumed you'd confess when he left. Now he's finding it tough to forgive himself for what you've done.'

'I am sorry, Lana. I know the words sound a bit trite.'

She didn't intend to say it, but she blurted it out anyway; was it a feeble attempt at revenge, wanting to hurt her mother? 'He's still with the woman he left you for. Eleanor.'

Janet shook her head, muttering under her breath.

'I can't hear you.'

'I said he was never a good Catholic. He shouldn't be living in sin.'

Lana gave a tight laugh. 'I don't think you should expect to be canonized any time soon. And he's only living in sin because you won't divorce him.'

'Why should I? That man ruined my life.'

'And that gave you the right to ruin mine, did it?' She tutted. 'He didn't ruin your life. You were perfectly happy to marry him. You just grew apart.'

They talked for another hour, until the words were spinning around Lana's head so fast that she couldn't make sense of them, and there was nothing her mother could say that could make things better. Nothing would give Lana back those lost years. She needed to focus on the future. It was a peculiar thought: she could make choices without taking her mother's wants or needs into account. Where did Lana want to live? What did she want to do? Did she want to travel, take up a new hobby? Hemmed in by caring responsibilities, she'd never asked herself any of those questions. One thing she was sure about – Janet needed to move out.

*

In the morning, Lana let Janet, her new deputy housekeeper, into the entrance hall of the Ellis house. Her assistant's eyes popped wide, gaping at the height of the ceiling, the elaborate plasterwork round the edges, and the frivolous use of space. The hallway was as long as the entire basement flat, and nearly as wide as its reception room. The parquet flooring shone in the summer sunlight.

'How do they keep this so sparkly?' whispered Janet.

'There's a special wax. Come on, Mum,' said Lana, closing the front door and leading the way down to the kitchen. The table was laid for breakfast. Lana guessed Gwen had done that.

Together, in the pantry, they donned housecoats. Five crystal wine glasses sat by the sink, half full of water to prevent red wine staining the inside. Lana hadn't expected anyone to swish them out; that would be Gwen too.

Janet was still whispering, 'This room is bigger than our bathroom!'

Noticing the red light on the machine, Lana instructed her mother to empty the dishwasher, pulling down the door to show her where it was. *Gwen again.* 'I'll get breakfast started,' said Lana, 'and there's no need to whisper.'

As she walked to the fridge, Janet's voice followed her. 'Where does the cutlery live?'

'Opposite the kitchen table, middle drawer.'

Janet sloughed across Lana's path in a pair of diamante-studded jeans and Gucci loafers, a fork in one hand. Lana tore off a length of foil. It crackled as she wrapped it around the inside of the grill pan, which was apt for her mood. She laid out the sausages, then added the bacon. The Gucci loafers did another circuit – this time, a single spoon was rehomed.

The pinkness of the sausages reminded Lana of how red her own skin had been after her shower last night. She wondered how long it would take to stop resenting her mother. The sooner

Janet moved out the better. The church would have to help if the state didn't. Her phone vibrated in her pocket, and she fished it out. "Dad".

We're in London. Fancy pizza tonight? Be honest, is it too soon for you to meet Eleanor?

A voice crashed into her thoughts. 'And the crockery?'

Lana looked up, pressing the phone to her chest. Janet was holding a cereal bowl, smiling warmly as if she was a guest who'd risen early and offered to help her hostess. Lana pointed with the tongs. 'Third cupboard along,' she muttered, slipping the phone back into her pocket. She pulled out the grill pan and flipped the bacon over. Janet could be as charming as she liked, but she wasn't forgiven. Lana wanted to see her father, but was it too early to meet Eleanor? She would think it over, reply later.

The front door slammed, and footsteps rang out overhead. Lana transferred the crisp rashers onto a warm platter and reined in her thoughts. Mark jogged into the kitchen, walked over and stole a piece of bacon.

'What time is the taxi booked for?' he asked, nibbling his bounty.

'Ten o'clock. This is my mother, Janet. She's helping.'

'Pleased to meet you, Janet!' said Mark, waving the remains of the rasher at her. 'Very kind of you.' He gave a soft chuckle. 'I can see she's got you as organized as she's got the rest of us. I'm off for a shower.'

And he was gone.

'Was that the rude, arrogant Mr Ellis?' asked Janet, smiling. 'Where does this mug live?'

She threw the oven gloves at her mother. 'Oh, Mum, you look after the sausages, and make coffee – the beans are on the counter. Machine's the same as ours. I'll deal with the dishes.'

Lana finished emptying the dishwasher, listening to the high-pitched whirr of the coffee grinder. Good. Mark would be gasping for caffeine. She started washing up the wine glasses. Above the sound of running water, Lana heard Janet introducing herself to Alex and Ginge, telling them to help themselves to coffee, and that breakfast was nearly ready. Lana picked up a cloth, dried a glass then polished it, and carried it through to the kitchen.

'Ugh!' said Alex. He was holding a mug near his mouth, spitting coffee back into it. 'Svetlana, what have you done to this coffee?' His eyes were narrow slits. 'It's filthy . . . so bloody strong.'

Janet was fidgeting with the oven gloves.

'I'll make a fresh pot,' Lana said, snatching up the offending brew and pushing her mother to one side.

Gwen walked in, leaning heavily on her stick.

'Gwen, this is my mother Janet. She's helping out this morning,' Lana said, then hissed at her mother, 'Dad may have taught you to like coffee like that, but most Brits don't like coffee as strong as the Polish.' She poured the coffee down the sink. 'Just put the platter on the table so they can help themselves and check how everyone wants their eggs.'

By the time Lana had made fresh – weaker – coffee and fried the eggs, Emily was in the kitchen, complimenting Janet on her outfit. 'I used to have a pair of loafers just like those, Janet. Two poached eggs for me, please.'

*Doesn't she recognize her own cast-offs?* Lana wondered.

Emily slid into a seat next to Alex, but he picked up his plate and moved to sit between Gwen and Ginge.

'Svetlana,' called out Mark as he came back in, freshly showered. 'Could you check I've plugged my phone in to recharge, please?'

'On my way,' she said, tossing a tea towel at Janet. 'Soft poached eggs for Emily. The water's ready.'

It took five minutes to track down Mark's phone by the side of the sink in his shower room. She slipped out her own phone and messaged her father.

Love to join you both tonight. Pizza Pomodoro on Beauchamp Place, eight o'clock?

The reply was instantaneous.

"Perfect xxx".

Lana returned to the kitchen. Gwen was standing beside Janet, her walking stick hooked over the eye-level oven door behind her. On the counter, there was a plate with a puddle of water and two eggs that looked like someone had drowned and shredded them. Gwen was swirling a pan of water, bubbling on the hob in front of her. 'See, it's ready now,' she said, cracking an egg on the side of the pan and releasing the contents into the water. 'Now watch that egg timer. Three minutes and she'll be done.'

Lana took the discarded plate into the pantry, dispatching the watery contents into the food caddy and snapping the lid shut. Today was arbitration day. She'd worked so hard to get to this point. She had spotted the discrimination angle, secured the best barrister, and helped Clare nudge Mark towards arbitration - but she couldn't go today, not with the house full. Emily would want lunch cooked, there were five beds to make, and five bathrooms to clean.

Her boss's voice floated in from the kitchen. 'Svetlana let's leave at nine. Don't want to risk traffic.'

Lana leaned around the side of the pantry. 'I'll change the taxi for you.'

'Hold on,' he said, putting down his mug. 'You'll change the taxi for *us* . . . I'm not going alone.'

'I'd love to,' she said, 'but . . .' She waved her hands at the table.

Mark pointed a finger at her. '*You* are coming with me. End of. Emily can cope.'

But Emily couldn't cope. It transpired she had the day blocked out to help at the dog sanctuary. Watching her employer's eggs poaching – Lana didn't share Gwen's confidence in her mother – she heard Emily say, 'They're short of volunteers . . . the kennels need cleaning . . . there's heaps to do. They rely on me.'

Well, there we go, thought Lana, draining a poached egg with a slotted spoon. Cinderella wasn't going to the ball after all. She fished out the other egg.

'I'm sorry, Mark, but I have commitments,' Emily wavered, 'just like you.' Hearing the faltering voice, Lana glanced up as Emily threw her son a pleading look. 'Everything all right, Alex darling?'

Alex turned to his father. 'Dad, can Ginge and I see you, please? We're looking for a strategic investor.'

Dabbing at his mouth with a napkin, Mark stood up. 'Not today, son, got a lot on. Speak to Svetlana and get a slot in my diary.'

Lana cleared Mark's plate, popping it onto the island.

'If Lana's busy, everyone can make their own bed,' suggested Gwen.

Emily dropped her cutlery, which clinked onto her plate. 'Did you just call her Lana?' She turned to face her housekeeper. 'Do you mind your name being shortened?'

Lana coughed out a laugh and picked up the greasy grill pan. 'You, Mark and Alex are the only people who call me Svetlana.'

'Leave that lot,' said Gwen. 'I can clear up in here when we've finished and run a mop over the floor. I've already done my room.'

'No, you won't!' said Mark.

A timid voice spoke up. 'Let me do it,' offered Janet. 'I can stay and clear away, tidy the bedrooms and bathrooms.'

'Thank you, Janet, that's very kind,' said Emily.

Lana carried the greasy grill pan into the pantry, smiling to herself – she would be at the arbitration meeting.

The parties had chosen a female arbitrator with impeccable credentials. Sheila Masterton – a tall lady with a long neck, prominent nose, and a sharp voice – had over ten years' experience including refereeing disputes between unnamed banks and equally anonymous former senior employees. The meeting took place on neutral territory at serviced offices paid for by the bank. There was a large conference room, a slightly smaller room, and a very small room. Mark and his team were allocated the smallest room, and he and Clare debated tactics for thirty minutes while Lana took notes, but she found keeping her mind in the present challenging. All morning, she kept drifting back and forth between the previous night's discussion with her mother, and the impending meeting with her quasi-stepmother that evening.

At eleven o'clock everyone trooped into the conference room. Sheila sat at the head of the table and invited everyone to introduce themselves. The bank's team – which, to Lana, resembled a small army – was squashed down one side, their elbows tucked in so they could all fit. Her boss knew everyone on that side of the table, except the outside lawyers. Lana recognized no one.

She counted, as the opposition introduced themselves: eight lawyers, compared to Team Revenge's one. Two in-house and six from the firm representing the bank. There were a couple of women from the HR department, and another from the PR department, whose name she didn't catch. Had they drafted in PR to deal with the aftermath of Tom's article?

There was an obvious hierarchy on the bank's team: the greyer the hair, the closer they sat to the leader, a man called Harold Caruthers, who clearly enjoyed his business lunches a little too much. Harold wasn't much taller than Lana, but his stomach protruded over his waistband and the buttons of his white shirt were straining to stay fastened, exposing flashes of pink hairy skin whenever he shuffled in his seat. Lana focused her attention on Sheila.

On their side of the table, her boss sat directly opposite Harold, flanked by Lana and Clare. Mark introduced his lawyer, then his assistant, and Lana felt a tingle of pride. Unlike her, being vastly outnumbered didn't seem to bother Mark. She sat upright, ignoring her fluttering heart.

Sheila's neck unfurled like a giraffe reaching up to nibble a leaf. She turned first to Harold, then Mark. 'Arbitration is a process designed to produce a settlement which both parties can accept,' she said, emphasizing the last word. Her eyes danced between the two principals. 'Neither of you will leave this building with the deal you want. You're too far apart for that, but I urge you to start thinking about what you are willing to accept to make this matter go away and get on with your lives.' She paused, as if allowing time for this message to sink in. 'Shall we begin?'

Opposite Lana, eleven pairs of eyes turned inwards. The leader of the pack gave a curt nod. Lana tried to imagine sitting on that side of the table. Why were there eight lawyers? And did any of them, to borrow a phrase her boss often used, think they were dancing on a pinhead, interpreting the law narrowly to suit the bank's ambitions? Had any of them ever questioned if Mark had been treated fairly? And did the outside lawyers care about the outcome? Wasn't it in their interests to prolong this dispute, continue charging the client at hourly rates over a hundred times the minimum wage, their fees picked up by an indifferent corporate cheque book? Shielding behind their squadron of advisors and the protective cloak of the law, the opposition had filibustered, repeatedly responding to Clare's letters with a simple:

Our client rejects your allegations.

The message was clear – come and fight me, all of me, if you dare. There must be a weak spot somewhere, someone with a shred of decency who would atone for what Effing Paul did.

'I suggest Mr Ellis starts by explaining his position,' said Sheila.

Mark spoke eloquently of his reputation as a master deal-maker and of his dedication to the bank. He reeled off project names that earned staggering advisory fees, and even larger additional sums from leveraging his relationships with clients, cross-selling other bank products. Lana wrote copious notes. It sounded impressive, even if she didn't know what the Equity Capital Markets division or Securitization desk did. She was beginning to understand how her employers lived such a privileged life. If this was what her boss had done, if he'd regularly pulled in these vast sums, he should never have lost his job.

Mark challenged Harold to name someone with a comparable track record. He mentioned a cross-border acquisition he'd advised on where he had pitched the idea to the client, secured the advisory mandate, and then earned a multiple of his own fee by arranging the foreign exchange to finance the deal. No doubt that had involved Bazza, thought Lana. Finally, Mark summed up by asking a simple question: 'So, why was I selected for redundancy?'

Harold rested his hands on his tummy. He had a deep voice and spoke confidently, claiming the process was conducted fairly. He refuted the allegation that a bonus was part of a banker's package. 'Mark, you know it's discretionary, and doesn't count when we calculate severance pay.' Harold claimed that part of the selection criteria was an assessment of an employee's collegiate spirit, in which Mark had scored low.

'Harold, let's cut the official party line crap,' said Mark evenly. 'Paul chose me because he felt threatened, but that's a reflection of his own management style, not mine. Give me one name, anyone in the bank, who you think will stand up in court and say they found me difficult to work with.'

Lana underlined the word “court”. She’d been told to record each time her boss mentioned the word; his goal was six. Earlier, in the small room, striding round the tiny table and gulping down coffee, he’d explained his strategy. ‘We need to keep reminding them that Team Revenge expects to end up in court.’

‘Why?’ asked Clare.

‘Undermine their confidence. The art of negotiation is to paint the downside clearly for the opposition. I want to demonstrate that we’re the ones going through the motions today, not them.’

One down, five to go, thought Lana. How would her father be around Eleanor tonight? Had Lana made a mistake – was it too early to meet? Stop it, she scolded herself. It was only a pizza, and if Eleanor captured his heart and still had it thirty years later, it’s unlikely she and Lana wouldn’t like each other. *Remember, it was Eleanor who encouraged him to track you down. Concentrate on this meeting!*

Harold patted his tummy. ‘Hey, Mark, don’t be so confident of your former colleagues. I still work with them.’

‘And they know who the paymaster is. But they have integrity and they know when to say ‘no’. Sometimes, the best advice I gave a client was to not do a deal. Honesty is one of the keys to a successful advisory career.’ Mark smiled, the smug smile of someone who knows they are on solid ground. ‘These guys won’t lie for you, Harold, not under oath.’

Did that count as court, wondered Lana. Deciding it did, she underlined the word oath.

A sharp voice cut in. ‘Right, let’s take a ten minute break, shall we?’ suggested Sheila.

Following her boss out of the room, Lana asked herself if Mark was right. Was this all a waste of time? She hoped not: she wanted that commission.

# Fifteen

More than a week after Mary had left her pithy messages, Tom called. Returning home from her regular Wednesday gym session, she listened to his voicemail. There was no apology; he didn't even mention the article. His message was jovial, like catching up after a holiday. The bloody cheek of the man.

She must return his money; she'd contemplated posting it to him but wanted him to promise not to rat on her. Paul suspected she was involved. She couldn't risk anyone discovering what she'd done before she plucked up the courage to confess to Charles . . . and Emily. This was her chance. She bit down on her anger, cancelled her afternoon classes, and invited Tom round for lunch.

Preparing a freekeh salad – she didn't want to risk temptation by offering anything solid which she might throw at him – she hacked away at the pile of herbs. With each slice, she felt her overworked triceps protesting, and channelled the pain, imagining Tom standing in front of her as she verbally tore him to shreds, mentally storing choice phrases that popped into her mind in the imaginary tirade. Tom had tricked her, used her and abused his friendship with Charles. She swept the herbs into the salad, her eyes falling on the fat envelope stuffed with Tom's money – her own thirty pieces of silver, the bribe by which she had inadvertently betrayed Emily.

She didn't bother to change. He didn't deserve the effort. The doorbell rang, and she waited long enough to force him to ring a second time. Mary opened the door, letting in a blast of rap music – the roofers were finished, but the decorators seemed to be working at a glacial pace – the beat chiming with her own rage. Tom was wearing the same outfit he'd worn to the dinner in January, and he'd brought wine. She wrenched the bottle out of his hands, as if removing a stick from Biscuit's jaws and turned her back to avoid the customary kiss.

'Lunch is in the kitchen,' she said with as much grace as she could muster.

He closed the front door softly behind him. 'Sounds cool. Thanks. You've timed the decorators well with this fine weather . . .'

She blanked out his voice; she was in no mood for small talk. Their trainers squeaked down the polished stairs. As they entered the kitchen, Biscuit got up to investigate. 'Basket!' shouted Mary.

The kitchen table was laid, glasses of water poured. She put down the bottle.

'Shall I open that?' Tom offered. 'I'm gasping for a glass of wine.'

She pulled out the salad, plonking it on the table, then added wine glasses and a corkscrew, slamming it next to the bottle. 'Help yourself,' she muttered.

'Are you still cross?' he asked, a faint smile tugging at the corners of his mouth. 'I thought you'd be over it by now. Remember you were paid for your trouble.'

*How could she forget?*

'You invented half the story,' she spat.

He winked at her. 'Poetic licence,' he said, twisting the corkscrew and extracting the cork with a sharp pop. She listened to the glugging sound of the wine being poured, telling herself she didn't care if she blew up his friendship with Charles. No friend should do what Tom had done. Suddenly she didn't feel hungry, but she wanted wine. She picked up her glass, watching Tom spooning salad onto his plate.

'Come on, Mary,' he said. 'It's all blown over. I did a good job, got paid, and so did you.'

She clenched her jaw. Why did he have to keep reminding her of that? 'Well, as that's clearly what motivates you, here's some more money for you,' she snapped, slapping the envelope on the table.

'What's this?' he asked, prodding it with his knife.

'It's the money you gave me.'

'Oh no, that's yours.' He grinned at her. 'You earned it. I'd never have got anywhere without your help.'

Unable to prevent her cheeks from flushing, she scowled at him. 'Go on, rub it in, make me feel even worse than I already do. I don't want your money. I want you to promise you won't tell anyone I helped you.'

'You've got nothing to fear on that score. I never reveal my sources.'

She took a gulp of wine to hide her relief.

'Mary, you're overreacting. Come on, in six months' time, no one will remember anyone's name.'

'But it's permanently there, isn't it? If anyone googles either of them – a potential new client of Mark's, or someone who's just met them socially – it's the first thing they'll see.'

Tom forked food into his mouth; the sound of his chewing was grating. Why had she offered the man lunch? Why hadn't she just posted back the money with a rude note? She should've guessed he wouldn't reveal her secret – he wouldn't want Charles to know what he'd done.

'You don't even care, do you? You used me.'

'Hey, a man's got to make a living. And I didn't use you, we did this together. It was a good story, and people need to know what goes on in the City. There's not enough prosecution for insider dealing.'

'The City has always traded on inside knowledge; it's how fortunes used to be made. It only became illegal after the Big Bang in 1985.'

Tom sniggered. 'Is that how your family made its fortune?'

Mary's stomach started churning; she was thankful Tom's article had focused on contemporary practice. 'Don't try to divert me. Your readers don't care about insider dealing.'

'After the banking crisis, most people worked out for themselves that the City was full of crooks,' said Tom.

She pushed her empty plate away. She would gag if she ate anything. She wanted to strangle this arrogant man.

'Lucky Paul, though,' he murmured. 'That friend of yours . . .'

'Don't go there, Tom,' she warned, glowering at him.

'You should get cross more often!' he said, laughing. He pushed himself upright, walked round to her side of the table, and leaned over her. She looked up. His eyes were closed. He lowered his head. She smelled spring onion on his breath and twisted her head as he kissed her hair.

Mary jumped up, picked up her chair, and pointed the legs at Tom. 'Out, now!' she shouted. Biscuit scrambled upright and growled. Mary felt a surge of love for her dog.

'Come on, Mary, birds of a feather . . . You're just as bored as Emily. I bet you could do with someone to spice up your sex life.'

Mary was speechless. He was supposed to be Charles's friend! And Emily didn't have an affair because she was bored; it was an attempt to force Mark to choose his wife over work.

Tom was still talking. 'All you idle City wives love to dabble with danger . . .'

'I am not idle! And I'm not bored, and even if I was, I certainly wouldn't fill my time by screwing you. I'd do something worthwhile, like more canvassing for the Labour Party.'

'If you were a real socialist, you'd give your money away, sell this house and donate the proceeds to charity.'

She glared at him. 'Not that it's any of your business, but it's not mine to sell. That's the point of having a Trust. I only get to live here, I'm a tenant, the house is tied up for the next generation.' Why was she justifying her life to this man? 'Get out!' She couldn't bring herself to add the word please.

Pulling his jacket off the back of the chair, he drained his wine, picked up the envelope of cash, winked at her, and left.

She heard the front door slam. Was this how people saw her, as a Trust Fund kid? She knew she was lucky to have a home, but it wasn't free. She and Charles spent tens of thousands of pounds maintaining the house, something she suspected he was beginning to resent, and she was hardly a classic Trust Fund kid. The trickle of income was spent mostly on trustees' fees.

Mary tipped the remains of the salad into a dish, poured herself a glass of wine and went upstairs, curling up with Biscuit on a sofa by the television, and letting a comforting voice take her on a tour of the gold medal winning gardens from the recent Chelsea Flower Show.

She took a sip of wine and reached for the remote, muting the reporter, and sat silently for a few moments, stroking Biscuit. She didn't enjoy gardening; she knew nothing about plants, so why was she even watching this? She had so much to do, not just preparing for tomorrow's lessons, but working out how to pay for the hallway renovations without Tom's money, and she still had July's meal plans to do.

Her brow wrinkled. Why was she doing either of those last two things – Charles didn't need to know what he was eating next month, and she would never make enough money to restore this house. Not without winning the lottery. And why should she? The house wasn't her problem. She didn't own it; she only had the right to live here for life. Tenants weren't responsible for the upkeep of a house – if the Trust couldn't afford to repair the hallway, why was she taking on their problem? Her father had been dead for twenty years, why was she still trying to live up to his expectations?

She slapped a hand against her forehead telling herself to be honest – she was inventing chores for herself, still doing homework in her fifties! What really gave her joy? Certainly not coaxing reluctant pupils; she enjoyed teaching those who wanted to learn, but not the others. And she didn't get a kick from planning meals to fulfil the latest dietary fad for "touching thirty plants each week". She got a buzz out of keeping fit and delivering leaflets for the Labour Party; she enjoyed cooking for friends, but not cramming in all the preparation. And there was no need as Charles would happily help, freeing her up to reach the bottom of her chore list. When did she ever relax, unwind, chill a bit, other than in Devon with Emily?

She leaned over and kissed Biscuit's snout, her thoughts drifting as she replayed Tom's pass. Should she tell Charles? It had been so clumsy it was almost forgivable, like someone squaring up to take on Usain Bolt in the 100 metre Olympics final while wearing a pair of wellington boots. She couldn't take it seriously, but why had he done it? He didn't really think she was bored and looking for a thrill, did he? Even if he did, that was no excuse. She patted Biscuit's side and got up to refill her wine glass. At least one good thing had come from her lunch with Tom – she didn't have to worry about her secret getting out anymore.

*

Outside the entrance to Pizza Pomodoro, suspended over the pavement and looking like a peculiar petrol forecourt sign, was a shiny silver tomato. Still buzzing from the adrenaline of her day, Lana was pacing up and down beneath the sign, hands stuffed in her jacket pockets. She walked to the end of the street, turned around and, for the third time, retraced her steps. Beneath the tomato she stopped, rubbed her hands down her face then strode up the stairs into the rather bleak, brightly lit corridor behind the sign.

On the staircase, she took her time, pausing to look at the framed photos of the rock 'n' roll celebrities and film stars who'd eaten in the pizza equivalent of the Hard Rock Café since its doors opened in the Seventies. Each step was accompanied by a tingle of nerves; her father hadn't left Janet for Eleanor – her parents' relationship was over before the two met – but he had left his daughter for her. Lana accepted that, at the time, he didn't think he was choosing between the two women. Her mother admitted he had written over a dozen letters which she had destroyed, but that thought wasn't enough to restore Lana's confidence. She dialled down her anxiety by reminding herself it was Eleanor who'd encouraged her father to track his daughter down, Eleanor's ticket that took Lana to the Chelsea Flower Show, and Eleanor who wanted to meet Lana – hardly hallmarks of the classic wicked stepmother.

Lana opened the door to the basement restaurant. The room was small and smelled faintly of garlic; there was a tapestry of celebrities covering the walls, spotlights over each picture lighting the room. Her father stood up, and a second later, the woman sitting opposite him also rose and turned to face the entrance. She was younger than Lana's father, maybe mid-fifties, and physically she was very different from petite Janet. Eleanor's chestnut-coloured hair was cut in a bob, and she was taller than

Janet, and stockier, but not like Lana. Eleanor's was the sort of physique that Lana assumed Emily would have in ten years' time – her father's partner had looked after herself, and it showed. She was wearing a short-sleeved dress – no bingo wings – which swept over a figure that still went in and out in all the right places. How did this woman eat pizza and still look like that? Lana took a breath.

Eleanor spoke first. The voice was gentle and encouraging, as if coaxing a suspicious rescue dog towards a piece of food. 'You must be Lana . . . May I call you Lana, or do you prefer Svetlana?' she asked.

'Lana, please.' she replied, cautiously.

'I'm Eleanor, and it's just wonderful to meet you. Your father has told me so much about you. I've never seen him happier than he's been since he found you. I can't tell you how pleased that makes me!'

Lana was conscious of her father, silently watching her and Eleanor. There was no trace of anxiety on his face. He knew them both; this was going to be fine. She sidled round to the empty space next to him. He hugged her, saying, 'You look very smart. Have you come straight from work?'

'Yes. It's been busy today.'

Lana hadn't been home. She'd messaged Janet to say she would be late, implying she was still at the arbitration meeting. She didn't like obfuscation, but she didn't owe her mother total honesty anymore, and she wasn't going to discuss Eleanor with anyone until she'd had time to process her own thoughts.

'We ordered drinks, but not food, in case you were running late,' said her father, pouring Lana a glass of wine. She took a gulp, swallowing down the last of her nerves.

'What is it that you do that you get to wear a suit?' asked Eleanor. 'I'm a nurse, always in scrubs.'

Good question, thought Lana. What was her job title? Was she a PA who did the housekeeping on the side, or the other way around? 'I've been at an arbitration meeting all day, and likely to be there most of tomorrow too.'

'Gosh, that sounds high-powered,' said Eleanor. 'And I understand that in your spare time you share your father's love of gardening.'

They ordered food – Eleanor opting for a salad – and talked about gardens. Eleanor mostly listened, allowing Lana and her father to talk, occasionally interjecting with lighthearted comments and questions to keep the conversation flowing. Lana thanked Eleanor for the ticket to the Chelsea Flower Show and for her suggestion that he bought her the jacket, saying how much she loved it. Her father started talking about the couple's garden in Manchester, and they swapped tips for keeping pests away from their vegetables.

As the food arrived, and with it the greasy aroma of melted cheese, Lana realized how hungry she was.

'Do you suffer with aphids in London?' asked Eleanor. 'I keep finding them hiding on the underside of my swede leaves. I hate using pesticides.'

'I've got a tip for that, 'said Lana excitedly. 'Mix 750ml of water with a few drops of vegetable oil and washing-up liquid. Spray the leaves daily.'

Eleanor laughed. 'That sounds like a neat cheap trick.'

'It works too. I get them in my greenhouse sometimes. It's my own fault. I always cram too much in there.'

'I am in awe of you getting lemongrass to germinate – what's the secret?' asked her father.

'Patience, I think,' said Lana. 'Mine took over a month. It's easy to give up and assume it's failed.'

'That's the truth with a lot of gardening, I guess,' said Eleanor.

'It takes time for your efforts to be rewarded. I do love it though. And it's brilliant for your health, both physical and mental. When I'm weeding, it's like a mindfulness session, your head just empties . . .'

Her father cut a sliver off his pizza and transferred it to Eleanor's plate. Lana watched as the other woman dissected the slice into tiny pieces, picked up a bit with her fingers, nibbled at the edge, and popped it back on her plate, chewing, as if to make the taste last.

'You don't keep your shape just through gardening!' said Lana.

'No, I've always enjoyed keeping fit. Weight training. Never too late to start, I could show you around our local gym when you come and stay . . .' She smiled, and Lana noticed the warmth in the other woman's eyes. 'You will come and stay, won't you? Your father would love to show off the garden.'

'Don't rush her, Eleanor,' said Lana's father.

Detecting a hint of tension in his voice, Lana said, 'Dad, it's fine. I'd love to come, and it's generous of Eleanor to be the one to suggest it.'

She wanted to ask why they hadn't had children. Eleanor would've been in her mid-twenties when she met Lana's father, but that was too personal a question for a first meeting. Instead, she asked if Eleanor always wanted to be a nurse.

'I did. I was lucky my parents encouraged me.'

'And you're doing what you always wanted to do now, aren't you, Lana?' said her father.

'Yes and no, Dad,' she said, shaking her head.

'But you must follow your dreams,' said Eleanor, a tinge of pushiness in her voice. Was this how she was around her patients, wondered Lana.

'Have you followed yours?' she asked, then wished she hadn't; she didn't want to ruin the atmosphere.

'Yes . . . Yes, I have. I'm a nurse and . . .' Eleanor stretched out her arm, wrapping a hand around Lana's father's, '. . . I got to spend my life with the man I love.'

Emboldened, Lana said, 'But you didn't marry or have children.'

'I always wanted a home and a family, and I assumed that would involve getting married and having children. But things change and I adapted. Being with your father was more important to me than being married. He didn't want a second family and he was honest enough to tell me, so my garden is my family. What about you?'

'Oh,' said Lana, coughing a laugh. 'I gave up on my dreams decades ago.'

Eleanor gave a soft tut. 'Don't do that, Lana. You've still got so much of your life to live. Live the one you want, the one that will make you happy. Work out what that is – if you don't work out what you want, you'll never get it.'

'That's easy for you to say,' said Lana tersely. Eleanor looked hurt, making Lana regret her outburst

The other woman took a moment to recover, then said, 'And it's easy for you to do. Make a decision tonight. To work out what's important, ask yourself: how do I want to live? Make a list; be selfish.'

'Eleanor,' said her father, his voice low but firm, 'she's not one of your patients. Lana's only recently found out what her mother has done. She's still processing what to do about that.'

'But there's only one thing to do,' Eleanor said, shifting her gaze to Lana. 'You must forgive her and move on.'

Lana spluttered into laughter. 'I'm not sure I can.'

The next morning started with Sheila gathering everyone in the conference room. 'I will remind you all that, for this to work, you must both be flexible. Neither of you budged yesterday. Mr Ellis, you are claiming compensation of £5 million . . .'

*HOW MUCH!*

Lana's pen dug into the page; she couldn't even write the figure down. She didn't need to - there was no way she would forget. Nor did she need a calculator to work out what she would earn if he won. Was this the art of negotiation in practice? Had her boss pitched his demand at this staggering level to convince the bank they'd done a good deal when he settled for a fraction of that sum? She reminded herself that Mark knew what he was doing. For decades he'd earned fees which eclipsed that number, negotiating transactions worth billions.

Sheila was still talking. 'And you,' she said, angling her words towards Harold, 'have offered a tenth of that sum.' A shiver ran down Lana's spine. Was her boss not tempted by half a million pounds? That would give Lana £50,000. Eighteen months' salary.

'Before we begin, remember what I said yesterday. Decide what you can *accept* and forget what you *want*. No judge will look kindly on this matter unless you demonstrably try to cut a deal.'

Chairs scraped across the floor, notebooks snapped shut, and papers rustled as they were gathered. Lana and Clare rose and followed the bank's army of advisors out, leaving Sheila and the two principals in the conference room.

The two women holed up in the Project Revenge base camp. The tiny room wasn't air conditioned, and, in the stifling summer heat Lana soon took off her Moloh jacket, pushed up her sleeves, and angled her face towards a fan, allowing it to waft waves of tepid air over her cheeks.

Throughout the morning, whenever Mark and Harold reached an impasse, her boss burst into the room for a catch-up. When they didn't see him for over an hour, Lana wondered if he was making progress. She started replaying the previous evening in her mind, allowing snatches of the conversation to take over her thoughts. Eleanor was right, she should work out what she wanted from life. She wasn't even fifty yet.

The door creaked open, letting in a gush of warm air, and Mark.

'Progress?' asked Clare.

'Nah,' said Mark. 'Anything left in that flask?'

'I thought they'd have given a bit of ground by now,' said Clare, shaking the flask and nodding. Mark put down his papers and held out a cup.

'Harold wasn't going to budge yesterday. He knows what he's up against. Yesterday was about working out how determined I am. There was never going to be any negotiation. Last night he would have met with the CEO, and Effing Paul would've been in the hot seat.'

The breeze from the fan sent Mark's papers fluttering. He clamped them down with his hand.

'Do you think he got permission last night to improve the offer?' asked Clare.

'He had that yesterday,' said Mark, 'but today is the day we'll see a bit of movement. Not too early. My money's on about lunchtime. He wants this wrapped up; he doesn't want to be here tomorrow.'

'Is that why you didn't move at all yesterday?' asked Clare. 'You were waiting for him to budge first, so you could gauge his wiggle room?'

'The art of negotiation isn't to extract the last pound off the other side. It's knowing your opposition so well you pitch your ask at a level they will accept. When he demonstrates he's ready to budge, I'm pretty sure I know what he's been advised to settle at.'

After a sandwich lunch, Harold upped his offer to £1 million. Mark reported this to his team, adding that he'd rejected it. Lana's mouth opened, wanting to ask why, then she clamped it shut. With a sly wink, Mark said, 'Time for the spurious number, I reckon.'

The two women exchanged a glance.

'What's that?' asked Lana.

'I don't know how Harold got lumbered with this task,' he said, looking at Lana, 'he's got about as much negotiation experience as you, so let's have some fun.'

'OK,' said Lana suspiciously.

'What's your lucky number, Clare?' asked Mark.

The lawyer looked startled. 'Twenty-seven. My birthday and wedding anniversary are both on the twenty-seventh.'

Mark scribbled down the number. 'Lana, your shout.'

'Three,' she said without offering an explanation.

'And I was born in 1974. Right, give me a moment.'

The two women looked at each other. Clare shrugged, and Lana switched her gaze to her boss; there was a look of intense concentration on his face and his eyebrows were scrunched together.

'Got it. £3,971,274,' said Mark.

'What's that?' asked Clare.

'That's my settlement proposal.'

Lana and Clare spluttered with laughter. 'That's a bit specific, isn't it?' said the lawyer.

It was also an enormous sum of money, thought Lana, which would mean nearly £400,000 for her. She told herself not to get excited; Mark had said they were just having a bit of fun.

He was grinning. It was the same sort of care free look Lana recalled Alex wearing when he recounted surfing stories. 'Exactly,' said Mark, without offering an explanation. 'Watch this space.'

He was only out of the room for ten minutes.

'Let's get some fresh air,' he suggested. 'Harold will be mulling this over for hours.'

At six o'clock, the offer had doubled to £2 million, but Mark wouldn't shave a pound from his earlier number. Curious, Lana asked why he wasn't compromising.

'I want him to think that's my absolute bottom line.'

'But it's a made-up figure,' said Lana.

'He doesn't know that.' Mark replied, laughing.

There was a rat-a-tat at the door; it opened a crack, and Sheila's long neck curled round the gap, like an ostrich stretching to check on her chicks. 'Mr Ellis, the other side would like a word.'

'On my way,' said Mark, rising and following the arbitrator.

At ten o'clock, her boss returned to the small meeting room. 'Right. We're off.'

'You've agreed a settlement?' asked Clare, rising.

'No. I've told Harold I'll see him in court.'

If she earned it, what would Lana do with her commission? That was the question circling her mind the following morning as she fastened the dogs' leads. Mark hadn't revealed if Harold had upped the offer from £2 million, but even if that was the final offer, Lana could have earned £200,000.

Waiting for the lights to change on the Brompton Road, Lana wondered why Mark had given up on arbitration. Was this another tactic in the art of negotiation? She heard the persistent bleep-bleep warning, checked for traffic and set off. What would she do with two hundred grand? At the pond, she stopped halfway over the bridge to watch the ducks, beaks down, pecking the grassy banks. There was a whiff of rotten eggs from the stagnant water; she wrinkled her nose and, realizing she was thinking about Janet, chuckled softly to herself. She'd hardly seen her mother since she confronted her. Both nights, Janet had retired before Lana got home, but Lana knew they needed time apart: Lana to lick her wounds privately, Janet to plan a new life.

Lana strode on, choosing the path signposted Speakers' Corner. The dogs trotted along in front, occasionally tugging when they spotted a squirrel or a pigeon within lunging distance. Lana paused beneath an overhanging plane tree; the sweet smell made her think briefly of breakfast, but absorbed in her thoughts, she carried on walking. Twenty minutes later, she spun around to retrace her steps, no clearer about what she would do if she earned that commission. What was the point of having a life-changing amount of money if you didn't know how you wanted to change your life? She was unencumbered, she could do whatever she liked, live wherever she wanted. What though, and where?

Back at Ovington Square, a gust of wind carried the smell of her tomato plants, and she cast a fond glance over the railings – yes, her future should involve a garden, she was sure of that. She unhooked the dogs, watching them charge downstairs to the kitchen, and opened the door to the office. Someone had stacked the post on the table. She slit open three envelopes: two bills and a letter with a logo she didn't recognize. She heard the door behind her open, dropped the letter, and turned around. Emily rushed in, shutting the door quietly behind her, and spoke in a conspiratorial whisper.

'Lana, I need your help.'

'What can I do?'

'I can't wait any longer for Mark. I want to organize a special evening. For the two of us. Which is the best night this weekend?'

Lana logged in and pulled up Mark's diary. There were no evening engagements, but that didn't mean her boss wouldn't be working. 'Avoid Saturday. He's going to Gwen's early on Sunday for lunch.'

'What about tonight? Can you block out tonight for me?'

'OK. What do you want me to call it?'

'Friday night dinner with Emily,' she said, holding up both hands with her fingers crossed. 'I'll book a table somewhere, get him out.'

'It's in,' said Lana.

After Emily left, Lana picked up the letter and scanned it. Her brow creased. She folded the letter back up and stowed it in Mark's in-tray.

Ten minutes later, with no sign of her boss, Lana sneaked back and re-read the letter. It was from someone called the Financial Conduct Authority. They wanted to interview him. Who were they, and why did they want to speak to Mark? Was he in trouble? Angling her screen away from the door, she pulled up the FCA website; it was the regulatory body that oversaw financial institutions. Was this a standard meeting, something to do with setting up Ovington Advisory, or could it be a delaying tactic instigated by Effing Paul?

At noon the doorbell rang. Lana answered – it was Barry. There was nothing in Mark's diary. Bazza's beard was bushier, now closer in volume to the former Cuban leader Fidel Castro. Most of his face was covered in hair, but Lana still thought that Barry looked ill. His eyes were glassy, and what she could see of his face was the same washed-out grey as Gwen's on the morning they had discovered Tom's article. Barry seemed to have shrivelled inside his sweatpants and hoodie – where was his swagger, his infectious grin?

'Is he in?' he asked wearily. She held the door open wide. 'Give me a minute alone with him,' he said. He plodded ahead of her, dragging his feet, and scuffing the polished parquet floor, making Lana want to scold him for increasing her workload.

She gave Bazza five minutes, then took refreshments into the office. This meeting may have been unscheduled, but Lana always joined Barry's meetings, and she wasn't going to miss this one. The guest was holding his face in his hands, shaking it as if forcing himself to think. As Lana handed out coffee, Barry spoke.

'Bethan says the FCA will be conducting what she calls a twin-track investigation.'

Lana's hand froze around her cup, her mind seeing the FCA logo on the letter in Mark's in-tray.

'Who is Bethan?' asked Mark.

'My lawyer.'

*Why did Bazza need a lawyer?*

Barry took a gulp of coffee then continued. 'She says they'll decide *if* they are going to proceed, and if so, *how*. Meanwhile I put my life on hold.'

'What are the alternatives?' asked Mark.

'Keep it in-house, charge me with breaching Article 14 of the Market Abuse Regulation Act, or involve the police.'

Wow, thought Lana, no wonder he'd wanted time alone with her boss.

Barry mumbled, 'If they do that, then it becomes a criminal investigation under Section 52 of the Criminal Justice Act.'

'Has the FCA interviewed you?' asked Mark.

'Bethan says I've got to cooperate.'

'Why?'

Barry stroked his beard. Lana hoped the facial hair was just a phase which, like the FCA, was making a short unpleasant appearance in this man's life.

'They have a lot of power and can basically force me into an interview. If I don't cooperate, it only delays the investigation, it won't prevent it. And if I refuse, they can ban me from working in the industry.'

Mark repeated his question, this time forcefully. 'So, have you been to an interview?' Bazza nodded. 'How was it?'

Barry exhaled, making a spluttering sound. 'There were no cops. But they cautioned me, you know: "You have the right to remain silent" - all that malarkey.'

Mark reached out and took a letter from his in-tray. 'They want to interview me too,' he said, flapping it at Barry. 'Why do they want to see me, Bazza?' he asked, reaching for his coffee and taking a sip. His eyes were narrow, drilling into the smaller man. That letter spells trouble, Lana thought.

Bazza sat back in his chair. 'Sorry, mate.' He placed his elbows on the table and hung his head between his hands, muffling his voice. 'I've screwed up, and I'm sorry, but you may get dragged into the mess.' There was a pause, then Barry raised his head. 'Those tips I gave you . . .'

Her boss dropped his cup. It crashed onto the saucer, splashing coffee onto his papers, the table, and Barry. 'Go on.'

Coffee trickled down Barry's neck. Instead of wiping it away, he ran his hands through his hair, then spoke slowly, reluctantly, like a child owning up to playing with their mother's make-up. 'I got them from someone else . . . from another bank.'

Mark sat back so fast it was as if someone had pushed him. '*Fuck!* You've been passing on inside information? Did you know it was inside information?'

No one spoke. Outside, a police siren wailed, growing louder as the seconds passed – fabulous timing, thought Lana.

Her boss put his own head in his hands. 'Shit, shit, shit,' he muttered. Mark lifted his head and glared at the other man. 'Just go.'

Lana stared at the trader. She'd bought into some of those

tips. Would she be in trouble too? Barry rose, shot her a furtive look, and said, 'I'll see myself out,' before bolting from the room.

She mopped up the spilled coffee with a paper napkin, waited until she heard the click of the front door, then admitted what she'd done with her savings. Mark's head lurched towards her. 'You did what?'

Lana's heart thumped against her ribcage; had she messed up again? Was this another breach of that confidentiality clause in her contract? She must explain. 'I wasn't earning anything from my bank. Am I in trouble too? What should I do, sell?'

'Definitely not! Your postcode is the same as mine. Wait until I've cleared my name before you deal.'

She clicked her tongue. He'd done nothing to reassure her. Was he ensuring she didn't get herself into more trouble, or was he looking out for himself? She had an uncomfortable fluttery sensation in her stomach. Did he even care what happened to her?

Mark's finger was on the printout of his diary. 'Hey, what's this eleven thirty meeting?'

'Alex and Ginge,' she said firmly.

'Yes, I can see that.' He shook his head. 'I'm a bit busy today.'

'You told them to make an appointment.'

'Move it.'

'I can't. Ginge leaves this afternoon.'

Mark huffed. 'Cancel it then. I'm not in the mood for baby-sitting.'

Lana opened her mouth to speak, then shut it and took a deep breath. 'He's your son, make time.'

Mark's face started to colour. 'Lana, this is none of your effing business.'

She jabbed a finger at him. 'Barry didn't have a slot in your diary, and you made time for him. Make time for Alex.'

'How dare you?' he shouted, rising, and putting his hands on his hips. 'You're bossy enough, don't start telling me how to run my private life too.'

She studied his face, trying to decide if the red colour was like a tomato or a radish.

He pointed a finger at her. 'If you want to keep your job, I'm warning you, Lana, get back in your box. I don't take orders from the housekeeper.'

Later, she would ask herself why she did it. Was it the arrogant finger pointing, or maybe his cheap shot about her job title? Or was it the realization that after decades of being controlled by her mother, here was someone else wielding power over her with his casual reference to firing her.

Lana shouted back, 'Fuck off!' Feeling a frisson of pleasure at swearing at her boss, and fortified by the knowledge that she was free of responsibilities and didn't have to take this crap anymore, she said crisply, 'I resign.'

In the eerie silence that followed, Lana heard her own breathing, short and shallow.

'Accepted,' he said, sitting down and rustling a pile of papers. 'One month's notice.'

Lana rose, stalked out, slamming the door behind her, and stood in the corridor shaking. What had she just done? Why hadn't she waited for Mark to fire her? He would've had to give her three months' notice. Now, in four weeks she would be jobless *and* homeless, and she couldn't even fall back on her reserve fund without adding the FCA to her worry list. Finally freed from the shackles of Janet's lie and able to follow her own dreams, she'd squandered the opportunity by sticking up for someone else. She should've followed Eleanor's advice; if Lana had her own goals, she wouldn't have leapt to help Alex achieve his.

Realizing her monumental mistake, her brain started whipping up memories from decades ago; was she about to slide back down the career ladder, forced to beg for cleaning jobs again? She stared at her trembling hands. She must secure a decent reference from Emily before Mark clouded his wife's opinion. Would it be best to swallow her pride and apologize? Mark wouldn't allow her to retract her resignation, but he might allow her a longer notice period – he wouldn't easily find someone else to do both jobs.

It was nearly midnight when Mary let herself in. There was a sliver of light underneath Charles's study door; was he still working? Mentally, she was still replaying the last bridge hand; her partner had been right – after the bidding sequence, the Queen of Hearts must have been with West. Mary had played the finesse the wrong way around and gone one-off, scoring the pair a bottom. Scolding herself, she tossed her keys on the hall table.

The hall echoed with a sudden  a burst of laughter. She opened the study door a crack to find Charles and Paul sitting either end of a sofa with their shoes kicked off, their stockinged feet on the table where Charles usually stacked his business magazines. The air smelled sour. Mary couldn't identify what it was, then Paul lifted his head, glazed eyes wavering her way. *Alcohol.* Paul wafted his glass at her, slopping amber liquid onto his suit trousers. 'Mary! Come and join us.'

There was a tight sensation in her chest – had they been discussing Tom's story? "Hi,' she said warily.

Paul beamed at her, slightly cross-eyed. There were damp patches on his shirt, his braces hung around his waist and there was no sign of a tie. 'You're lucky to be married to this one,' he said, dribbling drink into his mouth, then swirling the contents of the glass, making the ice clink. 'I let my best opportunity slip me by.'

So, Emily was on Paul's agenda, not Mary's secret. 'What are you both drinking?' she asked, offering the sort of self-satisfied smile sober people give the drunk.

'Whisky,' slurred Paul. 'I'll always regret letting her get away. I'll always be paying for my mistake.'

Mary suspected she was supposed to ask who the missed opportunity was, but she didn't have to. It was Emily. Had Paul finally accepted it was over? She felt a stab of sympathy. 'There's a spare bed upstairs if you want it, Paul,' she said softly.

'Thanks, but I'd better shuffle off.' He tossed back his drink, grimacing.

'Malt,' said Charles. Then, speaking slowly as if trying to convince his wife he was sober, he added, 'Not . . . just . . . any old . . . whisky.'

'On an empty stomach,' she said, arching her eyebrows at Charles, thinking only the seriously inebriated believe they can disguise drunkenness.

After Mary called a taxi, she helped Charles gather up Paul's possessions. She found his jacket on the floor behind a chair, his bow tie in one of the pockets. 'Did you have a briefcase?' she asked.

Paul shrugged, then started laughing.

Mary was tired and wanted to get to bed. She tried to keep the tetchiness out of her voice. 'Charles, did Paul arrive with a briefcase?'

Charles's eyes wavered, as if trying to pin her down, and Mary tutted – if he was seeing double, there was little point asking which rooms the pair had been in.

'Charles, have a scout around.' As he tottered to the door, Mary called out, 'And check for a coat and umbrella!'

In the study, Paul was trying to balance on one leg, while slipping a shoe onto the other foot. He danced on the spot, toppled over, put an arm out and lurched towards an armchair, collapsing and falling head first into the seat.

*This was going to take a while.*

Paul grunted and slithered off the chair onto the floor, kneeling with his head drooping over the seat, looking as if he was bobbing for apples. Mary took his arm, hefted him upright, then shoved him backwards into the seat and knelt, pushing on each shoe in turn.

'Pig of a day,' muttered Paul. 'Got fired from the best mandate I've landed all year.'

'I'm sorry to hear that, Paul,' said Mary, doing up his shoelaces. 'There, all done. You can stand up now.'

Paul shot upright, saluted her, then fell backwards again, laughing. He started to hiccup. 'Blast, hate these things.' He pinched his nose between a finger and thumb and clamped his mouth shut. His voice came out in a high-pitched whine. 'Huge. It was huge . . .'

Charles was standing by Mary's side. 'He's much worse than me, isn't he? No sign of a briefcase.' He held up a raincoat. 'Found this in the hallway.'

'Biggest IPO next year,' squeaked Paul.

'He was lead advisor on a fintech float,' said Charles.

'Thank you, Charles,' Mary said primly. 'I may not work in the City, but I do know IPO stands for Initial Public Offering.'

Paul released his breath and spluttered, 'Timing couldn't be worse. I've got the CEO' – he gave another hiccup – 'on my back about that bastard Mark . . . and his bloody case against the bank.'

'I'll leave you both to it,' said Mary, moving towards the door. 'Taxi will be here any minute. Goodnight, Paul. Don't forget to drink some water before you go to bed.'

'She should've left him . . . hic . . . He's a tosser . . . and I'm much richer than he is.'

# Sixteen

Lana spent Saturday in Kew Gardens, and on Sunday morning told her mother to find somewhere else to live. Lana didn't mention that she too would be moving. She'd taken Friday afternoon off to visit four recruitment agencies, but unfortunately her outburst had coincided with a lull in the private staff market. Her strategy for next week was to focus on housework, with her aim to remind Emily what a perfect housekeeper she employed, and to beg for an extension to her notice period along with a decent reference. She was also planning to enlist a second ally: Mark's mother was coming to stay.

Despite living the closest, Lana was the last guest to arrive at Anne's Sunday lunch. She debated cancelling, but the event coincided with the gap between morning Mass and Janet's evening service, enabling her to avoid Janet all day. Kenny let her in.

'Good to see you again! How are things working out with your dad? Anne and I thought he was a nice guy.'

She stepped inside, reflecting on Kenny's words. 'He is. And his partner Eleanor is lovely too.' She handed over a slightly crumpled, brown paper bag. 'From my garden, broad beans, and I put a few baby carrots in there. They'd make a nice risotto for two.' What was she going to do with her plants in four weeks' time? Her father would rehome them, but he lived 200 miles away.

'Wow,' Kenny said, rustling the bag open and peering inside. 'That plant you bought us, the one with the funny name, alstry something, well, it's still clinging onto life – just – but I think it misses your mothering touch. In this flat, a pot of basil dies within a week. I'm super impressed you can grow stuff like this. Thanks!'

There were three other guests. Lana recognized Stephanie from the arbitration meetings, recalling she worked in the human resources department, and was introduced to Kenny's brother, Josh, and his girlfriend, Laura.

'How's Mark?' asked Stephanie. 'I suppose you probably guessed that the reason I was with Harold was cos I was the one who did the deed in January.'

Lana didn't want to talk about Mark!

'Are you talking about Anne's old boss?' asked Laura, waving a flute of Prosecco at Stephanie.

'Lana works for him now,' said Kenny.

Temporarily, thought Lana. Anne would be working for Mark again soon; he was bound to poach her. Anne was much better at the job, and she knew how to cope with Mark's prickly side.

'What's he like to work for?' asked Laura.

Lana didn't want to answer, so just smiled a reply.

'Did you read that piece in the paper?' asked Laura, 'Anne said it was mostly lies.'

'The PR department had to peddle like crazy to get the press to back off about insider dealing,' said Stephanie. 'I can't believe Mark would get involved in anything like that.'

Nor could Lana, but it looked like the FCA thought otherwise. Her stomach clenched – she didn't want to think about the FCA either. Was Lana about to be summoned for questioning? She might find out tomorrow; Mark had arranged his interview for Monday, and Lana was joining.

'Why ruin a good story by sticking to the truth?' Kenny arched his eyebrows and passed Lana a glass of bubbly.

The door to the kitchen opened, emitting a fragrant smell of garlic. Lana had fond memories of the room, cooking evening meals with Anne and Kenny. They might offer their spare room if she couldn't find another job, but she hoped something would come up as she'd circulated her CV widely. Her next position would probably be in the country. Would Anne keep in touch if Lana didn't live around the corner?

'I don't know why he was so angry,' said Anne, joining her guests. Kenny passed his wife a tumbler of sparkling water. 'It's not as if the piece was rude about him. Here, try some of these.' She held out a platter of cured meats. 'They're from that lovely old-fashioned Italian Deli on Walton Street, you know, La Picena.'

While the other guests talked about Tom's article, Lana pictured the grocery store where she shopped for salami, cheese and fresh meat. It was a small narrow shop, the entrance protected by a bright-blue awning, right beside an Italian restaurant Mark used for entertaining clients. She'd miss that side of her job.

'I reckon it was the bank being linked to insider dealing that annoyed Paul, especially as his own name was mentioned,' said Stephanie. 'Clients might read it. And even if they don't, the competition will, and they'll use it.'

'Do you think many people in the City read that sort of paper?' asked Josh. 'I thought they all read the pink one.'

Stephanie laughed. 'You won't find anyone who admits to having read that article, but they all did. I think one or two of the juniors were quite amused. It's not exactly typical of the rather staid image of the M&A department: extramarital affairs and steamy sex.'

The main course – a vegetarian lasagne–cooked by Kenny,

accompanied by a green salad. When everyone had finished eating, Lana helped Anne clear the dirty plates into the kitchen. Why wasn't her friend drinking?

'Late Saturday night?' Lana asked.

Anne passed her a carton of cream. 'Pour this into that jug on the side there for me,' she said, pulling food wrap from a bowl of fruit salad. 'No, I'm off the booze. Fingers crossed it'll be worth it.'

'Still dieting?'

'No, you wombat, we're trying, you know . . . Kenny and I.'

Lana frowned. 'Trying?'

'For a baby,' mouthed Anne.

'Oh! Fingers crossed for you,' said Lana, feeling a little rush of happiness. She'd never been included in such an intimate secret before. She considered telling Anne she'd resigned but decided not to; she didn't want to be labelled as the friend "always in need".

Over chocolates, which Stephanie had brought, the talk drifted back to the bank. Their jobs seemed to define who Stephanie and Anne were. They spoke with such pride; was this how Mark had spoken when he worked there? Stephanie and Anne were swapping gossip, who had blown how much of their bonus on what super car or exotic holiday.

'So, what did Effing Paul buy in the end?' asked Lana.

Anne giggled. 'I keep getting calls from recruitment agencies asking if he's ready to conduct interviews for his new housekeeper. Fancy applying, Lana?'

'Why does he need a housekeeper for a London bachelor pad?' asked Stephanie.

'Oh no, this isn't for his London pad. This is for the "country seat",' said Anne in a mocking voice. 'I think he fancies himself as the new Lord of the Manor. Must be quite a grand place. He's looking for a live-in housekeeper, and he wants a full-time handyman too.'

Stephanie helped herself to a chocolate. 'I didn't know he had a country house. Where is it?'

Lana didn't care where it was; her CV must not end up in Effing Paul's in-tray. She wasn't that desperate!

The first person to arrive for Gwen's Sunday lunch was Deidre. She came alone – her husband was playing bowls – half an hour early.

'I thought you'd like some help,' she said cheerfully.

'Why's that now? You think I can't cook Sunday lunch without your help?' said Gwen, taking the bottle of wine from her friend. 'I cook a roast often enough for Mark,' she said. 'He wouldn't get one if I didn't. I don't think Emily even knows how to make gravy.'

Deidre pursed her lips, tiny lines appearing around her mouth. 'Emily doesn't have to, does she?'

Gwen stepped back to let Deidre in. As her friend walked past, Gwen breathed in the scent of lily of the valley and told herself not to be so snappy. She was pleased to see her. She did want help – she needed her courage bolstering.

Gwen opened the kitchen door. Romeo was sitting close to the oven. 'I think we'll eat inside, just in case the weather changes.'

'Gwen Ellis don't try fobbing me off with snide digs at Emily. You all right, girl?' asked Deidre, putting a hand on Gwen's shoulder.

Gwen ran her hands down the front of her brown-checked housecoat. 'Do you think I should change?'

'Only if that's what you'd do if it was just Mark and Alex coming. Relax! Now, is there anything you want me to do? Why don't I lay the table?'

'I'll make us a cup of tea,' said Gwen, nudging Romeo away from the oven with her stick.

The second time the bell rang, Deidre answered, returning with Mark and Alex. Gwen tried to recall the last time her son and grandson had visited together. 'There's beer in the fridge,' Gwen told them. 'And Deidre has brought a bottle of wine. Help yourselves while I finish the gravy,' she said, trying to ignore the jittery sensation in her stomach.

'Can I get you something, Mum?' offered Mark, giving her a hug.

She shook her head. She'd be ill if she had something to drink. *Where was he? Mark would be so hurt if he didn't come, and he'd suffered enough pain this year.*

Alex was standing beside her, talking about his business. Gwen pasted an interested expression onto her face, tipped the roasting tin to one side, and drained the excess fat into a mug.

'What do you think, Gran?' asked Alex.

'It sounds complicated, Alex. But I'm proud of you. Sounds like you've found your feet.'

She measured a spoonful of flour into the pan, scraped the bits off the bottom, then added hot stock and stirred, listening to the gentle roar from the tin. She hadn't taken in a word Alex said. Had she said the right thing?

'Alex isn't really interested in business, are you, son?' Mark scoffed. 'Your real passion is surfing.'

'Dad - I am serious about this business.'

Mark laughed. 'When the surf's not up.'

The doorbell chimed, and Gwen's stomach lurched. Her hand shook, and she dropped the spoon into the roasting tin. 'Damn,' she muttered, trying to fish it out, burning her fingers on the hot gravy. Was that the first or the second mistake, she wondered? Should she have even organized this lunch?

'Want me to go, Mum?'

'Let me,' said Alex.

'I'll go,' said Deidre firmly.

Gwen spun around. 'Look after that for me, Deidre, please,' she said, passing the mucky spoon to her friend. 'I will answer my own front door.'

Steve had brought a four pack of beer and a box of chocolates. She left them in his hands and led the way, listening to his stilted speech that sounded as if he was reading from a script, about how grateful he was to be invited, how much he'd been looking forward to it. Gwen opened the door to a silent kitchen, feeling like a court clerk ushering in the star witness. 'You remember my friend, Deidre, don't you, Steve?'

Removing the now-clean spoon from Deidre's hand, Gwen started stirring the gravy again, watching the mixture bubble. Behind her, the men stumbled through small talk. Mark offered his father a cold beer, while Alex took the cans off his grandfather, exclaiming that Steve had chosen his favourite brand. Gwen heard the fridge door click open, then Mark asked too formally, like he was asking directions from a stranger, 'Mum, do you want us in the front room out of your way, or can we help?'

She switched the gas off and turned her back to the hob.

There was an awkward silence, and the heat from the oven on such a warm day magnified Gwen's discomfort. She looked at the three men in turn. Alex was lounging against the fridge, Mark beside him. Steve was by the table, clutching the box of chocolates, looking as if he'd turned up for a blind date and discovered it was the wrong day. She couldn't recall ever seeing him look so uncomfortable. Three pairs of eyes bored into hers, and there was a pleading expression on Steve's face. She felt a stab of irritation; she'd brought them together, why couldn't they get on with it? Did they expect her to choreograph this family reunion? With her *ex-husband*?

'Mum?' said Mark.

She realized none of the men knew what to do. Mark hadn't a clue how to behave around his father but didn't want to upset Gwen. Steve had no idea how to interact with either his son or grandson, and Mark and Alex were about as comfortable around each other as a pair of cock pheasants in mating season.

'Right, let's all sit down. Steve, you go at that end,' she said, pointing to the far end of the table. 'Alex and Mark can sit either side of you. Deidre, give me a hand, would you love?'

The men dived into position. Reminding herself she only had to get through this once, Gwen limped towards Steve, taking the chocolates off him. 'Ta for these, we'll have them later,' she said, giving him a friendly pat on the shoulder then returning to the oven and shooing Romeo to one side for a second time. After today, if the men wanted a relationship with each other, it was up to them.

Mary handed Charles a wine glass. 'Dry that while it's hot. Gets a better shine.'

'You don't say. I've never heard you suggest that before.' He laughed, taking the glass from her. 'He won't be here until next year. He's got six children!' Charles exclaimed. 'How can anyone afford that many kids?'

'Who's got six kids?' Mary asked.

'The new CEO! He's coming from New York. That's what's taking time: they need to find schools, and the right house. The wife's coming over for an exploratory visit next week. What's that scraping noise?'

'Biscuit pushing his bowl around,' said Mary. 'Do you mind putting him outside?'

She plunged her hands into the hot water, checking for unwashed cutlery. The back door opened, making a grinding noise, and letting in a fug of warm air.

'Paul wants to take us out for dinner,' said Charles. 'He had an interesting take on . . .'

While her husband talked about interest rates and bond yields, spurred by the mention of Paul, Mary's concentration wandered. She still hadn't found the right moment to tell Emily she'd sold Barry's contact details to Tom. At least now Emily wasn't seeing Paul, there was no danger of him mentioning anything to her.

Charles was waving a hand in front of her face, a quizzical expression in those blue eyes. 'Penny for them?'

'Waste of your money.'

'Mary, after decades of marriage, I know when something's bothering you. Out with it, what's eating you? Let's sit down and you can tell me.'

He steered her to the table, pulled out a chair, and sat her down. She dropped her face into her hands, releasing her breath through her fingers, and massaging the corners of her eyes with her little fingers.

'Come on, ugly truths are always better out than in.'

She looked through her splayed fingers. Charles was perched on the edge of the table, wearing an expression inviting her to speak.

She told him.

'Why?'

She sighed. 'Money. I thought it would help pay for the entrance hall.'

'This bloody house!'

'I wish I'd never done it. I gave Tom the money back. It made me feel better, but it doesn't change anything. Tom told me the story wouldn't have happened if I hadn't put him in touch with Barry.'

'Umm,' he said. 'Yes, I'm not surprised you're troubled. I'm cross with Tom – he shouldn't have tricked you. I can't really blame Barry; he's always been a loose cannon. Who else knows what you've done?'

'No one.'

Charles inhaled, letting the breath out in a noisy drawn-out exhalation. He tutted, then said, 'So you haven't told Emily.'

She shook her head.

Silently he rubbed his chin.

'I know,' she said, her voice wavering. 'I just can't find the right moment.'

'Probably because there won't ever be one. If it's any consolation, I think you're right to have waited. But own up, darling. Now, shall I say yes to dinner?'

'Eh?'

'Dinner with Paul . . . Shall I accept?'

Could she be polite for a whole evening? Mary didn't like Paul very much. She still suspected he was responsible for linking Mark's name with insider dealing.

'You like eating out, and he'll bung it on expenses, so it won't cost him anything.'

She gave a soft snort. Paul probably would claim their meal on expenses. Tom was right, they were a bunch of crooks.

On Monday, Lana caught a tube to Stratford with her boss. They were shown into a room with a view of Canary Wharf. Gazing at the towers, she thought of Anne. According to Anne, the reason the site was so visually appealing was because it wasn't a homogeneous design but a blend of different architects. Somewhere in one of those skyscrapers, her friend was sitting outside Effing Paul's corner office. The first evening they'd met, leaving the Parlour, Anne had pointed out where she worked, but from this angle, Lana couldn't identify the building.

Beside her, she noticed her boss also staring at Canary Wharf. Was he remembering how he felt when he'd worked there, and worn the team colours of a major bank?

The door opened, admitting a woman who reminded Lana a little of Clare. There was no physical resemblance – this woman was shorter, with shoulder-length, curly brown hair – but there was the same air of confidence. Introducing herself as Rose from the enforcement team, she looked as if she was going to enjoy conducting this interview.

'This is my assistant, Lana,' said Mark, explaining that she was there to take notes, as she did in all his meetings. When Lana found a new job, there'd be no note taking involved, just housekeeping; she'd miss it.

'I'd like to start by talking a little about Project Iris,' said Rose, taking a seat opposite Lana and setting up a tape-recording machine. 'There was some unusual trading activity in the run-up to the announcement of Project Iris, wasn't there?'

'Yes,' Mark replied. 'I was advising the target, and the share price ticked up. I came under pressure to get the client to release a holding statement. I resisted. The Panel's knee-jerk reaction is always to get potential offers into the public domain, kill off any risk of dodgy share trading. But the deal was looking wobbly. When we did announce, the Panel asked me to draw up a list of everyone who knew about it, why, and when they'd been made insiders. I'd already anticipated the request, so we had our list ready and sent it back the same day, together with the client's. I never heard anything more.' Mark wrinkled his nose. 'Was there a problem?'

The interviewer ignored his question, firing off on a different tack. 'Compliance records at your former employer show you have a history of share-buying. Did you take advice from a wealth manager?'

'No.'

'All your own ideas?'

'Yes.'

'Hmm, I see. Then in January this year, you suddenly became *remarkably* good at stock-picking. How so?'

'I was made redundant. I had to generate my own income,' he muttered.

'And your redundancy improved your ability to work out which companies would be the subject of takeover offers, did it?' She reeled off the names of three companies. Lana recognized them: they were all tips from Barry. 'Interesting choices. What made you invest in them?' Rose's eyes flickered to the tape recorder.

Mark didn't answer.

'Did Mr Hitchens suggest them?' Rose asked, tilting her head to one side, and arching her eyebrows.

'Barry might've mentioned them,' Mark stated flatly.

'So, it's *Barry*, is it? You're on first-name terms.'

'We're mates, we worked together for over a decade.'

'How long have you been swapping inside information with Barry?'

'I never passed any inside information to Barry.'

'But did Mr Hitchens pass any to you? '

'Not to my knowledge.'

'Interesting choice of words. Have you met with Barry since you left the bank?'

'Yes.'

'Why?› 'I told you, he's a mate.'

'And how many other friends who work for your former employer have you met recently?'

Mark didn't reply. He turned towards the window, gazing out at those skyscrapers, the longing evident in his eyes. Rose wrote something in her notebook – was it just for show, wondered

Lana, as every word was being recorded. But, she thought, not every action. Had Rose too caught that look in Mark's eyes, detected the almost inaudible sigh?

'Barry is the only one, isn't he?' said Rose.

'I've run into Paul Williams once or twice, unplanned . . .'

'Your old boss?' asked Rose, and Mark nodded. 'Anyone else?'

'I'm suing the bank. It could be a bit uncomfortable for them if someone senior was seen with me.'

That was true, thought Lana. What would Paul do if he saw an MD having a drink with the enemy?

'So, you met Barry - *your mate*. How many times did you meet and where?'

'He came to see me at the office.'

'Ah yes.' Rose glanced down at her notebook. 'Ovington Advisory. Business meetings, were they, at the office with your friend?'

'Yes. I asked him to keep me on the list for the bank's research. In hindsight, I probably shouldn't have, but it's not illegal. We discussed the markets, and this and that.'

'This and that,' said Rose. 'Sounds very technical . . . and did *this and that* involve "chit-chat" about specific companies?'

There was another pause. Lana could hear the faint ticking of a clock and cast around to find the noise, eventually tracking the sound to the wall behind her. When she spoke, Rose's voice was cold with a hint of menace. 'Are you claiming that, in the space of a few months, it's pure coincidence that you selected three companies, without any guidance, which had takeover bids launched for them within weeks of your investment?' Her voice rose, and she leaned towards him as she launched her final taunt. 'Those share prices rose considerably, subsequent to your investment.'

'I didn't notice.'

'You didn't notice,' said Rose. Her tone switched to sarcastic as she added, 'And no doubt *you didn't notice* the offer documents sent to you – we both know they go to every shareholder shortly after a takeover is announced. Come on, Mr Ellis, you were in M&A, you knew what those documents signified.'

Lana stifled a gasp. That's what those dull documents she'd tossed in the recycling box were.

'Pure luck? Or was this payback time, Mr Ellis?'

For a few moments, silence hung like a bad smell in a lift. No one looked at anyone else. Lana wanted to scream that it must be a coincidence, she'd done the research, typed up all the meeting notes, and Barry hadn't said a word about those companies being in takeover talks. But if Lana drew attention to herself, Rose might ask the obvious question, and Lana didn't want to make matters worse by revealing that the only other person who worked for Ovington Advisory had bought into Barry's tips too. She unscrewed a bottle of water and poured, letting the rhythmic sound of it trickling into her glass calm her nerves.

The questions kept coming, and each time Mark batted them back. But to Lana, it seemed as if Rose was convinced Mark and Barry had been in cahoots for years; with her boss alerting the trader to companies whose share prices would react once a transaction was announced, enabling Barry to trade ahead of the market. Lana recalled the two men explaining the concept of the bank's firewalls to her at that first meeting in the dining room. Bazza had quipped that he could've retired if he'd had a camera in the M&A department. Rose was alleging that the two men had ignored the firewall and that, after Mark had lost his job, Barry repaid him by informing him of deals he knew were about to be announced by other banks.

'Let's talk about something else.' Rose glanced at her notebook, then mentioned two companies Lana recognized from the article that had made her question if Barry had got his wires crossed.

Apparently, the American company the journalist rated as better, had bid for the London-listed company Barry had recommended. Had Barry known? Was that why he'd encouraged Mark to invest in the less impressive company?

'You can phrase the question any way you like,' said Mark, 'but the answer will always be the same. I have never passed on, nor knowingly been in receipt of, inside information. Never.'

Lana nibbled at her thumbnail; to her, that sentence sounded worryingly precise, as if carefully constructed by a lawyer. Mark loosened his tie a fraction, running a finger round his collar. 'Even if someone with inside information suggested I buy shares in those companies, we both know that for me to have committed an offence, that person would've had to tell me they had inside knowledge that the shares were about to rise. That didn't happen. Ask Lana,' he said, angling his head towards her. 'She attended all the meetings with Barry and can give you contemporaneous notes.'

It sounded complicated, but it seemed neither her boss nor Lana had done anything illegal. She pictured Bazza's straggly beard and impish grin, the cheeky wink as he reached for a biscuit and said, *Buy them, mate, cos I know they're about to be bid for.* That's what Rose was claiming took place, and Lana now understood it was what had to have happened for either her or Mark to be in trouble. But it hadn't been that way. Bazza never explained why he made his recommendations.

She had a sudden thought and reached for her glass of water . . . that wasn't quite true though. All she could be sure of was that Barry hadn't said anything when Lana was listening. What if Barry had called up after the meetings and told Mark there was a reason behind his tips, that he knew those companies were in takeover talks? Was Lana being duped? Were those meetings in the dining room just for show? Was that why she was invited along today, to reinforce the story that the Barry meetings were innocent?

Lana didn't read the financial press, and she hadn't read those documents she'd mistaken as welcome brochures. She would never have questioned why the share prices rose – she was just pleased when they did. But her boss was financially savvy. Even if he didn't read about the bids in the press, Lana had put two offer documents in her boss's in-tray, and although Lana tossed hers in the recycling bin, Rose was right, of course: Mark knew what they were. Could Rose also be right, that there was no coincidence, and Mark had invested expecting those shares to rise?

Standing beside her sitting room window, Mary could hear the clank of scaffold poles and boards hitting each other as they were tossed onto the back of a lorry. Finally. The lead flashing on the roof had been replaced months ago, and now the woodwork on the sash windows was repaired and repainted. Maybe she would throw a drinks party to celebrate.

She pulled the curtains shut, examining the frayed edges.

Charles leaned around the door. 'Darling, I'm making tea, would you like a mug?' he offered.

She smiled at him. 'I could get used to you chaperoning the new CEO's wife around rental prospects. It's lovely to have you home so early.'

'Tea then?'

'Please. Charles, come and look at this.' She held out one of the curtains, as if examining it for stains; the frayed edge revealed the white interlining fabric. 'These really are tatty. Emily says she knows a wonderful interior designer . . .'

'No.'

She let go of the curtain and walked towards him, smiling. 'Give me a budget, and I'll pay for the rest.'

He shook his head. 'No. No more money on this house.'

'Oh, Charles . . .' she wheedled, pouting.

He spoke kindly, but in a resigned tone. 'I don't think we should live here anymore, Mary. Don't pretend you enjoy it any more than I do. You're far happier when I speak to you in Devon.'

The mention of Devon transported Mary there in an instant. She pictured herself walking on Exmoor with bracken swooshing round her legs, the peaceful silence occasionally disturbed by the bleat of a sheep, or the soft sound of Biscuit panting beside her.

'I want to live somewhere we can afford,' said Charles. 'Think about it for a few days.' He gave a little nod then said, 'Now I'll make us both a cup of tea.'

Someone pushed past Gwen, swatting her aside with his newspaper. Her insides started to slither. Was this train about to set off back to Essex? With her dodgy hip, would she get off in time? This was a mistake. She should've caught the coach. Or not come at all. What was the flap about, and why had Mark insisted she come immediately to discuss this stent thing the cardiologist was advising? She lowered one foot onto the station platform, which was teeming with people.

'Need a hand?' asked a man in blue overalls.

She smiled at him. 'Ta.'

He picked up her trolley and his body tipped to one side, like a collapsing domino. 'Bloody hell, what've you got in here?' he asked, placing her luggage down beside her. She grasped the handle, thanking him, then raked her eyes across the crowd gathered by the gates. Mark wasn't there. Now Steve was part of his life, he was too busy. She heard the shrill squeal of a whistle, and people started running, jostling past her. Everyone seemed to be in such a rush, as if they needed to get home in time for a Wimbledon final.

Gwen stood her ground, letting the human wave wash round her. She fished out her mobile phone.

'I'm here!' she announced.

'So am I,' said Mark.

Her eyes criss-crossed the barrier before she caught sight of him, smiling and waving. Gwen and the trolley trundled down the platform. When she reached his side, he kissed her and said, 'Emily's looking forward to seeing you.'

Gwen wasn't looking forward to seeing Emily, but she had to if she was going to mend that fence. Deidre was right – everyone's relationship works differently, and she shouldn't assess someone else's partnership using her own rules.

'What's unacceptable in yours, Gwen, might work for others.'

Who was Gwen to judge? Fidelity may have been the cause of Mr Ellis the elder getting the boot, but Mark wasn't his father, and it was Mark's marriage. Gwen should mind her own business.

She relinquished the trolley, and he lifted it off the ground; there was a thump as he dropped it. 'Phew, Mum, what's in this bag?'

'Careful now,' Gwen admonished, watching her son manhandle her luggage into a cab. 'You don't want to break those Welsh cakes.'

She clung onto the roof strap as the cab accelerated down Bishopsgate, then pulled to a stop at a set of lights.

'Could you do something for me while you're here?' asked Mark.

'What's that, boyo?'

'I need your help with Alex. He's still avoiding his mother. This has been hard for him.'

'Do you want me to call him?'

'No, he's in London. He and Ginge arrived this afternoon.'

'Want me to have a word?'

'Could you?'

She patted his arm; she'd do anything to restore his happiness. As they crawled round Sloane Square, Mark leaned to one side and dug a brass key out of his pocket. 'This is yours,' he said, passing it to her. 'Let yourself in. I'll pay the cabbie.'

Folding the key securely into the palm of her hand as if it was a precious jewel, Gwen squeezed her eyes shut. Her son's familiar scent came closer, then she felt a gentle kiss on her cheek.

It was on Tuesday morning, when Emily asked for advice, that Mary finally confessed. They were lying on their backs, head to head on one of the plastic benches in the steam room at Emily's gym. Mary preferred the gentle moist temperature of steam rather than the stultifying heat of the sauna. Here, she could lie cocooned in a fog of steam, and doze in a semi-conscious heap. She licked a bead of moisture from her lip, tasted the salt, and asked, 'What sort of advice?'

'Tell me how you get Charles to be such a brilliant husband? How it is that you two are so close, and Mark and I are like two bookends with years of space between us.'

'Um,' said Mary, reflecting. Yes, she had chosen well in Charles.

There was a slithering noise. Mary arched her neck and peered backwards. Emily had spun round and was sitting upright, facing Mary with her knees bent, her arms cradling them to her chest. 'What's your secret?' Emily asked, giving Mary a penetrating look. 'Or are you two just made for each other?'

Mary lowered her head back to the slippery bench. 'There isn't a secret. Your problem is you've drawn the boundaries on your relationship which allows him to . . .' She paused, asking herself what Mark was doing. Was he avoiding Emily, neglecting her, or did he assume she was getting what she wanted from their marriage like he was? It didn't matter, the effect was the same. 'Tell him you want to redraw the boundaries and carve out some of his time for you. Properly. Give you the same attention he would a client. Mark wouldn't avoid meeting a client, so why does he think it's OK to do that to you?'

'I've tried,' said Emily, sounding miserable.

'Pin him down. Ask Svetlana to put it in his diary.'

'I've done that too.'

Mary thought about this. Mark was lucky his wife was so persistent – what else could she suggest that might tempt a workaholic away from his desk? 'Book a weekend away, confiscate his phone at the airport, and then be blunt. Or why not insist on a monthly date night?'

'Good idea,' chirped Emily. 'If I get him away from the house, I stand a better chance. I'll have a word with Lana, book a weekend somewhere romantic like Paris.'

There was a hissing noise, and the air clouded with fresh steam. Mary wriggled, her body squeaking as it slid against the plastic.

'Can I ask you a favour now, Emily?'

'Fire away.'

She sat up and faced her friend. 'Don't get cross, but I've got something to tell you about Tom's article. You remember at Mark's council of war, the first of his three questions: "how"?'

When Emily spoke, she dragged the single word out, 'Y-es.'

'It was me. *I* was the how. I put him in touch with Barry.'

'You did what!' Emily shouted, leaping off the bench, her face lurching towards Mary.

Mary's heart was beating loudly. Had she misjudged her timing? 'I'm sorry, I can't tell you how sorry I am.'

'Why?' asked Emily, eyes blazing. 'What made you do it?'

Mary couldn't look at her, but she couldn't do this twice, she must come clean. 'He paid me.'

'You took *money*. Why?'

'The house,' mumbled Mary.

'You need to move!' shouted Emily. 'You can't afford to live in that house.'

Mary felt a jolt of anger, and her voice came out in a hiss. 'How dare you. I'm a Standerwick, we've always lived in that house.'

'Come on, Mary,' scoffed Emily. 'You scrabble around like paupers trying to keep that house running. I don't know why Charles puts up with it. I wouldn't. Now look what that house has made you do. Betray a friend.' Emily's voice was low but filled with bitterness. 'I trusted you.' Then she picked up her towel and left.

Mark's visitor was a young woman named Holly – not that she introduced herself, she didn't even say good morning. Instead, she arrived bellowing instructions into her phone so loudly Lana suspected she might startle the pigeons in Hyde Park. Holly was dressed in a sharply cut, dark trouser suit and crimson silk blouse. Her hair was swept off her face and pinned to the top of her head with a large clip.

'Book me on the last flight to Paris. I must be at that meeting in person tomorrow. Cancel everything else,' she shouted into her mobile.

Lana flattened herself against the wall. Holly stomped in, as if walking through an automatic door, chuntering on, 'Well, that's your job! Rearrange things, and make sure none of those meetings happen without me.' She stabbed at her phone and glanced up, her eyes fiery. 'Where is he?' she barked.

Lana showed Holly into the office, saying sharply, 'I'll be back with coffee.'

'Black, one sugar,' said the guest.

*Were all the juniors at the bank as rude as Holly?* If Ovington

Advisory employees were going to be like this, she was glad she was leaving. Behind her, Lana heard the front door click open, then slam shut. Emily ran past wearing leopard-print Lycra, and without a word, raced up the stairs. On Saturday, Emily had been too spiky for Lana to mention extending her notice period; apparently Mark had cancelled their dinner date. Today didn't look promising either. Lana closed her eyes for a moment. Maybe she should ask Gwen for help instead. She had to do something, no one had asked to interview her. Lana had just over three weeks to find another job and somewhere to live.

'Just put it there, please,' said Gwen, pointing at the hob with a spatula. She stirred her Welsh cake batter, the spoon ringing out each time it hit the side of the bowl. The follow-up meeting with the cardiologist was this afternoon. She was a bit nervous; the night before, Mark had explained that, without a stent, she was risking a heart attack.

Alex heaved the cast-iron griddle onto the hob and grunted, 'Blimey, that's heavy.'

'What've you been up to?' Gwen asked.

'Steve's going to come down to see me in Devon.'

She listened to Alex talk about Steve. She'd had a similar conversation with Mark. Both wanted advice about getting to know him better. She'd also had Steve on the phone, under the guise of thanking her for Sunday lunch, praising Mark and Alex, saying how much he hoped they'd both stay in touch. It was like running an undercover dating agency.

'Now, how's business?' she asked.

'Fantastic, Gran. We've identified some software which will transform the business, take it to a whole new level.'

As Alex eulogized about software, her thoughts wandered. She might have to reconsider her relationship with Steve. Be a bit friendlier. She'd been tempted to delete his telephone number, but maybe she'd wait.

Gwen brushed her finger on the griddle – hot. 'Mind out now, Alex, she's ready.'

'Ten grand.'

'What's that, love?' she asked, dropping a spoonful of mixture onto the griddle. It sizzled, and she scooped up another portion.

'Ten grand, that's what we need from a strategic investor,' he replied, hands on his hips. She grinned. Alex may have thought he was nothing like his father, that he never emulated him, but that stance was pure Mark. 'I'm going to ask Dad for the money.'

Entering the kitchen, Lana breathed in the rich smell of baking and heard her stomach rumble. She should eat something before Mark complained about the noise.

Gwen was standing by the oven, a mixing bowl to one side, and the aroma was coming from a flat black plate, half an inch thick, which was resting on the hob. Alex was hovering close by. Now wouldn't be the ideal time to ask the other woman for help. Her boss was right, the relationship between him and his son was none of her business – she'd stuck her neck out for the boy and had it severed. Mark wouldn't give her a decent reference after such impertinence. Lana must beg Gwen for help.

Gwen held a spoon close to the griddle, tipped it, and the mixture hit the plate with a gentle hiss.

'Alex, why not see if Ginge and your mother want a cup of coffee,' suggested Lana.

'Ginge is out,' said Alex. He looked Lana's way and added, 'Don't worry, he promised to be back before eleven.'

Lana hesitated – she was always the one to break the bad news. 'I'm sorry, Alex. Your father's cancelled your slot.'

'Again! *Why?*'

'He's too busy. Your mother's just back from the gym, she might like a hot drink,' said Lana, refilling the kettle.

'If she's thirsty, she knows where the kitchen is,' spat Alex.

Gwen and Lana's eyes met over the hob. 'Help yourself to a Welsh cake, luv,' said Gwen cheerfully. Lana picked one up; it was still warm, like a newly laid egg, but she wasn't hungry.

'Take some through to Mark and his guest,' suggested Gwen. 'And why don't you run one up to your mother, Alex?'

Lana bristled – the cakes were too good to waste on Ms Haughty; Alex didn't move.

Gwen measured out another spoonful of batter. 'It must've been very unpleasant for you reading all that nonsense in the newspaper, Alex luv.'

'I don't want to talk about it,' Alex snipped back.

'Most of it was invented. Lies,' said Gwen.

'She had an affair.'

Lana opened her mouth to speak. If she could help reconcile Alex and Emily, it would secure her a glowing reference. No, she thought, this was too private, and she'd already been bitten once for sticking her oar in uninvited. Gwen's eyes settled on her. 'Go on, Lana.'

Lana blushed. 'I was going to suggest that Alex talk to his father.'

'Why?' said Alex sulkily. 'Not even the master of the big deal can roll back time, and magic away an affair.'

Lana rushed on. 'People make mistakes. Sometimes it's difficult to understand why they do things that hurt you, but if you love them, you must forgive them. She's your mother, and she loves you.'

Loading the tray, Lana thought about what she'd just said. Last night, Janet had announced she was moving out – the Church had come to her rescue again. A fellow worshipper was decamping to

Sydney for nine months; her daughter-in-law had been diagnosed with breast cancer, and she was going to help with the two children. In her absence, Janet would house-sit. Maybe Lana would feel more forgiving towards Janet in nine months.

Outside the dining room, Lana balanced the tray in one hand. Without knocking, she let herself in. Holly wasn't a client; she was here for a mentoring session. On the whiteboard was a list of words in red marker pen; as she unloaded the tray, Lana read a few – *rude; offhand; dismissive* – before scanning a second list in black. She didn't get past *polite.*

'I think you've met my assistant, Lana.'

Slowly, Holly turned Lana's way. The face broke into a smile, the kind reserved for wedding photos when repeatedly prompted to "say cheese".

'Remember what we were just discussing?' Mark continued. 'Don't assume the worst outcome is inevitable.'

'Er . . . thanks very much for the coffee. Sorry, I was in a bit of a tailspin earlier when you let me in.'

'Forget it,' said Lana, backing out of the room.

Further down the hallway, the front door opened, letting in Ginge and the shrill sound of multiple police sirens. Ginge was shaking an umbrella. He closed it and placed it in the stand, leaving the door wide open behind him. A police car was framed by the architrave, its flashing light spinning. Lana clutched the empty tray to her chest, feeling her heart pounding against it. Two police officers ran up the steps. The tray clattered to the floor.

# Seventeen

**Four months later**

Mary hadn't intended to watch the trial, but Emily's plea for support was both a cris de coeur, and another opportunity to bolster their friendship, and Mary still snatched at any chance to rekindle that bond. After confessing her role in Tom's article, even after the arrest it was three days before Emily returned Mary's calls.

Sitting beside her friend, Mary watched the Counsel for the Prosecution – a tall lady with podgy hands – rise, gather the folds of her black gown, and clasp its lapels.

'Ladies and gentlemen of the jury, the defendant knew exactly what he was doing. This is a cunning, clever man, who took advantage of his seniority, and manipulated an innocent junior person employed by a competitor bank.'

She paused, running her eyes slowly across the members of the jury, as if belatedly scoring their suitability for service, then raised one plump hand to point at the dock behind her. Mary tracked the hand to the expressionless face; the defendant either wasn't listening to the barrister or had his emotions under control. She glanced at Emily, concerned to find her rubbing her hands together as if trying to keep warm.

The barrister's voice rumbled on. 'We shall prove that this scenario was going on for years. Not content with the vast sums earned legitimately, this unscrupulously wealthy man gorged on information and used it to play the markets and line his pockets with the proceeds.' She paused again and turned round, gesticulating at the accused, as if the jury might have forgotten who was on trial, then peered down at her notes.

Mary was surprised to feel her stomach fluttering; she'd hosted this man, laughed with him, listened to his entertaining stories, and endured him boasting about his bonus – what could he possibly have wanted that his City package couldn't buy?

'We shall prove that the defendant used his contacts, built up over decades of working in the City. He knew the value of the information he persuaded people to part with and built a fortune off the back of it.'

Beside her, Emily gave a soft, drawn-out groan. Mary agreed with her: this sounded dreadful. She glanced up at the dock, wanting to throw an encouraging look, but couldn't catch the defendant's eye.

'Insider dealing is a crime,' said the barrister. 'Ladies and gentlemen of the jury, let me explain the theory behind it. We'll invent two companies whose shares are listed on the London Stock Exchange, call them Target and Bidder. Bidder wants to buy Target and is willing to pay a price higher than Target's current share price. You and I are unaware of this potential deal. However, the senior employees of both Bidder and Target, and their respective teams of advisers, are aware. The people in the know are technically called "insiders", and the information they possess – that Bidder might buy Target for a price above the current share price – is called "inside information".'

She stopped, picked up her glass of water, and drank, studying the jury over its rim. 'Now', she said, setting down the glass. 'Let's pretend this deal is being finalized today. At this point, an official announcement would be made. In my fictitious example, the share price of Target will rise because the information that

Bidder is offering to pay more than Target's shares are trading at before the announcement will be factored into the price. The people who own shares in Target will expect to sell them for the higher price, so anyone who bought shares at a lower price will make a profit. Lucky them. All sounds fair, you say. But . . .' continued the barrister, waving a hand at the dock, '. . . how fair would it be if an insider told someone that this bid was about to be announced, and that person then purchased a vast number of shares in Target immediately before the announcement? If that happened, it wouldn't be luck,' she faced the jury box and raised a finger. 'That would be insider dealing, which is illegal. And that, ladies and gentlemen of the jury' - she faced the jury with one hand pointing behind her at the dock – 'is exactly what this man has been doing for years. Getting hold of inside information and trading shares to make his fortune.'

Mary sensed Emily stiffen beside her. She glared at the prosecution barrister, trying to tell herself to relax, this wasn't evidence. The lawyer was just explaining the crime of insider dealing in layman's terms.

The thrust of the case against the accused was that he had a contact employed as a director in the M&A department of another bank – the prosecution's key witness. They claimed that this director had been choreographed by the wealthy, middle-aged, highly experienced banker. That he used his powerful position, dangling the prospect of a better job at his own bank, promising both promotion and a fat sign-on fee in exchange for the information.

'The defendant's contact knew which deals were significant enough, that when they were announced' – there was that podgy hand again, waving at the dock – 'would cause share prices to rocket. He asked for the names of those companies. He demanded them, in exchange for a leg up the career ladder.' The barrister grasped the sides of her gown and rocked back and forwards on her feet. 'Ladies and gentlemen of the jury, the defendant does not deny purchasing shares in those companies, nor profiting, on one occasion, when a transaction was announced and the shares soared.' There was a pause, then the lawyer added, 'By more than 30 per cent.' The barrister pulled a quizzical face. 'He just claims he was *lucky*. We will prove that this wasn't luck: this man knew precisely what to buy, and when, because he had inside information.'

The Counsel for the Prosecution shuffled a few papers resting on the lectern in front of her, then rested her eyes momentarily on each jury member in turn, as if she was appearing on *Strictly* and was waiting for them to hold up score cards for her performance, before sitting down. It was looking grim for the accused if this woman was to be believed.

Mary crossed her fingers as the Counsel for the Defence rose. She was slim and much shorter than her opposition. Her gown and white wig looked oversized, as if she was a child wearing her mother's clothes. She spoke confidently, addressing her words – as her opposition had – directly to the jury.

'This is an unfortunate misunderstanding,' she said. 'The accused did nothing wrong. His job was to network. In a war for talent, he was expected to spot people working for competitors – not just in his own field – and entice them to his bank.'

Listening, Mary thought it was sad that the barrister spoke in the past tense, but when the accusation of insider dealing hangs over a banker, they no longer have a career.

'The defendant,' said his barrister, 'is not denying an association with the director to whom my learned friend refers. But their meetings were about recruitment. He never once asked for, nor received, confidential information. He has a portfolio of shares, and trades actively. He understands the financial markets – it was an essential part of his job. He was perfectly entitled to spot undervalued companies and speculate on them. Yes, he has an extravagant lifestyle. Yes, he has a second home, a smart car and a live-in housekeeper. Members of the jury might squirm at this lavish lifestyle, at the overt demonstration of wealth in the teeth of a cost of living crisis, but the defendant's money was earned legally. He is not on trial for his extravagant lifestyle. My client is not guilty.'

It sounded like the defence was in capable hands. It needed to be, thought Mary.

Earlier, as she arrived at court, dragging a pale Emily behind her, Mary spotted the defence team huddled on the top step. The barrister was holding her wig in her hands and wore the sort of expression Charles adopted if she asked the score during an Ashes Test cricket match, a sort of stoic attempt at positivity.

'There's been an unfortunate development,' said the lawyer, fingering her wig.

*Oh no,* thought Mary. *Are our best batsmen out already?*

'What's happened?' gasped Emily, sagging against Mary. 'He's not changing his plea to guilty?' Mary tensed to take the weight of her friend, but Emily wasn't as heavy as she'd expected. She had lost a lot of weight. Unsurprising, given that over the last few months, Emily seemed to have adopted a cost of living crisis version of Patsy's diet from *Absolutely Fabulous* – white wine.

'No,' said the barrister, shaking her head. 'He's still denying the charges. It's one of the witnesses for the prosecution. The director has changed their story and now admits to giving him confidential information.'

'Why?' asked Mary. 'Surely that incriminates them both?'

The barrister explained that the director would only face the lesser charge of passing on; they weren't accused of profiting from inside knowledge, trading in shares, or from accepting money for revealing price-sensitive information. The director was unlikely to go down, especially if they showed contrition, and helped convict someone more senior.

'S-so . . . this is bad news?' stammered Emily.

'It's unhelpful,' said the lawyer. 'It enables the prosecution to establish that price-sensitive information was given, but . . .' she added, '. . . the jury won't consider the witness to be some kind of saint. Our only hope is if we can undermine the director's credibility, sow a seed of doubt, imply they are simply trying to save their own skin, or trying to seek revenge.'

On the second day of the trial, Gwen joined Emily and Mary. It was the last place in London she wanted to be – she was sure she wouldn't understand what the lawyers were saying. She was in town for a pre-op meeting for her stent operation, and when Emily suggested she bolster the numbers – explaining the importance of demonstrating to the jury that it wasn't just the defence legal team who believed in the accused's innocence – Gwen knew she had no choice. She had to go, sit next to her daughter-in-law, set an example for her grandson.

Today, Gwen was dressed in her belted coat and cloche hat. As she'd feared, there was a lot of technical evidence and, although the terms differed, it was a bit like trying to follow one of Alex's monologues about his business. She had no idea what went on in the City – her son never explained his job. So, she switched her attention to the jury, people randomly selected from the electoral register. What were they thinking? She didn't fancy the chances of support from any of the women: all four looked shocked whenever the lawyer with the podgy hands referred to the defendant's lavish lifestyle. Maybe the men would have more sympathy. But since the financial crash, there was little of that to be found for any banker, let alone one who had allegedly partied his way through the decade of austerity and, if he walked free, would continue to party his way through the cost of living crisis.

Lana didn't have a lot of compassion for the man in the dock and avoided the first two days of the trial. But when, on the third day, Emily begged her to go, she relented. She owed Emily. Big time.

Four months ago, the morning after the police raid, when Lana let herself in for work, Emily was waiting in the entrance hall, chewing a fingernail, dressed in the same leopard-print Lycra she'd been wearing the day before. There were dark smudges of mascara below her eyes, and her hair looked unbrushed. 'We need to talk,' said Emily, leading the way down to the kitchen. Silently, Lana followed.

Lana brewed tea, and they sat at the kitchen counter, Emily toying with her hair, Lana replaying yesterday's drama in her mind.

'You saw what happened. This wasn't the only place they raided. It seems there was some kind of cartel . . .'

'I know, Alex told me.' She didn't add that Alex had gloated over the news.

'Mark is in a mess, he's made some big mistakes,' said Emily.

*Was Lana being invited to comment?*

Before she could decide, Emily rushed on, 'Last night, he told me you'd resigned.'

Lana gave a slow nod.

'He said it was a misunderstanding, that you were trying to stick up for Alex.' Emily sighed. 'Look, it doesn't matter what it was about, he regrets accepting your resignation. Could you forgive him and stay? Please? I need someone to talk to.'

'What about Mary?'

'She's the last person I want to talk to,' huffed Emily. 'Yesterday, my so-called best friend told me she sold Tom, that journalist,

Bazza's contact details. It was entirely her fault that story appeared and I can't forgive her for that.'

'Wow,' said Lana. So that was why Emily was so upset yesterday morning. It also explained why Mary had been at Tom's dinner.

Emily threw a beseeching look at Lana and said, 'It would be a weight off my mind if you'd stay.'

And mine, thought Lana, smiling brightly. But she wasn't only thinking of herself; Lana didn't want to leave Emily to fight this battle alone.

Today, Lana couldn't look at the dock. Considering it rude to stare at the jury, she focused her attention instead on the witness box. The prosecution called several people to the stand. A policeman explained his investigation into the defendant's finances, how he'd followed the money, tracing the defendant's share purchases and then the proceeds from the sale of those shares. A woman from the bank's compliance department was questioned about the bank's procedures. Is that what should have happened, wondered Lana. Was all personal share trading supposed to be sanctioned by a compliance officer?

Later in the morning, the court clerk swore in the final witness for the prosecution. A woman. The witness raised her right hand, the sleeve of a baggy jumper slipping down past her elbow. 'I swear to tell the truth, the whole truth, and nothing but the truth . . .' Lana did a double-take. She hadn't expected to recognize any of the witnesses for the prosecution, but she would always remember this face. Back then, the day she came for her mentoring appointment, Lana had assumed Holly worked for Mark's former bank.

Lana listened as the witness was led through her evidence by the silken tongue of Counsel for the Prosecution. With her hair tied up in a ponytail, wearing no makeup, and dressed in a plain knee-length skirt and oversized jumper – a sharp contrast to the crisp, tailored trouser suit and crimson blouse she'd worn to Ovington Square – Holly looked young and a little vulnerable. Lana guessed that this was deliberate. To paint her as a victim, preyed upon by the experienced older banker.

The barrister established the pattern of Holly's relationship with the defendant: expensive restaurants, boxes at Ascot, seats at the Royal Opera House – it was a description of a luxurious lifestyle. From the raised eyes in the jury box, Lana didn't think the accused was winning any fans.

'Were you in love with the defendant?' asked the barrister.

Lana couldn't look at the witness anymore, and she didn't want to see Emily's reaction to this accusation, so Lana sneaked a look at the dock. The defendant was nursing his head in his hands. How did it feel listening to evidence that might convict you? Was it about to get a whole lot worse? Was Holly going to claim that they were lovers, or worse, suggest that he'd taken advantage of her?

The witness nibbled on a thumbnail, raised her eyes at the dock and whispered, 'I was besotted.'

'And did you believe he felt the same way about you?'

In a tiny voice, she told the court that she did.

Holly admitted giving the defendant information she knew was price sensitive. Lana grimaced; the first nail of insider trading had been hammered home. The barrister asked if the defendant was aware he was being given inside information. Recalling Mark's interview with the FCA, Lana knew this was a crucial question. To be guilty of insider dealing, the perpetrator must be aware they are being passed price sensitive information. The witness opened and closed her mouth like a fish in a poorly oxygenated tank.

Lana held her breath. There was a hushed silence. A barrister shuffled papers, and Lana thought she heard a groan from the heating system. Someone coughed. The witness didn't speak.

'I'm not sure,' Holly said, and Lana exhaled.

The barrister tried again, rephrasing the same question, adding, 'Take your time, this is important. Did the accused know he was being given inside information?'

Lana risked a glance at the dock; the defendant was leaning forward, resting his elbows on the bar at the front of the dock. The seconds ticked by, and Holly gnawed at her thumbnail, but didn't answer. Lana ran her tongue over dry lips.

Again, Holly said she wasn't sure.

The barrister repeated the question a third time: 'Did the defendant know he was receiving inside information?'

This time the witness mumbled that she might have made an error and maybe she *had* told him the information was special.

On either side of her, Mary and Emily gasped. There was a subtle stiffening in all twelve bodies in the jury box, as if the court clerk had warned them to stop slouching.

'You told the accused that the information was price sensitive.'

'Yes.'

The defence counsel bounced to her feet, looking imperious despite her slight stature. 'Objection, my lord,' she said. 'My learned friend is leading the witness.'

The judge agreed. 'Sustained.'

'My lord, I do apologize,' said the prosecuting counsel.

It was a mortal wound, thought Lana. The apology wouldn't change anything. Holly had just hammered in a second nail, and the accused wasn't denying the third – buying shares in the relevant companies.

Moments later, the defence counsel was on her feet again, complaining about her learned friend, pointing out that Holly was not giving evidence as an expert on the stock market, and shouldn't be asked if she thought a share price would rise once a takeover was announced. The judge agreed, reprimanding the opposing counsel, who hung her head, managing simultaneously to look smug and apologetic. The judge did his best. 'Ladies and gentlemen of the jury, I must instruct you to forget what you have just heard.'

*Too late!* Lana wanted to scream.

In the afternoon, Holly was once again on the stand, but this time it was the defence counsel's turn to ask questions.

'How long have you worked in the field of mergers and acquisitions?' asked the barrister.

'Ten years.'

'And you were a director. Impressive after only ten years. Did you always work for the same bank?'

'No, I was headhunted five years ago.'

'And were you happy in your role?'

Holly didn't hesitate. 'Yes.'

'But you are no longer employed by the bank, are you?'

'No,' she replied, timidly.

'You were dismissed, weren't you?'

'Yes.'

'To draw on a military analogy, you were dishonourably discharged. And how did your recent employer compare to the bank the defendant worked for? Would you say both banks are in the same league?'

The witness shifted her stance. She mumbled something, and Lana concentrated, straining to hear.

'Could you speak up, please, so the members of the jury can hear you?'

'No,' she whispered.

The barrister addressed the jury. 'No, the witness's former employer, and that of the defendant, are not in the same league. Let's draw an analogy people might be more familiar with than investment banks . . . Let's talk about football. Which division would you say each of these banks plays in? We'll start with the bank where the defendant worked. Is that in the First Division?'

'Premier League,' replied the witness.

The next question was asked with the barrister facing the jury. 'And the bank where you were employed?' The counsel pursed her lips. 'Is that also in the Premier league?'

'First Division . . . Maybe at the top of the Second Division,' mumbled Holly.

The barrister turned back to the witness box. 'You'd jumped ships before. You're quite familiar with the way the City works: loyalty goes to the highest bidder. Were you surprised, maybe even flattered when, working for a Second Division bank, someone approached you to play for a Premier League team?'

'I . . . I guess so.'

'You weren't besotted with the defendant; you were besotted with the idea of working at the top of your game. But then something went wrong, didn't it? He heard rumours you were a bully and broke off discussions. Stopped returning your calls, shattered your dreams.'

The witness remained silent. Her eyes were narrow slits.

Lana allowed herself a little smile. She glanced at Emily, whose head was bobbing in agreement. This sounded far more plausible. The barrister leaned on her lectern to deliver the final blow. 'He never requested, and you never gave him any price sensitive information. This is revenge, Holly, pure and simple, a woman scorned; not in love, but in something as close to love as some City workers ever get. Money.'

'I blame myself. This is all my fault!' Emily wailed, squeezing a sodden tissue in her hands.

'No,' said Mary, removing the soggy tissue and replacing it

with two fresh ones. 'You cannot take the blame. If he is guilty, it was his decision, it had nothing to do with you.'

All evening, Emily had sat in a Lycra-clad heap, a box of tissues by her side, downing wine like a marathon runner gulping water at the finishing line. They were in Mary's sitting room, and she'd put on the expensive oil fired radiator, and laid out a selection of homemade salads, a bowl of olives and a cheeseboard. But Emily wasn't eating.

There was a loud sniff. 'I should never have had an affair.'

'Stop right there. This started years ago, way before your affair.' She caught the startled look in Emily's eyes and rushed on. 'If . . . I mean, *if* it was going on at all. I only meant . . . he's been playing the stock market for years. I'm sure he's innocent. Plenty of people who work in the City have a portfolio of shares. He didn't start investing because of your affair.'

As the hours dragged past, the salads grew warm, the olives mushy, the soft cheeses began to ooze, and the hard ones became sweaty. Mary tried to encourage her friend to eat, telling her she would feel awful in the morning if she didn't, but Emily was only interested in quaffing wine, and given her friend's tiny frame, it wasn't long before Mary was struggling to decipher what she was saying. At eleven o'clock, Mary staggered across the Square, her friend slumped against her shoulder.

Back home, she was wrapping up the cheeses and scraping the salads into Tupperware boxes, as she pondered what Emily was going to do if he was found guilty. She poured herself a glass of wine and took it back up to the sitting room. Flopping onto a sofa with her feet on one of the arm rests and a hand ruffling Biscuit's fur, Mary wished she could wheedle her way out of accompanying Emily in the morning. But she had to go. Emily had forgiven her for selling Barry's contact details to Tom, and Mary must atone for that sin.

Shortly before midnight, she heard a key in the lock and dashed into the entrance hall. 'How did it go?' she asked.

Charles tossed his keys onto the table where they made a tinkling sound before sliding across the marble. 'It was like escorting the condemned man to his final meal.' He shook his head. 'I tried to have the "what do you want me to do if it all goes pear-shaped?" chat. How can I help *etcetera*, but he kept banging on about his innocence, and where he was going to live, and how he's going to change his life when this nightmare is over. Not work so hard, make time for the more important things in life . . . He even talked about going to live in Portugal in the sun.' Charles slipped off his coat. 'How did you get on?'

'No better. She still blames herself, says if she hadn't been a trophy wife gorging on money that it would never have happened. Says *she* should be in the dock not him.'

'That's a bit dramatic!'

'I'm worried about her. She looks so vulnerable, like a gust of wind would blow her away.'

Charles gripped Mary by the arms. She felt the strength in his hands, and her shoulders relaxed. 'Are you going again in the morning?' he asked.

'Yes,' she sighed, 'but I don't want to.'

'A friend in need can be a blooming nuisance,' he said, chuckling softly. 'I wish I'd been there to support him the last two days, but it's been tricky enough getting away just for tomorrow, what with the auditors . . . And now the bond markets have gone haywire since Kwarteng announced his plans. I pity any poor souls with variable-rate mortgages. Somehow, I've still got to find time to escort the new CEO's wife around yet more estate agents.' He tutted. 'On and on he spoke about where he was going to live, and I couldn't banish the thought that soon he might not have to worry about accommodation, that he may find himself housed on an all-inclusive basis, albeit not quite in the style he's accustomed to.'

'Is that what you'd be worried about?'

'Yes,' said Charles, pulling a grim face. 'I'd be worried sick about where you and the girls were going to live. You couldn't afford the upkeep on this house on the money from your lessons.' He squeezed her shoulder. 'Buck up, old girl. Last day tomorrow.'

'Yes. Verdict day,' said Mary, her stomach clenching.

The next day, the defendant took the stand. He made a good witness, stuck to his brief, and wasn't thrown when the prosecuting counsel cross-examined him. He even managed to bring a rumble of laughter into the courtroom when he joked that the only difference between gambling on the horses and investing in the stock market was the size of the bet. His defence was simple: through experience, skill, and research – *not inside information* – the defendant identified potential takeover targets and took calculated investment risks. He was good at his job, and it was no surprise he'd chosen the right companies. Mostly. The defence produced a record of the accused's investments for the last three years, drawing attention to a few underperformers.

Sitting between Lana and Emily, Mary was unconvinced. She knew from Charles that just because a company was undervalued, it didn't automatically follow it would receive a takeover offer. Listening to all those tedious stories trotted out by Mark, Barry and Paul, she understood that even if an approach was made, it could take months of talks between chief executives, followed by weeks of due diligence by teams of accountants and lawyers, before a formal offer was launched; and even then, at any moment the deal could falter. It was only in the last few weeks of negotiations when the likelihood of success tipped onto more solid ground. The chances of someone striking lucky four times in the same year, which was what the defendant claimed, was a bit far-fetched. Fortuitously, it appeared the prosecuting counsel wasn't aware of the protracted art of a public company takeover, or if she was, chose not to explain it to the jury.

Feeling warm in the centrally heated courtroom and minding her elbows didn't poke either Lana or Emily, Mary shrugged off her jacket and folded it on her lap. Maybe all was not lost for the defendant.

There was only one other witness for the defence – a character witness. Charles. Mary was pleased her husband was able to speak up for his friend, but she wondered if it was the right decision. One banker speaking up for another was like an alibi for a late night out from a convicted burglar: it might not play well with the jury.

Charles marched to the witness box, and stood stiffly as he was sworn in, holding his right hand rigidly upright as if he were preparing to salute. He spoke in a calm authoritative voice, explaining how he'd known the accused for over twenty years, and praising his friend. Would it sway the jury?

Just before lunch, both barristers summed up. Listening to the closing speeches, Mary watched each member of the jury in turn, wondering what it was like to judge a white-collar crime. There was no obvious victim. Was it easier if you could focus on someone's suffering or loss when you condemned the accused? She looked from one impassive face to the next, but they were all inscrutable. She had no idea which side they believed.

'All rise,' instructed the clerk.

Standing, Mary caught a glimpse of someone she didn't want to see. Was that . . .? She peered over her shoulder and, two rows back, Tom grinned at her. She glared at him. If it hadn't been for his article, the bank's investigation would never have started.

Mary must warn Emily. 'Don't turn around,' she whispered. 'Tom's here.'

Emily looked puzzled. 'Tom?'

How could she forget? Mary never would! 'You know . . . Tom Withers, the journalist, Charles's ex-friend,' hissed Mary.

'Come to gloat, has he? The journalist that blew the lid on the corrupt City. Why am I not surprised he's here?' said Emily.

Tom trotted down the stairs towards the women.

'Go away,' said Mary curtly.

'Come on, Mary. I was right all along. Stop bearing a grudge and at least let me meet Charles for a beer!'

'No,' said Mary firmly.

'I'll deal with Tom,' muttered Lana. 'You two go on ahead.'

They gathered in the unofficial defence basecamp, a nearby café. While the other women picked at sandwiches, Mary complained about the rain, the accelerating price of oil, and how she wasn't looking forward to another cold winter. She talked about anything but the verdict. After an hour, the defence legal team joined them.

'How do you think it went?' asked Emily.

The barrister removed her wig and shook her hair. 'Holly gave us a bit of a mountain to climb when she changed her story. I hope I've given the jury an alternative explanation to chew over.'

Mary patted Emily's arm. 'Come on, girl, stop dwelling. What will be, will be.'

'I think he did well,' said Emily.

'He did his best,' said Mary. 'And I enjoyed Holly being given a dressing-down. Suggesting she was besotted with him.'

'She was right, Holly is a bully,' said Lana. 'She came to the house once. I've known cuddlier piranha fish.'

Mary laughed, and Emily managed a faint smile, saying, 'I'm so glad I persuaded you to withdraw your resignation, Lana. I don't know how I'd have coped without you these last few months.'

'Has he ever told you why he did it?' Mary asked the barrister.

The lawyer looked startled. 'He has never admitted his guilt.'

'I'm not saying he's guilty. I'm asking why he would risk being *accused* of insider dealing – why was he speculating in shares he expected to become takeover targets? That was a hell of a risky way to top up his massive income,' said Mary.

The barrister cocked her head to one side. 'He says he likes being in control of his money. He accepts it would've been more sensible to delegate investment decisions, especially as, sadly for him, he was obviously good at picking winners.'

A phone rang. Mary, Lana and Emily sat up straight like schoolgirls when the headmistress walks in. The barrister answered, averting her eyes. Mary cupped Emily's hands between her own. They were cold, and she rubbed them between hers trying to restore warmth. The barrister stood up, her chair making a rasping noise on the café's floor tiles. 'Jury's ready,' she said.

'Charles always tells me you can get a no quickly, but a yes takes a little longer,' said Mary.

'Let's wait and see,' said the barrister, non-committedly.

They trooped back into the courtroom and sat together at the front of the gallery. Mary leaned forward and gripped the guardrail, tracking each jury member filing in to take their seat, wishing it was Charles, not her, waiting to hear his friend's fate. The judge instructed the defendant to stand. The clerk crossed to the jury box, invited the foreperson to rise, then asked if the jury had reached a decision they were unanimously agreed upon.

'No,' said the foreperson.

Mary shot a look at the dock. The defendant was gazing her way, not so much at Mary, more at Emily. Mary couldn't recall seeing sags under his eyes before. She squeezed her friend's hand, imagining Charles's loving eyes casting her a forlorn glance from the dock, waiting to discover if strangers thought he was guilty under Section 52 of the Criminal Justice Act. How would she feel if it was Charles standing there?

The Judge addressed the foreperson. 'Do you think you would be able to reach a unanimous decision if you were given more time to deliberate?'

'No.'

'Have you reached a decision on which at least ten of you are agreed?' questioned the judge.

'Yes.'

Mary sucked her breath in over her teeth. She felt a little queasy. She looked back up at the dock, at the defendant standing with his back straight, his head held high, looking handsome but desperately tired. He was standing to attention, staring straight ahead, preventing her from catching his eye.

'How do you find the accused – guilty or not guilty?'

Mary closed her eyes.

'Guilty.'

Mary groaned, puckering her face. Beside her, she heard a sob and saw Lana putting her arms around Emily. Mary looked up at the dock, at Paul's impassive face, then down at Emily's blotchy one.

'It wasn't your fault,' said Mary, handing Emily a tissue. 'Paul didn't do it for you. He did it for himself.'

# Eighteen

**A week later**

It was a crisp autumn day, the sort that makes you want to get outside and trample through piles of fallen leaves. Gwen and Steve were returning from walking Romeo on the beach. They'd taken it in turns to hurl a ball, watching the corgi's little legs canter after it, kicking clods of damp sand into the air, before returning, jaws clenched around the prize. Deciding that Romeo might never tire of the game, Gwen wrestled the ball off the dog, clipped the lead on, and they set off home for tea and Welsh cakes.

Since October, when Steve had secured a six month winter let on a holiday flat in Chalkwell, the pair had fallen into a pattern of an early morning constitutional. They weren't friends, but Gwen was proud of herself for accepting that it was better to forget their dismal marriage and be amicable. Her forgiveness was a gift to Mark, enabling her son and grandson to forge a relationship with Steve without worrying about her feelings.

The pain started when Gwen turned the final corner into her street. A searing pain which left her gasping, fighting for breath.

'Oooh!' groaned, Gwen, staggering and dropping Romeo's lead. 'The pain . . . Help me, please help.'

Steve's eyes closed on hers. She smelled the lime of his scent, saw concern etched on his brow, and felt his warm breath on her cheeks. Was this the last face she was going to see on Earth?

'It's . . . like a vice.' she gasped.

'Sit down, Gwen,' he said, grasping her arm and lowering her to the pavement. His phone was in his hand. 'I'm dialling 999. Hang on, they won't be long. Ambulance please.' he said in a steady voice. 'I think someone is having a heart attack.'

He was kneeling beside her, Romeo's lead wrapped round his torso. He ripped off his gloves, and she saw him fumbling with her coat, then her jumper was lifted. She heard her blouse tearing open and just before she passed out, felt warm hands on her chest, pressing hard against her ribcage.

With her key in the lock, Lana could hear a phone ringing inside – Mark would be out jogging or in the shower. She flipped the key, shoved the door open, and ran, tossing her coat onto the floor. For the last week, she'd been virtually living in the office, often eating dinner at the table opposite Mark if he wasn't entertaining.

The power of the pen, thought Lana, reaching for the phone. It was Lana who had convinced Tom to include a line in the article covering Paul's trial, confirming the FCA was not investigating Mark. She suggested this might earn him forgiveness from the Standerwicks. Mark's diary soon became as full as an eligible debutante's dance card, resulting in Mark reinstating Lana as his PA.

Tom did not know what he was exposing when he wrote his first article hinting at insider dealing. It unleashed a wave of compliance officers who crawled through records, exposing share trading which had escaped compliance checks, including some of Paul's. That led to a fingertip search through Paul's expense claims linking him to Holly. Hours after the police officers marched Holly from the Ovington Square dining room, Paul was arrested. The bank's investigation also revealed Barry's connection with Holly, but she confirmed that the trader was unaware she was passing him inside information, which cleared him.

The phone rang off. Lana checked the caller ID – Gwen – and printed out Mark's diary, popping it near his laptop. Her own phone rang: Anne.

'I'm on my way to work, but I wanted to tell you,' she whispered. 'Keep this under your hat, but last night, Kenny and I decided I'm not coming back after maternity leave. I can't face the prospect of a third boss in less than two years.'

'I'm not sure you're cut out to be a stay at home mum!'

Her friend laughed. 'I will go back to work, but, maybe something a bit less stressful.'

'I can't talk now,' said Lana. 'Mark will be here any minute, and I haven't finished with the post.'

'Meet me at The Enterprise at six o'clock?'

'Not sure we'll be finished that early. Make it seven?'

'You're hooked, aren't you! Seven it is. Mine's a sparkling water.'

Lana chuckled and ended the call. Mark walked in running his hands through his wet hair. He picked up his diary page. 'What's this nine thirty meeting? It just says, new IPO.'

'It's a new IPO.'

Mark waggled the sheet at her. 'Come on, Lana, you're better than this. How big is it? What does the business do? Who are the quoted comparators, and which stock exchange are they listed on? People think because we're a boutique advisory business, I'll be flattered to be asked to float businesses the big banks won't take on.'

She stood her ground. 'They said they'd explain everything in the meeting.'

'They all say that. Cancel it.'

'Just meet with them,' she huffed.

His face twitched into a smile. 'OK.'

The phone was ringing again. Mark glanced at his screen. 'It's Clare,' he said, turning up the volume. Putting a hand either side of his computer, he leaned closer.

Project Revenge. For the last four months, Clare had been tying up Mark's former employer, demanding reams of documents, sifting through each for evidence to bolster his case.

The lawyer's familiar voice rang out. 'Morning, Mark. Got a minute?'

'For you, I've got ten!' he said, chuckling. 'Found something helpful?'

'I just got off the phone with your least favourite lawyer.'

Lana glanced across at her boss, her heart beating faster. What had the other side said? He threw her a confident look. 'And?'

'They've made a new offer.'

Lana's heart soared. Mark had already rejected £2 million, which meant that she would be in line for at least two hundred thousand quid. She would have to pay tax, but what a Christmas present! And she knew exactly what to do with it.

'Hacked off scurrying around dealing with your disclosure list, are they? Well done! What's the offer?' he asked.

'I've asked for it in writing, because it's quite complicated.'

'I'm not taking shares.'

'I hear you. Now listen to this.'

Clare outlined the bank's proposal. Mark laughed. Lana's heart sank.

Ovington Advisory's nine thirty clients were punctual. Lana escorted them into the office, still pondering Clare's news; Mark had said he would think about it for the day. Lana was sure he would accept. It was over, he had won, but Lana wouldn't be earning the deposit on a flat – she would be looking for a new job.

'What are they doing here?' asked Mark tetchily. 'Five minutes,' he said, glaring at Lana. She slipped out to fetch refreshments; she knew how everyone took their coffee.

As she left the office, the front door opened, letting in a blast of frosty air, and giving Lana a view of the communal square gardens, looking bedraggled; the leaves were stripped from the trees and lay on the pavement in slippery patches of orange and brown. Her mother, dressed in a pale blue Chanel tracksuit, knelt on the front steps, wiping first Tosca, then Floria's paws with a towel. Janet had settled into the role of the Ellis house-keeper, her first job at the age of sixty-four! When her house-sit ended, Janet would move back into the basement flat, and it would be Lana and her vegetables who were squatting. The dogs trotted past, paws clitter-clattering on the floorboards. Lana followed, an uneasy feeling churning in her tummy. Why? Eleven months ago, she'd have been thrilled. Get onto *the Lady* magazine website or call Alice, ask her to find your dream job. It's out there waiting. The Ellises will give you a sparkling reference. She plodded downstairs, trying to work out why she felt so deflated.

Standing in the corridor, Lana listened to the excited babble of voices behind the dining room door. Would she miss this? Did she want to continue with office work? With a good reference, she would find another post. As she let herself back in, Mark glanced up, running his hands through his hair. Lana had grown to recognize that look, the frown lines, his dark eyebrows virtually meeting in the middle. After months of working in the same room, she understood it better.

'Lana, you'd better take notes.' Mark turned to his son. 'Why didn't you tell me?'

'Dad, we did try! Twice. You cancelled both times. After we fired Paul – I couldn't stand the sight of him when I read that article – he begged us to reconsider, told us we were the most interesting fintech start-up coming to market next year.'

The last meeting her boss cancelled had been scheduled to follow Mark's mentoring session with Holly. The one the police interrupted. They'd been to Holly's bank first, discovered where she was, and then tracked her down to Ovington Square. With her hands cuffed, Holly had been frog-marched past a dazed Lana – relieved it wasn't Mark the police were after – and then past a bemused Ginge, cringing by the Ellis front door. What a day that had been, thought Lana, collecting her laptop, and tuning in to the meeting.

'Who are the major shareholders?' asked Mark.

A lever-arch file clicked open. Alex pulled out a sheet and laid it in front of his father. 'Ginge and his dad are the key investors.'

Mark rubbed his chin. 'You're going to be a millionaire too, son.'

'No, I don't own much.'

'Yes, you do. Says here you own 5 per cent.'

'That's not me, Dad.'

'Well, it says Ellis, and it's not me.'

'That's Gwen,' said Ginge.

Lana took a sip of coffee, hiding a smirk. She must remember to tell Mark that she had called earlier.

'My mother!'

'Yes, she stumped up ten grand for the software that transformed the business.'

Across the Square, Mary was in her entrance hall, balanced on the top step of a tall ladder. In her right hand was a dog toy, a piece of plastic designed to hurl a ball for Biscuit to chase. Mary clenched her stomach muscles to steady herself and reached out with the toy, stabbing at the dangling piece of wallpaper, trapping it against the wall and flattening it, grunting with the effort as she chivvied it into position.

The ladder rattled as she climbed back down and surveyed her handiwork. While elevated, Mary had spotted a few wrinkles where the glue she'd dolloped onto the wall had smudged. She squinted upwards; no one would notice. She looked down at the rug she'd bought for £50 in a local charity shop. Not bad. Only a diligent housekeeper would look beneath it.

Mary switched her thoughts from DIY to her husband. Charles was seeing Paul for the second time today. After his first visit, Charles reported Paul was protesting his innocence, claiming he'd been set up by Holly. Apparently, it was Bazza who'd alerted Paul to Holly as a possible recruit – just as he'd recommended her to Mark. Although initially impressed with Holly, Paul's due diligence picked up hints that she was a bully, and he stopped chasing her. That was when she began calling him and tried to recruit him to her cabal of M&A bankers, each one passing tips to the other, and all trading off the back of the others' knowledge. Paul told Charles he assumed Holly was trying to embarrass him; he was horrified by her suggestion and unwilling to believe crooks existed in the rarefied atmosphere of his M&A world.

If his story was true, it was Paul's fault he was locked up – if he knew what Holly was up to, he should've told the police, rather than staying silent in some misplaced nineteenth-century sense of honour to protect a woman. Holly was more than capable of fighting her own battles. As Lana had said on the day of Holly's testimony, some piranha fish are cuddlier than others. Maybe Paul was so confident he wouldn't be found guilty, he didn't think he needed to shop her. Had Holly set up Paul in revenge, or to save her own skin? Who was lying: Holly, Paul, or both?

Returning from that first trip, Charles told Mary that Paul

had begged him to get Emily to visit. Mary refused to pass on the message. Paul had misconstrued Emily's attendance at his trial. Emily went to assuage her own guilt, suspecting Paul committed the crime to woo her, not as a gesture of love.

Thinking of Emily made Mary's mind drift back to Devon. She heard a lorry reversing outside. Through the fanlight window above her front door, she saw the orange hazard lights spinning; the staccato warning bleeps echoed through the hallway, but despite the noise, she felt a sense of calm just imagining herself by the sea. If they sub-let the London house, she and Charles could afford something quite special in Devon. Charles wouldn't mind working a few days a week from home. In fact, if Charles's new CEO was still searching for a central London house with lots of bedrooms . . .

# *Nineteen*

Lana would always remember the December day when Clare called with the bank's revised offer. The meeting with Ginge and Alex took up most of the morning, discussing which lawyers to invite to pitch, the need for specialist financial PR advisers, and reporting accountants. 'I can't believe my mum gave you the money,' said Mark.

'She didn't *give* us the money. She invested in the business,' said Ginge.

Mark shook his head. 'My mum a millionaire, that sounds ridiculous!' He was quiet, pensive, then he asked, 'Where did she get ten thousand quid from?'

Alex answered that one. 'She said you've been sending her money for years. She never touched it. Told me to take it if I had a good use for it.'

Mark addressed most of his advice to Ginge, as he was the majority shareholder, but the look he gave his son was full of respect, and under his father's admiring gaze, Alex's shoulders lost their rounded look, and his face brightened.

The meeting wrapped up at noon. Mark shuffled his papers together into a neat pile. 'You know I'm going to accept, don't you?' he said to Lana.

'Yup.'

Lana understood the lure: replacing Effing Paul as Head of

M&A. Mark would withdraw his discrimination claim, the bank would reinstate him, backdate his salary, and pay him a bonus – entirely in shares. Lana wouldn't earn a penny, but she was proud of what they'd achieved; she'd helped take on a powerful organization and their army of lawyers, and they'd come out on top. Had Mark engineered this? Was this the goal of Project Revenge all along, to somehow disgrace and replace his former boss? Was money never the objective?

'Accepting shares is different if you're employed there. I'm happy for you,' she said. 'You won!'

'No. I didn't win. *We* did. Discrimination was your idea.'

'That's not why you won though.'

'*We* won because we worked as a team. We brought our combined strengths to the fight and cornered them. You secured the top KC, and that's when they started to take us seriously.'

'You don't have to massage my ego, and I know you don't owe me anything.' She cast her eyes around the room, at the printer – setting that up was her first win – her rose-gold-coloured laptop, the whiteboard. She'd miss this office.

'We certainly wiped that smile off Paul's face, didn't we?'

'If he knows what the bank's done. But I'm not sure he's been smiling much lately anyway. Can I ask for something, as a sort of thank you?'

Mark rolled his eyes. 'Of course.'

'Would you give me a decent reference, so I can apply for a similar job?'

'No,' he said firmly, shaking his head. 'I can't do that.'

She frowned. Had he taken umbrage over her outburst when she resigned? 'Why not?' she asked.

'We're a team. If they want me to work for them, they must take you too.'

She laughed. 'Seriously? Me?' Mark would still be her boss!

She would swap the dining room for her own cubicle – Anne's cubicle – outside a corner glass office with a view of the Canary Wharf skyline. 'Will they take me on?'

He gave a loud tut. 'Lana, haven't you learned *anything* about negotiation this past year? I wouldn't mention it unless I was certain they'd agree.'

'When would I start?'

'No point messing with the middlemen, I'm calling Harold,' he said, reaching for his phone. 'Ask Janet to clear up in here, will you? And by the way . . .'

'Yes?'

'I'm pleased we're not going to fall out over Project Revenge. I don't owe you anything, and I appreciate you acknowledging that.'

'The job is a fabulous compromise, thank you,' she said. 'I'll go and find my mother.'

'Hold on. If you join me, you'll lose your rights to a redundancy payment from this position. You've been here fifteen years; you'd be owed close to £10,000.'

Inwardly, Lana laughed at herself. Not so long ago, she'd thought that Mark was trying to get rid of her and avoid paying that money. How could she have doubted this man's integrity? Why had she wasted energy on a misplaced grudge for what happened to Janet – it had never been his fault her mother was cold.

'I'd rather work for you than take the money.'

He smiled. 'Are you happy for me to negotiate your new package?'

'What's your fee?' she asked, returning his smile. Then added, 'Your mother called earlier. I missed the call, so I don't know what she wanted.'

'Thanks, I'll call her this evening,' he said.

*

By the second week in December, Lana was working in Canary Wharf. She ate breakfast before dawn. She showered and dressed listening to the rapid-fire delivery of the Bloomberg presenters reporting the overnight financial market news, then elbowed fellow commuters out of the way to claim a seat on the Tube. She liked listening to the screech and rattle of the train, reading the pages of *City A.M.*, the free newspaper she'd previously used to line the dogs' travel crates.

On the first day in her new office, she recognized Stephanie from human resources, and of course, Anne, who showed her around the department, introducing her to a bewildering number of people.

During her second week – on Anne's last day before her maternity leave started – the pair arranged to meet for lunch. Lana was typing up an agenda, thinking that today Alex was arriving from Devon and the Christmas tree would be delivered to Ovington Square. For the first time in fifteen years, Lana wouldn't be toasting the tree with Alex and Emily, nor helping to decorate it – Janet would be. She wondered how her mother would react to such a glitzy celebration of the birth of Jesus.

Her desk phone buzzed. It was Emily.

'Hi, Lana, just calling to check he's going to make it to Mary's dinner party tonight.'

Lana bit her lip; she hated taking these calls. She pulled up Mark's diary. The dinner party wasn't even in it, but there was a client meeting at 7 p.m. and a Zoom appointment an hour later. 'He won't get there much before nine,' she said. Looking through the glass partition at her boss Lana added the dinner to the diary. Mark's feet were up on his desk, his chair tipped back, his phone in his hand, and there was an intense expression on his face. 'I can't disturb him now, but as soon as he's free, I'll check and call you back.'

'Thanks, Lana. Tonight is Mary's farewell dinner before they go to Devon, and I'd really like him to be there, even if he's late. Tell him if he makes it, even if we've already sat down for dinner, he's forgiven for cancelling last weekend's trip to Paris.'

Lana's insides squirmed. She didn't think Mark would remember anything about the Paris trip. Bouncing out of the office last Wednesday, his eyebrows one long dark smudge, her boss had told her to book him on a flight to New York on Friday. When she mentioned he was supposed to be flying to Paris with Emily that morning, he gave her a thumbs-up, saying, 'Fantastic, the diary's free.'

Lana had been speechless.

'I need to be in New York for a dinner, but I'd prefer to drop in at the office first for a briefing. Earliest flight, please.'

She nearly didn't ask, but then thought it was naive to assume Mark would do it, and she felt so sorry for Emily; Lana knew how much planning had gone into the Paris weekend. 'Will you tell Emily, or . . .'

He rubbed his chin. 'Probably best if you give her the heads-up. I might be late tonight, and I wouldn't want her to start packing.'

Lana hadn't mentioned any of that conversation to Emily, just told her that Mark was gutted, but he had been summoned to New York. Should she tell Emily the truth? She decided to fudge the issue saying, 'When I speak to him, I'll dangle that as a reward.'

'The Christmas tree has arrived,' said Emily. 'It's not the same without you here helping.'

Lana's second phone line was flashing. 'Got to go, Emily,' she said, stabbing at the red light and ending the call.

'Can you let me in, please?' said a familiar voice she couldn't quite place.

Walking towards the glass entrance door, she heard someone rapping on it, then recognized the face smudged up against the glass. The last time she'd seen that face it was hairy.

'Barry!' she said, pushing the release button. 'In case no one has told you this, don't grow it back.'

He roared with laughter. 'Don't worry, I've been cleared by compliance. Take me to the new leader . . . You'd think he could've found a more professional assistant . . .'

She felt a little ripple of pleasure at his back-handed compliment. 'No peeking,' she instructed, walking him through the hum of activity.

He glanced left and right. 'Much better. This place was like a morgue when Paul was in charge.'

Lunch was at The Parlour. Lana stopped off at the cashpoint machine. She punched in her pin, checked her balance, and stood chewing her lip.

'What's wrong?' asked Anne, stamping her feet, and rubbing her hands up and down her arms. 'Come on, I'm cold.'

'I don't understand,' said Lana, tapping a fingernail against the screen.

'We don't get paid until later this week. Do you need to borrow some money?'

'No, you're all right, but thanks anyway. I'll sort this later,' said Lana, retrieving her cash and the card.

Back from lunch, Lana logged onto her banking portal. Her brow wrinkled. Someone had made a mistake; she would call the bank. She heard a throat being cleared.

'Good lunch?' asked Mark. 'Is that 2 p.m. call with Milan confirmed?'

Lana closed the portal and switched her attention to her boss. 'Yes, all sorted. I've arranged a pre-briefing for the team in your office at 1.45 p.m. Emily wants to know if you're going to make the dinner tonight.'

A quizzical expression crossed his face. 'What dinner?'

'Mary's farewell dinner before they leave for Devon.'

He groaned and shook his head. 'Could you send flowers, please?' He was backing away from her cubicle. 'Order them from Moyses Stevens and get them to deliver before this evening. Use my credit card,' he said, tossing it onto her desk.

'For Emily?'

'No, of course not,' he replied, giving a little laugh. 'For Mary, Oh, and call her and make my grovelling apologies,' he added before shutting himself in his office.

Logging off that evening, the lights of East London and Canary Wharf were not soothing Lana. She was concerned about her banking problem. She'd spoken to the bank's helpdesk, but they couldn't give her any more information than she could see online.

'You off for the night?' asked Mark, dumping a pile of papers on her desk. 'This will all keep until tomorrow.'

'Mark, I need to ask you something.'

'Fire away.'

Lana had read about these cases, where the wrong payment was made, too many zeros added in error. 'There's been a deposit of £250,000 into my bank account.'

'Well, it is Christmas,' he said with a self-satisfied smile.

'But . . .' she hesitated, the penny dropping. 'You don't owe me anything, you're being paid in shares not cash.'

'It's all yours,' said Mark. 'You've earned it. And anyway, I didn't pay it, the bank did. It's your signing-on fee. You work for a Premier League team now. Enjoy!'

'But what about tax?' she demanded.

'I was never going to accept less than two and a half mil after tax. You were always in line for a net £250k.'

'But . . . why so much?'

'Remember the golden rule about negotiation? Get into the mind of the opposition and steer them towards a deal they will accept. I think it's a fair cut for you, and knowing you as well as I do, I think it's what you want. Should be enough for a deposit on a garden flat.'

Four months after making an offer, Lana moved in. The new flat was in Pimlico, a short stroll from the Tube station, far enough away from Janet to convince Lana she'd left home, but still close to Anne and the London Lana knew well.

The kitchen was her favourite room. It was tiny, more a corridor than a room; if she stood in the centre with her arms spread wide, there was barely six inches between her fingertips and the two walls. The previous occupants had painted the walls a vivid yellow. It was ghastly, reminding Lana of the flashing lights she used to get from her migraines. She hadn't had one of those for months.

Accompanying Lana on a second viewing, Anne, heavily pregnant with a hand supporting her back, had joked, 'Yuck, not what you want with a crashing hangover. But hey, this room's so small, you'll be able to improve the colour with a tester paint pot.'

The units were plain white, the counter beige plastic. But none of that mattered – this was her room, where she cooked what she wanted, just for herself. The kitchen's redeeming feature was the door – a stout one with Banham security locks – which opened on to Lana's own courtyard garden. It was south-facing, and large for the area, nearly as big as the Ellis kitchen.

She was blown away on her first viewing, but on her second, on that dreary, damp December morning, standing outside in the drizzle – Anne remained inside, claiming she could see the garden perfectly well through the kitchen window – surrounded by upturned plastic pots of decaying dandelions, she knew it was perfect. Weeds grew in gaps where the grouting between the paving stones had washed away, and the back fence sagged inwards under the weight of a tangle of ivy. But she didn't care. This courtyard could be hers, and there was the perfect spot to relocate her tiny greenhouse. Lana wiped the rain off her face. She could hear water dripping and tracked it down to a gutter; it was probably clogged with leaves blown off a nearby sycamore tree. She'd keep that pipe clear, buy a water butt, catch the rain, recycle it for her plants.

Within days of moving in, Janet's welcome present arrived. A glass greenhouse. Two weeks later, on a warm Saturday, the doors to that gift were open, allowing easy access for the bees hovering at the entrance, tempted there by the pots of daffodils, tulips and early alliums. Lana was rearranging her vegetable seedlings on a slated table. She tore off a handful of rocket, nibbled at it, then pushed pots of eight inch tall red and orange pepper plants hard against the glass, lining up her cauliflowers in front of them. One more week of sunshine and she'd plant them outside.

She took a moment to examine her cucumber plant, the corkscrew-like tendrils wound around a bamboo stick angled against the ceiling. There was a single yellow flower attached to the plant by a fledgling two inch cucumber. Any week now, she'd be in production. She'd never had room to grow cucumbers before. Lana felt protective of these seedlings and now understood what Eleanor meant the night they first met; this was a little bit like nurturing her own family.

Lana had been to stay with her father and Eleanor twice since their meal at Pizza Pomodoro. The first time, in January, Lana didn't tell Janet where she was going – she didn't want to invite snarky comments about bad Catholics. Eleanor made such an effort to make the weekend appear effortless, rearranging her shifts so she wasn't working, and precooking all the meals. The three of them spent Saturday touring the RHS Garden at Bridgewater. Even though it was winter, they spent over an hour in the Kitchen Garden, before her father dragged the two women away to explore the winding paths of the Chinese Streamside Garden. Her second visit was last weekend, and she had mentioned that one to her mother. Janet didn't ask Lana to send her love, but she did tell her to enjoy herself.

A white butterfly fluttered past Lana, and she picked up a length of netting and wrapped it over her cauliflower seedlings. It could find somewhere else to lay its eggs.

She checked the time. She must get cracking; she was due at Janet's in an hour.

While they tucked into one of her mother's sausage casseroles, Janet regaled her with stories about Emily's new puppy, Spoletta, a miniature bull terrier. Spoletta was entirely white, save for a small black patch over each diamond-shaped eye, and like all terrier puppies, viewed everything he encountered as a potential toy.

'He's a menace, chews anything. Last Saturday, he was after poor Romeo's tail; Romeo didn't think it was as funny as Gwen and I did! Even when Romeo sat on it, the little villain was still pawing at his tail. We had to lock the pup in one of the travel crates to give that poor corgi a bit of peace.'

Lana smiled at the image of Spoletta chasing the corgi's tail. Lana already knew that Gwen and her dog were in London last weekend. Since the heart attack, Mark's mother spent every other weekend with him – it was recorded in his diary. Gwen now had a stent, but if Steve hadn't been with her the outcome might have been very different. Lana ate her last sausage, reflecting on how different her relationship with her own mother was now. Months apart had been good for them, allowing Lana time to mourn historic dreams and focus on new ones.

'I found the remains of the oven gloves in Spoletta's basket this afternoon. He'd chewed them in half! Emily just laughed and threw them away. She's fun, isn't she, Emily? I think she misses you.'

Lana thought Emily missed her husband more. Why wouldn't Mark make time for his wife? She was often tasked with rearranging meetings, so Mark could take a client for lunch or dinner, or attend a pitch – why couldn't he do the same to squeeze in time for his wife? Other than his mother's weekend visits, social engagements weren't recorded in his diary. Lana would suggest Emily told her about them, instead of Mark.

'We had a lovely natter while I cooked Emily's supper,' said Janet.

Listening to her mother speaking about Emily, Lana recalled her own girly sessions at the breakfast bar. Apparently, that afternoon Emily had entertained Janet with the latest tidbit on Paul's case. Holly had been rearrested and confessed to framing Paul to save her own skin. Holly was the mastermind behind the insider dealing ring, and her bank accounts would prove it. Her trial wouldn't be for months - they were holding her on remand - but they had released Paul from prison. His name would be cleared, enabling him to resurrect his career. Lana recoiled at this news: would Paul demand his job back?

Her mother was clearing away and Lana was putting on her raincoat when Janet removed a bottle of champagne from the fridge. 'Stay for a glass,' she said holding it up. 'I've never opened champagne. Would you do it, please?'

Lana shrugged off her coat.

'Nor have I, but I've opened plenty of Prosecco,' she said, grasping the cold bottle with both hands. She ripped off the foil, then the metal cage, and wiggled the cork with one hand. 'Just what are we celebrating?'

'My divorce.'

The cork exploded in Lana's hand. 'Your what?' she asked, filling two flutes with the frothy liquid and passing one to her mother. *Her parents were getting divorced.* 'But, your faith . . .'

'That's not what stopped me. The sin is in remarrying, not divorce, and I'm never going to do that.' Janet clamped her mouth shut. When she spoke next, her tone was softer. 'I wanted to stop your father from remarrying. Spiteful, really.'

'Why now?'

Janet explained that, just before Christmas, Gwen had persuaded her to draw a line under it and move on.

'Your father did the right thing by you, and this Eleanor, and well . . . she can't be all bad if she encouraged him to use his savings to help you buy your flat. I reckon it's time to set him free. Gwen says it will set me free, too. Not sure about that.'

Lana picked up her glass, sniffed, then looked at the bubbles; they seemed softer and smaller than she was used to. She took a sip, savouring the richer, buttery taste. She could get used to this! She wondered why her father hadn't told her about the divorce when she was with him last weekend – was he being kind, allowing her mother to break the news, or not wanting to celebrate until he was certain Janet hadn't changed her mind?

'The divorce may set me free from him, but I'll never be free of the guilt. Not after what I did to you.'

'Oh, Mum! Would I be drinking champagne with you if I hadn't moved on?'

Janet gulped. 'Thank you,' she said, her voice wavering. 'That means the world to me.' She raised her glass, clinking it against Lana's. 'To you and your future. You are happy with your life now, Lana, aren't you?'

'Yes . . . Yes, I think I am,' she said, then searched around for a neutral topic.

After finishing the entire bottle of champagne, toasting each other, their new lives, forgiveness and the future, Lana borrowed her mother's toothbrush while Janet made up the sofa bed.

Lana woke, yawned, then lay still, her ears straining to identify what was making her feel uneasy. She couldn't hear a thing, and she realized that was the problem: where was the traffic? She ran her tongue around her mouth and reached over for the glass of water she always left on the bedside table, then she remembered she'd spent the night on her old sofa bed, in the quiet of Ovington Square. She glanced at her wrist – six o'clock – it was difficult to lie in at weekends. She plumped up the pillows and settled back against them, planning her weekend. Later today she was meeting Anne for lunch. She'd go home and change first, she didn't want to turn up in her office clothes and raincoat, especially not when she'd bought a new outfit.

She asked herself what she would do if the bank reinstated Effing Paul. Anne hadn't liked working for him. She decided if Paul was reinstated, Lana would follow Mark wherever he went; they were a team. She threw the duvet back. She was hot. And thirsty. She got up and made herself a cup of tea then crawled back into bed, watching the steam rising from the mug, trying to decide if she should risk wearing her new shoes to meet Anne. She didn't want to have to hobble home.

In front of her, a yellow glow tracked across the curtains from right to left, then stopped. Was it the headlights of a taxi for Mark? His chauffeur didn't work at weekends, but it was unlikely. Lana hadn't booked one. But last night she had left before her boss; there might've been a late night drama, causing him to book a taxi himself.

She put down her mug, walked to the window and jerked back the curtain. Up at street level, the driver's door of a car swung open, setting off the interior light. There was only one person inside. It looked like a man in a suit, so it must be a chauffeured limousine, the sort she arranged to collect Mark if his driver was unwell. It couldn't be for Emily; she would've told Janet if she was going away for the weekend. The dogs would need looking after, Mark was catching a plane to Chicago on Sunday.

Hearing a dog yapping, Lana looked up past the steps she'd trodden almost every day for the last fifteen years. The Ellises's porch light was on . . . Had Mark let the puppy escape?

The driver got out of the car, walked in front of the car's headlights, and Lana's eyes popped. He was wearing emerald green braces. She dropped the curtain, grabbed her raincoat, ran to the door and yanked it open. Emily was on the doorstep in her cream cashmere trouser suit. She was holding a white puppy, which was squirming to get free, Floria and Tosca at her feet, their leads secured to a fence spike. As she watched, Paul took the wriggling puppy from Emily, tucked it under one arm, where it kicked and writhed, then engulfed Emily with his other arm, kissing her.

Lana gasped. The pair unfurled. Paul handed the puppy back, jogged down the steps and opened the car's passenger door. Emily climbed in.

Barefoot, Lana padded up the cold stone staircase. On the pavement, Paul ran past her, panting, seemingly oblivious to her presence. He heaved two suitcases into the boot, then rushed back into the house.

'Emily!' Lana called out.

The other woman leaned out of the car window. She pushed a hand through her hair and gave her former housekeeper a faint smile. 'You're up early,' said Emily.

'Why?' asked Lana.

'Mark is in his own slice of heaven. He hasn't changed, and he's never going to. He's married to the job . . . always has been, always will be. I *have* tried, but he hasn't. I don't think he can.'

She was right. His expense account proved it. Over the last month, Mark had spent every evening entertaining clients, with London colleagues, or on Zoom with senior team members in New York. Not once had he suggested Lana ring-fence an evening for him to eat with his wife. He hadn't even tried to make Mary's dinner party before Christmas. He didn't want to. He preferred work to socializing.

'Take care of him for me, Lana,' said Emily.

Lana scoffed to herself. He was the boss - why should she take care of him?

Paul ran back towards the car, dogs scuttling down the steps either side of him.

He raised a hand and gave a short wave before sliding into the driver's seat, the door slamming shut behind him.

Just before the car pulled away, Lana mouthed to Emily, 'I will.'

Lana watched the tail lights disappear wondering why she'd just said that. The car turned right onto Walton Street, and it came to her - Mark needed looking after!

# A Thank You from Debbie Morrison

Thank you so much for reading *A Perfect Chelsea Townhouse*. I truly appreciate it. With so many wonderful choices out there in women's fiction, I'm incredibly grateful that you chose to spend your time (and money!) on my book.

I hope you enjoyed getting to know Lana as she was pushed headfirst out of her comfort zone. Trying to find her feet while grappling with new tasks and responsibilities—and all the while under immense pressure—it wasn't easy for her, was it? But it's often those tricky, uncomfortable moments that reveal what we're truly made of, and I think Lana discovered that, too.

Writing about London was such a joy. It's an incredible city, filled with energy, surprises, and countless stories waiting to be told. There were so many funny and poignant moments I couldn't fit in, but who knows? Maybe I'll get a chance to share them next time!

If you haven't already, do pop over to my website at www.debbiemorrison.co.uk to grab your free copy of an exclusive new e-book, coming your way in late 2024 (it's a little gift, and won't be available anywhere else!).

And if you have a moment, I'd be thrilled if you could leave a review on Amazon, Goodreads, or wherever you like to share your thoughts about books. It means the world to me, and it really helps other readers discover my stories.

Thank you again!

*Did you love A Perfect Chelsea Townhouse?*

Have you ever wondered what would have happened if life took a different turn? If you made a different decision, to set off on an adventure instead of stick with the life you have?

What would have happened if Mark and Emily used Mark's redundancy as a chance to completely change their lives?

Let's rewind all the way back to the start and find out:

Can two different beginnings lead to the same happy ending?

Read on for your exclusive preview of

*A Perfect Algarve Villa...*

# Two

On Tuesday morning, Emily woke again to the chirp of crickets. She snuffled, turned on her side, and allowed the sound to conjure memories of sitting on romantic terraces, the heat of the evening on her bare arms. Twenty seconds later the crickets were still singing. She rolled back to face her husband and grunted, 'Mark, alarm.'

A hand shot out. The room fell silent. She drifted back to sleep.

An hour later, Emily rose, showered, and dressed before breakfast, then rode the lift to the basement. The door slid open. She breathed in the smell of chlorine and grinned. Svetlana was bustling about, jabbing fingers, and issuing instructions to an army of men gathered around her pool. They were dressed in light-blue overalls with a picture of a wave on their breast pockets, the words "Blue Dreams" picked out in white.

The housekeeper's eyes switched from the men to her employer. 'You want me to walk dogs, or sort men?'

'Men please, Svetlana,' Emily said, her eyes dancing with excitement.

An automatic pool cover, how thrilling, she thought, her mind racing through the rest of the "shopping list of treats". Now she'd given the list to Mark, she was in for a wonderful week of fun.

The night before, Mark had come home earlier than usual, for a Monday. At 8 o'clock, she'd unfurled herself from a sofa as the door clicked shut. 'Darling, what a lovely surprise,' she said, bouncing into the hallway, a glass of wine cupped between her hands like a communion goblet.

He hung up his overcoat and plodded towards her. He looked exhausted, like it was already the end of the week. She put down her glass and hugged him. 'Tough day?'

He sagged against her, eyes closed. 'You've no idea,' he said. 'Bloody effing Paul.'

Her hands tightened round his arms. 'Paul?'

'Forget it,' he mumbled. 'I'd like to.'

'Poor you.' She took his hand and led him downstairs to the kitchen. Her Blakes kitchen, with its bank of moss-green cupboards and shiny, marble central island where she liked to sit and gossip with Svetlana. Emily opened the door to the concealed American fridge. 'Let's get you a beer.'

Flipping the top off the bottle, she passed him the drink then lowered her eyes. As demure as a young child handing their letter to Santa, she'd handed him her shopping list.

'What's this?' He held the paper limply in his hands and raised his beer to his lips.

She batted her eyes at him. 'I've given you the quotes for everything except the holiday villa, but I guess you won't set the budget for that until we've done a bit more research.' Emily stood behind him as he read, massaging his shoulders; it was like trying to knead stone. 'Wow, you're tense. Is that helping?'

He screwed up the list, tucked it into his trouser pocket, finished his beer in one long pull, then turned around, and folded her into his arms. 'Come here, you,' he mumbled softly into her hair. He kissed her, and she tasted the earthy sour flavour of lager.

'Let me have a shower. Fancy an early night?' he asked, nibbling her earlobe.

Her eyes answered for her as she led him out of the kitchen.

It was a busy week at Ovington Square. On Wednesday, under the watchful eyes of Svetlana, the new gym equipment was installed in the precise spots dictated by the diagram Emily left with the housekeeper. The old machines were taken away to a local homeless shelter – there was nothing wrong with them, and the manager was optimistic they would entice some of the homeless former soldiers into the centre. Emily found time to transfer more money to Alex, and in between a Pilates class and visiting a facial clinic, she called round to see her girlfriends, sounding them out on a trip to the Californian health spa. By the evening, she was tired and cancelled her dinner arrangements.

On Thursday, before a shopping expedition on Sloane Street, Emily rearranged her wardrobe with Svetlana, who walked away with three designer handbags for herself and two black bags full of virtually unworn clothes for a specified charity shop. Emily rang her girlfriends, coaxing them into buying tickets for an upcoming charity ball. Emily had paid for the whole table already and would donate any spare tickets to the Dogs Trust – a treat for a fellow dog lover who couldn't afford £500 to attend an event.

At nine-thirty on Friday morning, Emily opened the door to her husband's dressing room. It was pitch dark. She flicked on the lights and spotted a lump under the bedclothes. There must have been a late-night drama on that deal; Mark always slept in his dressing room if he came home after she'd gone to bed.

'Darling, you're still here. Svetlana thought so.'

The lump pushed itself into a sitting position. Mark's head was drooping – poor lamb, he was having a 'mare of a week. He'd returned in a foul mood on Tuesday night and Wednesday. Her heart went out to him, but her mind was focused on the overseas property show the following day. How would she get him there if he could justify spending the weekend in Canary Wharf instead?

Mark raised his head and blinked a few times. 'I've hardly slept.' He ran his tongue slowly over his lips. 'That client lunch poisoned me.'

'Ugh, should I call a doctor?'

He scrunched his eyes closed. 'No, I just need sleep. I can work from home today.'

Her eyes widened; the only time Emily could recall Mark working from home was during lockdown or on holiday. 'Gosh it must be bad.' She gave a short burst of laughter. 'It's not the day today, is it? You don't want to miss that, boyo.'

'Do you ever think about anything but money?' he asked in a flat voice.

'Don't be like that. My life is always on hold at this time of year.'

'How tragic, being asked to wait a few weeks before you can spend chunks of money that would keep a normal family ecstatic for a lifetime.'

She toyed with the door handle, pouted, and said in a slightly petulant voice, 'You've no idea what it's like waiting.'

He glared at her. 'You haven't waited. I've seen the pool cover.'

She recoiled, hiding half her face behind the door. 'I had to do that. I was worried the dogs might fall in.'

'They've managed the last few years,' he snapped. 'And what about those flattened cardboard boxes I clocked on Wednesday evening? There was nothing wrong with our gym equipment. Jumped the gun a bit this year, haven't you?'

She swallowed and stepped into the room, closing the door behind her. 'What's wrong? What's happened?' she whispered, crossing to her husband.

'Nothing,' he mumbled, lying back down. 'I just don't feel well. I'll stay here today.'

'I just want to get on with things!'

'Well, you can't. No more spending. Please.'

Her voice croaked. 'Why?'

'Because I say so.' He thumped onto his side, pulling the duvet over his head, adding in a muffled voice, 'Now turn off the lights and let me rest.'

Emily withdrew. She'd been the verbal punchbag for roller-coaster deals before. Once Mark got the transaction back on track, he'd apologize.

Shaking out the Saturday edition of the Financial Times and propping it against the cafetière, Mark sniffed. Bacon. Svetlana was expensive – with payroll taxes, over £3,000 a month – but Emily didn't cook anymore. He wasn't sure what she did on weekdays when he was entertaining clients, but at weekends, the couple invariably ate out. He tried to concentrate on an article speculating about the direction of interest rates – inflation was picking up, but economists expected it to be temporary – but like a bee stuck in the tempting nectar-filled flowers of a snap-dragon, his mind drifted back to the topic of domestic costs: on top of Svetlana, Emily had announced a new gardening team was starting soon.

He was still perusing the pink pages, worrying at the problem like a dog at a favourite toy, when Emily walked in, dressed in pale-blue Lycra. He rustled the paper shut.

'Sleep well? You look great in that!'

Emily stroked her sides, wriggling her body suggestively. 'It's a new range. I only bought it yesterday.'

She spooned raspberries and strawberries onto her plate. Recalling his own childhood bowls of porridge and stewed apple, Mark remembered he hadn't spoken to his mother all week.

A dollop of yoghurt was added to the fruit. 'It's supposed to be more flattering to us older gym bunnies!' she said. 'Shall I give you a quick run through the weekend agenda?'

Fuck, please not a charity ball where he was expected to bid thousands to secure some overpriced piece of shit!

'Today it's the Overseas Property Show! Let's leave about ten-thirty. Give you plenty of time to work first.'

Mark dropped his cutlery and pushed his plate aside, unable to finish his food. There was a rat-a-tat sound, and Svetlana walked in, stacked a tray, then melted away, shutting the door behind her.

Emily lowered her voice. 'Do you know which day it is yet?'

'What?' he snapped.

She leaned closer. 'Come on, boyo,' she teased.

He felt a ripple of pleasure at the use of her pet name for him; she'd even copied his mother's Welsh accent.

'You know what I mean! I love this time of year! I've such plans. I gave you the big list, but I've got so many other ideas to discuss with you.'

He chewed his lower lip. 'No,' he said, refilling his coffee cup.

She arched her eyebrows at him and leaned over, batting her eyelashes. 'But it must be soon,' she coaxed.

'Think I might take that blue Lycra off you,' he offered, standing up and holding out a hand.

She laughed, pushing herself away from the table. 'Later, darling. I'm giving Mary a lift to Pilates!'

Having devoured every page of every section of the newspaper, Mark tossed it aside. Over the previous twenty years, gradually, everything except work had been eliminated from his life. Emily ran domestic affairs, and he had no outside interests. Hobbies and a career as a mergers and acquisitions banker were a contradiction. Tennis, friendships, they'd all been sacrificed at the altar of his career and shrivelled to nothing, like an untended houseplant that struggles, parched, then curls up and dies.

He rang his mother.

'Gwen Ellis,' purred the voice he'd loved all his life.

Despite living in Essex for nearly fifty years, his mother still spoke with a Bargoed accent, the soft lilt of the Welsh mining town she was born into, where she'd lived happily until she was eighteen, before being enticed away by the exotic future promised by Mark's wayward father. For the first decade of Mark's life, the wastrel had played a walk-on part, confusing the young boy for those occasional periods when, briefly, a father figure was present at the cramped kitchen table. He bellowed out instructions and advice to both son and wife, who, it seemed to Mark, coped remarkably well without any interference from this comparative stranger. When Mark was ten, his parents divorced; no one stepped in to be a father figure.

'Mum. It's me.'

'Oh, lovely boy. Where you to then? I know you're busy, but I love to hear from you.'

He fished around for things to say, listening to his mother jolly along about her little triumphs in the garden, then talk about her corgi Romeo's latest bid for fatherhood, and how he'd been returned by a glowering neighbour with a red setter. Mark let the words rumble on, comparing his mother's life to his wife's. One spent all the money he could earn, the other hardly any.

'Gotta dash, Mum. Emily's organized tickets to a show, and I've got some work to finish first.'

The couple left the house at ten-thirty. Mark hailed a taxi and held the door open for his wife who was chattering like a schoolgirl reunited with friends after the long summer holidays. He climbed in behind her, dodging the gushing words by pulling out his phone.

At Olympia, they passed through security and into the main hall, where exhibitors had gone to extraordinary lengths to metaphorically transport potential clients to the sunny shores they were selling. There were exotic plants, fat terracotta pots, straw hats, and brightly coloured pool towels. There were huge posters featuring powder-blue skies, landscapes filled with olive groves or vineyards, and sandy beaches with happy swimsuit-wearing families, hand in hand, enjoying the brilliant sunshine.

Banners advertised the hotspot each stand specialized in. Exhibitors were clustered geographically, the more off-beat locations relegated to the outskirts. The couple passed stands for Turkey and Croatia. Mark even noticed a few trying to tempt customers as far afield as Florida. There was a buzz of excited conversations, and he caught snatches of laughter as he was steered towards Spain and a firm of estate agents. Emily announced that she had an appointment with Margery.

Margery – "call me Marge" – was identified, and the couple were fawned over for half an hour. Marge worked her way down a questionnaire pinned to a clipboard, directing the pitch entirely Emily's way. Was access to a golf course important? How crucial was it to be close to the airport? Marge's sales patter didn't falter when, after twenty minutes discussing the merits of buying on or off a condominium, Mark announced he needed to make a phone call and left.

Emily did falter. She'd earned this villa; Mark wasn't going to wriggle off this hook. But there was no mileage in fighting the phone: maybe the big deal was still teetering. It would explain why he'd yet to apologize for being downright rude yesterday, sniping at her for spending less than £100,000 on gym equipment. And he was keeping Bonus Day a tight secret. She was pretty sure it had been yesterday; even if her source was fibbing, Mark must know the date – the boss always tipped the wink to his star MD.

After another ten minutes of Marge and still no sign of Mark, she went husband-hunting, clutching a wodge of brochures and promising to be in touch with dates for a house-hunting trip. Where was Mark? Surely, he must be off the phone by now. Not considering French property, she concluded, circling the stands twice. After walking through Italy and Greece, she saw him, in animated conversation wearing that focused look, typically reserved for relating tedious war stories about City deals. As she watched, her husband threw his head back and laughed. Her eyes searching for clues, spotted a banner: PORTUGAL. Ok, that's tacked onto the side of Spain. The happier he was, the bigger the budget.

She made her way over. Mark stood up and pulled out a chair like an attentive maître d'. 'Emily, meet Peter Mathews, my new best friend.'

'I think your new best friend is the NHR scheme,' said Peter, winking.

Both men erupted in laughter. This was no polite forced titter: Mark was guffawing.

'I'm sorry, guys, you're going to have to share the code,' she said, standing beside her husband. He was reaching out a hand for one of hers. Emily shot the estate agent a quizzical look, before arching her eyebrows at Mark, who was still grinning like a child on Christmas morning. He put his arms around her.

'It's time for an adventure. We are emigrating to Portugal.'

No consultation, no explanation. Her husband – the architect of their game plan for over 20 years – expected her to uproot her perfect life in London and decamp to a country she'd never even been to.

Why?

She was given a loving look, but no explanation. Emily stood to one side, her mind a scrambled mess of worries – she didn't want to leave London permanently, just occasionally. She watched Mark scoop up a pile of papers, pump Peter's arm, and with her hand in his, he kissed her forehead, promising to explain everything over lunch. Where would she like to go? Money no object. He whisked her out of the exhibition, bouncing like a teenage Alex on the first day of a half-term trip to Devon, anticipating hitting the surf after weeks away.

It was shortly after noon and the exhibition was open until late. In the entrance lobby Emily and Mark were heading against the tide, forcing them to weave their way through a throng of incoming customers. Once they escaped that obstacle, the couple emerged onto the forecourt into a teeming mass of excited arrivals who were not looking where they were going, shaking off umbrellas and stumbling into departing customers. None of these normally intensely irritating encounters with the public provoked a reaction from Mark.

Fifteen minutes later they were being shown to a table. Vintage champagne was ordered, that's a little presumptive. The bottle was opened, poured, then left on a nearby trolley in an ice bucket.

Mark raised his glass. 'To you.' He reached across the white linen tablecloth, and she felt his fingers stroking the back of her hand, then he took a deep breath, leaned back in his chair, and said, 'I have quite a lot to say.'

It was forty-five minutes since he'd announced they were emigrating, Emily thought, and the verb 'to discuss' was yet to make an appearance. Her stomach clenched as her mind circled through possibilities. Was he ill? Was there more to working from home yesterday than he'd led her believe? Was there another woman? She reached for her glass, took a gulp of champagne, swishing it round her mouth and allowing it to dribble down her throat, before taking another slug.

'The first piece of news is . . .' He drained his own glass before rushing on – 'I've left the bank and I'm not joining another one.'

Emily swallowed her mouthful of champagne, coughing as the bubbles swamped her throat and fizzed uncomfortably at the tip of her nose.

'I've decided on a new career. One that gives me more time to spend with you and Alex.'

Emily glared at her husband as she hissed across the linen. 'Oh, please,' she said, drawing out the words. 'You've just told me we're relocating to Portugal, a country we've yet to even visit, and now you announce you've decided to cast aside your job, which certainly for the first twenty-three years of our marriage has been your entire life.' She shook her head. 'And this selfless act of sacrifice has been motivated by your sudden desire to spend more time with our son, with whom you can't hold a civilized conversation?' Fixing Mark with a pitiless gaze, she demanded a little respect, and 'a little more of the truth, please.'

His lips pulled into an unattractive grimace. He ran a hand through his hair, then down his face, and around the back of his neck. Emily felt her heart fluttering, like a trapped butterfly. She twisted the stem of her glass. What was the truth?

Mark ran his tongue around his dry lips, blinked, then looked across at the woman he loved. She was sitting upright, her spine straight, and he had a fleeting memory of Emily's father, ever the military tactician, and his favourite piece of advice: Always face your foe with conviction, shoulders back, chest out, show them you can handle whatever they throw your way. What would his father-in-law – if he was still alive – have to say about this mess?

'OK. The truth is my luck has run out.' He spoke calmly, his voice disguising his inner angst. 'The enemy has outmanoeuvred me.' He clicked his tongue and huffed. 'I've been skewered. I need to let the dust settle for a few years. The shit who shafted me isn't half as good as he thinks he is.'

Mark groaned as he recalled Monday morning. Like most Mondays, it had started with him sitting in the back of a black taxi, working his way methodically through overnight emails. He was firing off replies as the cab sped down the Embankment, past early morning joggers puffing out their weekend extravagances, and the straggling reluctant commuters bundled into thick winter padding, heading for the shelter of the comparatively warm tube stations. The taxi arrived at its destination without so much as a grunt passing between driver and passenger, and Mark joined the silent army filing through the doors, all keen to reclaim their foothold on the financial opportunities beyond the security turnpikes.

Using his electronic security pass for a second time gained Mark entrance to the Mergers and Acquisitions department and the haven of his own office. His lair was spotless, just as he had left it, reluctantly, late on Friday evening. He remembered the stilted conversation with Paul about shooting – had that man been inwardly gloating, knowing Mark's fate? Then preparing for the call, the knock on the door . . . but it wasn't the director with his second coffee. It was Stephanie from the Human Resources department. He liked Stephanie; she was from Essex too.

'Not now, Steph, I've got a call. I thought you were the director; she's gone AWOL. Buzz off, and I'll call you when I've got a moment, probably won't be until this afternoon.'

'I'm sorry, Mark, but I need you to accompany me to Boardroom 3.'

Mark was good at hiding emotions, but not that good. His head shot forward, his mouth gaping wide, his eyes large gawping at Steph like a child at a movie star. He closed his mouth, but discovered he couldn't swallow. Was he being sacked? Mark Ellis, Managing Director, and biggest fee-earner in the department, a casualty of the January cull? He couldn't be. Not with his track record!

As an M&A banker, Mark was trained to remain calm during a crisis, to think clearly through all options. Lawyers, accountants, financial PR advisors, even the client, could panic, but that luxury was never an option for the lead banker. He inhaled, counted to six, then exhaled slowly, unobtrusively. It wasn't working. He could almost hear his heart thumping like an ancient boiler. His throat constricted as tendrils of fear shot through him. It was a few minutes before he found his voice.

'You can't do this. You've got fuck all grounds to sack me. I'll see you in court.'

He stood up and kicked his chair which rolled backwards towards the window. Steph stepped closer, bringing with her the cloying sent of jasmine, which made Mark's stomach churn.

'You're not being sacked, Mark. A few positions are being made redundant. Yours is one of them.'

'Piss off. That's just a legal fucking loophole.'

Mark was cursing himself for squandering his opportunity. He had become too comfortable, too confident . . . he'd forgotten that ability is not the driver of success in the top echelons of an investment bank. That's why he'd been tipped off about Paul's promotion: he was being warned to move to a competitor while there was still time! His former boss had probably engineered those calls from head-hunters, recorded on message slips which Mark tossed in the bin with misplaced arrogance.

Colour was returning to Mark's face. He concentrated on what Steph was saying – she did this every year, she probably wasn't enjoying it any more than he was.

She spoke kindly, 'I know this is a shock for you. I'll take your phone and laptop off you when we get upstairs – they're bank property. You probably don't have a personal phone. Why would you? No one in M&A has any personal time.' She drilled him with her eyes as she added, 'If asked, I'll deny this, but you might want to jot down a few phone numbers while I speak to a few more . . .' She licked her lips.

'A few more . . . ?' Mark repeated, lips drawn back in a look of disdain. 'People,' muttered Steph.

'People,' he said sarcastically, rolling the word around as if testing it out. 'I think technically we're still employees, aren't we? Just.'

Steph withdrew, leaving behind that hint of jasmine as a reminder of her visit. Would the smell of jasmine forever remind him of that humiliating day? He screwed his eyes shut, freeing himself of the memory and focused his gaze on Emily. She leaned closer, resting her arms on the table. She shook her head, whispering, 'Henry dumped you? I can't believe he would do that.'

Mark tutted loudly. 'No, of course not. Henry would never do that. We are – well, more accurately, we were – close. I think that was the problem.'

Mark pulled the drinks trolley closer and retrieved the champagne, refilling their glasses, and glaring at the wine waiter who stepped forward to claim the bottle.

'Henry lost out in a power struggle he was never equipped to win. His wife insisted they relocate back to Sydney, and that enabled my archenemy, Paul, to bag pole position. I was ambushed.'

She spluttered into her drink. 'Paul fired you?'

'Yes. I know you like him cos he was in the same regiment as your father, but the man's a fucking piece of upper-class shit.' She frowned, running a hand round the back of her neck. 'He's always hated me. Why are you frowning?'

There was a moment's silence, then Emily said, 'This could be awkward. He's friends with Mary and Charles.'

It's more than effing awkward, thought Mark, scowling at her. 'Unlike you and Mary, I'm not taken in by his smarmy manners and regimental tie.'

Cocking her head to one side, she asked meekly, 'Was it just you and him in his office?'

Mark downed his champagne. 'Paul didn't do it. He's not brave enough to do his own dirty work, so HR did it for him.'

Her questions were dragging him back to Monday. Was it less than a week since Steph had relieved him of his phone and laptop? He closed his eyes, trying to blank out the memory of one of the worst days of his life. He recalled the way his heart pounded, his breathing so fast and noisy it felt like he'd just returned from a brisk jog. At least he'd remembered how to swallow again. He didn't utter a word as, one by one, his electronic gadgets – symbols that marked him out as a successful banker – were claimed by Steph before she showed him into a small meeting room which he'd often used himself as a breakout space to negotiate those last few crucial sticking points with his opposite number.

Only this time, it wasn't a top-notch rival banker sitting opposite him. Instead, one of the bank's in-house legal flunkies sat casually shuffling a wad of envelopes as if they were a deck of cards, marking off names, destroying lives with a swift tick, as casually as Mark checked off routine items on his bank statement. This backroom functionary had never met a client, far less battled to win a pitch. He had never nurtured a deal through its sometimes-tumultuous life to land a fee.

'This is for you, Mr Ellis,' said the lawyer.

Mark didn't acknowledge the envelope being thrust his way. He pressed his lips shut and kept his eyes trained on the man opposite. For a few moments the only sound was the soft drumming of Mark's fingers on the edge of the table, then the lawyer spoke.

'It has some important information about . . .' There was a pause.

Listening to his own breathing, biting back his temper, Mark didn't blink. The lawyer adjusted his glasses and fidgeted with the envelope. Mark sat bolt upright, his eyes narrow, still, and steady as any spaniel waiting for the command to pick-up. The envelope fell to the desk, the lawyer lowered his head and stuttered his way through a pre-prepared speech, without once looking up at the latest casualty of the morning slaughter.

Emily interrupted Mark's train of thought, asking why he thought Paul was responsible, suggesting it may be someone more senior based in New York.

Mark felt his hackles rising. 'A hundred percent Paul. The shit even stopped by my office to check I was around.' Once this was sorted, Mark was going to skewer that man. He'd tie his hands together with his bloody regimental tie, then wrap his effing stripy braces round his neck and gag him with them.

Seeing her husband staring wistfully at the restaurant ceiling, Emily felt a surge of pity. But this was unnecessary torture – she'd spent enough evenings in the company of Mark's boss, she knew her husband was brilliant at his job. She leaned across the table and said, 'I know you've worked there your entire career, but just move to another bank.'

She watched him close his eyes. He reopened them and stared at the ceiling. The muffled sound of a phone came from her handbag, and Mark trained his eyes on her.

'Emily,' Mark hissed. 'Not now!'

She reached down and scrabbled through the contents of her handbag, tracking down the sound, thinking it might be Alex.

She glanced at the screen, felt a surge of anger, and let it go to voicemail, then switched it off and dropped the phone into her lap.

'It can wait,' she said firmly. 'You were saying?'

'I can't just jump ship. Believe you me, that was plan A, and I was enjoying plotting revenge against that bastard, but I can't.' He paused, jutted his chin, then said, 'not yet.' He took a gulp of champagne. 'Not content with orchestrating my downfall, Paul poisoned the well, spread rumours and I can't even get to the bottom of what he's effing said.'

Emily gasped, her eyes gaping wide. What was happening to her perfect life? She ran her hands down her face, feeling her torso shaking with rage. She licked her lips and looked up at Mark, 'Are you telling me you're unemployed? Do we have savings? I know we have oceans of debt.' She took a deep breath and asked, 'Ok I need to know. How much is the debt?'

She saw his Adam's apple bobbing. This was not going to be good news. Why hadn't she kept in touch with their finances? Because money was never a problem. He earned it, she spent it.

He licked his lips. She held her breath.

'Devon is manageable. The debt is only five hundred K, and when we kick Alex out and start charging proper rates, it will cover all its costs.'

She ignored the jibe against Alex.

'London,' he said, his voice faltering.

'Yes?' Her voice squeaked.

'London's about two and a half million.'

'What?' She gave a strangled laugh. 'How?'

'We borrowed over a million to buy it, took out money to buy my mother's house – I did explain Chalkwell had to be debt free; it's too expensive to borrow with Mum living there – and then we borrowed another million to fund the basement dig.'

How would they pay the mortgage without his salary? She raised her voice. 'So how much does this ginormous mortgage cost?' She emptied her glass, slamming it back down. 'Am I expected to get a job? I will not be like my mother!'

He reached for her hand, but she withdrew it.

'The mortgage is six and a half grand a month. Then there's Svetlana.'

She stiffened. 'We are not sacking Svetlana!'

'Calm down,' he said soothingly. 'I haven't suggested that. When you add on utility bills, the run rate is about ten K a month. I got an exit package: three months' salary in lieu of notice, and redundancy. After the taxman, it's over sixty grand, which covers six months, and I can sort this if you give me a chance.' He refilled her glass.

She took a large sip; this wasn't a discussion to have sober. Everything would be OK. Mark had a plan. 'Well, as you City guys say, if you will insist on hanging out with gunslingers and hatchet merchants, eventually you're bound to get hurt.' He huffed a tiny laugh. 'I presume this happened sometime last week,' she said. 'I'm only sorry you didn't want to share it with me. It must've been agony going through it alone.' She set her glass back down, this time gently, and asked, 'What have you been doing? Where did you go?'

'Balham,' he confessed, peering over the rim of his glass at her. 'I had to buy a phone and I didn't want any of our friends speculating what I was doing in a phone shop in Knightsbridge on a weekday.'

'I didn't think you even knew where Balham was!'

His eyes seemed to brighten. Mark reached across the table for her hand. She inched forward and felt his warm fingers enclose hers, almost clinging to them as he said, 'Hey, I know you've built your life around helping your chosen causes and spending what I earn. I know the deal. That doesn't need to alter much if we move to Portugal.'

She wasn't moving to Portugal. He could go and work there if he wanted, but she was staying in London. She pulled an incredulous face. 'Well, that's the first piece of good news. What is this miraculous part-time Portuguese job which allows you to spend more time with your family without interrupting the money flow? Diversifying into gunrunning?'

Their first course arrived. Mark ordered a second bottle.

'It's not the job, it's the taxman,' Mark whispered.

Her forkful of food stopped halfway to her mouth. 'The Portuguese taxman is going to supplement our income?'

He put down his own cutlery. 'Well, both the British and the Portuguese, but yes, that's about the size of it.'

Without interrupting, she let Mark outline the plan, or "our new adventure" as he referred to it. The route to financial security relied upon them selling their London and Devon houses. She could cope with selling the gorgeous house in Croyde built on the cliff road with a long terrace facing the sea, but selling Ovington Square would be a wrench. Mark explained that it wasn't as simple as just selling up; there was a wrinkle. A few years ago, they'd claimed a cottage in Devon – owned since before they were married – as their principal private residence, avoiding tax when they sold it. That little wheeze meant their London house was a second home, and the taxman's axe would slice off a third of the proceeds. But they'd never intended to sell it.

'Portugal has a little-known tax loophole called the non-habitual residence scheme – the NHR. It's totally legit. Avoidance, not evasion,' he explained.

'That doesn't make it right.' There was a note of concern in Emily's voice.

He slid a brochure across the table.

Portugal's 'non-habitual residents' (NHR) scheme offers preferential tax treatment to new residents for their first 10 years in the country. If employed in Portugal in a 'high value' activity, your tax rate is set at an attractively low 20%. The scheme also allows you to receive some foreign income tax-free.

'That means virtually no tax from the UK, or Portugal.' His voice rose, bubbling with excitement. 'Once we are on the NHR, we can sell Ovington Square tax-free, which saves us £2 million of capital gains tax. We can tell everyone that, with Alex grown up, we're downsizing and buying somewhere smaller.'

Emily didn't mind downsizing. She wasn't sure about dodging the tax bill – Alex would hate the idea – but neither did she want to part with that much money.

Mark salved her conscience, saying, 'The rules aren't meant to catch Ovington Square. It's our home. If we'd paid a hundred grand in tax on the Devon cottage, we wouldn't have to pay tax when we sell London.'

That made her feel better. They were just finding a way of escaping a whopping tax bill they shouldn't be paying in the first place and wouldn't be facing if Mark hadn't been fired. And he didn't deserve to be fired.

'Let me get this straight. The goal is to sell our home tax-free and then come home to a slightly smaller house, still in Knightsbridge, and I can live the same way as I do now, and we won't be doing anything dodgy?'

'Yes.'

'But until we come back, what do we live off? You say our basic costs are ten grand a month, but I must blow an additional ten.'

He coughed a laugh. 'Sometimes more than that! I'm going to take on a couple of noddy roles.'

'Noddy?'

'Sorry, slang, non-executive directorships.'

'Will that fund our current lifestyle?' she asked, eyebrows raised.

'Not on their own, no.'

'So, what will?'

He sat back, a confident expression on his face. 'Simple. Until it sells, we rent out Ovington Square, just like Croyde.'

Her bottom lip quivered. 'No! Not London. Where would we live?'

He pulled something from his jacket pocket, beaming at her. 'I'm buying this house for you. It will drain our entire reserve fund though.'

She took the page, unfolded it. 'Wow,' she said, her gaze bouncing back and forth between the pictures and him.

'It's got two acres of garden,' gushed Mark, 'all fenced off for your dogs. It's next door to a tennis club, and it's in the heart of what the estate agents call the golden triangle.'

There were four bedrooms, all with en-suite bathrooms – two upstairs and two on the ground floor – a small study, outdoor pool, built-in barbeque surrounded by terraces, manicured lawns, flower beds bursting with colour. Every photo showed blazing sunshine. She shivered at the thought of all that heat. This would be fine. She could just base herself in Portugal, come home whenever she wanted to.

'Boyo, this is stunning!'

'She comes fully furnished, so we can move straight in. The sellers are even leaving the linen!'

'Not so sure about that idea.' She wrinkled her nose. 'I don't want to pack up the London house, it's our home.'

'You won't be packing it up. We can still use it when it's not booked, and Svetlana will still be here. She can run it as a holiday let, short-term bookings like Croyde. Anyway, think what you'll be swapping it for.' He tapped the brochure with his fingertips. 'Look at the sun, there are over three hundred days of sunshine every year in Portugal.'

She finished her food then dabbed her lips with the napkin. 'I don't want to burst the bubble, but when I got up this morning, I thought we were buying a holiday home in Spain. Now you're telling me you've lost your job, you want me to leave all my friends, my entire life, and emigrate to a country I've never been to, as well as sell a home I adore and never planned to move out of. Forgive me if I'm not as enthusiastic as you are. What's the alternative adventure, please, darling?'

He clicked his tongue and looked away. 'There isn't one.'

Emily listened as Mark told her how he'd spent days flailing about, saying – a little melodramatically, she thought – that he'd felt like a deep-sea diver low on air trying to find an escape hatch, searching for a way out of the shipwreck of their lives, before he miraculously discovered this solution.

'You go,' she said. 'Leave me here. I can come and visit.'

He pointed a finger at her. 'Nope, that's not possible. We both need to get out of the UK tax system for five years and, if you like it in Portugal, we can take advantage of the NHR for an additional five.'

Listening to her husband, it dawned on Emily that she could either opt for an adventure in the sun or divorce a man she loved and lead a modest life in London with her share of the proceeds from selling up – after deducting a vast tax bill. She didn't want to lead a modest life. For over twenty years she'd lived like a queen bee, and a queen bee can't exist on a budget.

Emily sucked in a deep breath, then forced a smile. 'So, it's Portugal or bust, is it?'

He gave a tiny nod. 'Shit happens.'

She'd hankered after a house in the sun for years. She would do as he asked and support him. She might love living in Portugal. And if she didn't, she would find a way to come home.

In sunny Portugal, a fresh start beckons . . .

**Escape on a sun-soaked journey to Portugal's Algarve with this heartwarming and gripping holiday read.**

Can Emily learn to love her new home, embrace her family's imperfections and rediscover what truly matters in life?

# Available now

# Acknowledgements

Writing *A Perfect Chelsea Townhouse* has been an incredible journey, and I'm so grateful to the wonderful team who have helped me along the way.

First, my heartfelt thanks to Laura Palmer for her publishing expertise and fabulous guidance. Your encouragement and sharp editorial insight have been invaluable—this book wouldn't be the same without you. Thank you for believing in this story (and in me!) from day one.

To Hannah George and the team at Meiklejohn: what can I say? The cover illustration is a dream! You've captured the spirit of the story and Ovington Square in particular so perfectly—right down to the smallest details. It's a joy to see Lana's world come to life so beautifully.

A huge thank you to Jessie Sullivan, my brilliant social media guru. Your creativity and talent have been invaluable in helping me connect with readers and share my love for storytelling. From clever posts to navigating the complex world of online platforms, your enthusiasm and expertise have made the process not only manageable but fun. I couldn't have done it without you.

A big shout-out to my fantastic early editorial team, Susannah Walters, Gale Winskill, and Denise Spencer. Your thoughtful feedback and unwavering support kept me going when I was knee-deep in drafts and edits. Your attention to detail, patience, and eagle eyes have made this book shine.

Finally, thank you to my meticulous proofreader Katherine Biggs, whose keen eye and careful reading have ensured every page is polished and ready for readers. Your work behind the scenes is so appreciated.

To everyone who has helped shape *A Perfect Chelsea Townhouse*: thank you. This book is as much yours as it is mine!

# About Debbie Morrison

**Debbie Morrison** was always meant to write, but real life held her back. She studied law, then qualified as an accountant, and went on to work for twenty years in the City. Now, finally freed from the shackles of the day job, she has moved from London to rural Devon to pursue her childhood passion and become an author, writing the kind of books she loves to read: fast-paced, escapist and visual with credible and relatable characters.

When Debbie is not writing, she can be found playing tennis (badly), bridge (a little better), walking her dogs, or tending to her garden. She also loves cooking her own home-grown produce for friends and family. She lives on the edge of Exmoor with her husband, miniature bull terriers and small flock of free-range hens.

Printed in Great Britain
by Amazon

61947963R00211